STALKING the PLUMED SERPENT

and Other Adventures in Herpetology

D. Bruce Means

Pineapple Press, Inc.
Sarasota, Florida

Photographs not otherwise credited are by the author.

Inquiries should be addressed to:

Pineapple Press, Inc.
P.O. Box 3889
Sarasota, Florida 34230

www.pineapplepress.com

Library of Congress Cataloging-in-Publication Data

Means, D. Bruce.
Stalking the plumed serpent and other adventures in herpetology / D. Bruce Means. -- 1st ed.
    p. cm.
Includes index.
ISBN 978-1-56164-433-9 (hardback : alk. paper)
1. Reptiles. 2. Amphibians. I. Title.
QL641.M39 2007
597.9--dc22

                              2008015153

First Edition
10 9 8 7 6 5 4 3 2 1

Design by Shé Heaton
Printed in the United States of America

TABLE OF CONTENTS

Color photographs between pages 148 and 149

Foreword by Edward O. Wilson   v
Preface   vii
Acknowledgments   ix

1. The Eastern Diamondback: Gentle Ben
   of Rattlesnakes   1
2. River of May: New World's First Snake   6
3. Diamonds in the Rough: Afternoon Delight   13
4. Herpetophobia: Roundups or Festivals?   22
5. Herpetophilia: Apalachicola Kingsnake   30
6. Blue Indigo: Forest Ruler   38
7. *Phaeognathus:* Secrets in the Red Hills   52
8. The Feared Cottonmouth: Is It Aggressive?   61
9. Cotton Rat: Base of the Food Web   70
10. Alligator Snapping Turtle: Leviathan of
    Southern Rivers   75
11. Ouachita Earthworms: A Glowing Story   82
12. Bushmasters and the Volcano: Silent Death,
    Violent Death   93
13. Is Tzabcan Kukulcan? Stalking the
    Plumed Serpent   102
14. Island Treasures: Nosy Mangabe   118
15. Treefrog Dines on Bats: Prey Turns Predator   131
16. Wonambi: Quest for the Rainbow Serpent   138
17. Black Tiger Snake: Glutton of Chappell   154
18. Hunt for the Roughie: Rare Kimberley Relict   162
19. The Fiercey: World's Deadliest   173
20. Coastal Taipans: A Dream Realized   183
21. Greenies and the Cape York Python Trove   194
22. Okefenokee Alligators: Congratulatory Bellows   212

Epilogue   216
Bibliography   223
Index   227

FOREWORD

EVERY NATURALIST, I AM INCLINED TO BELIEVE, DREAMS occasionally of what it would be like to be another naturalist. Endless goals, fresh adventures, and exciting discoveries might then be savored. I can easily imagine myself an expert searching for ferns in the Karakorum, rare mammals along unexplored Orinoco headwaters, and new species of coral on Pacific seamounts. But the fantasy I most enjoy is to enter the life of my friend Bruce Means.

Keep in mind that Bruce is a scientist—the real thing. His painstaking (and, on occasion, painful) studies on the natural history of the eastern diamondback rattlesnake have made him the leading expert on that important species. He is a premier student of the desmognath salamanders. He has contributed hard-won and valuable information on the ecology, life cycle, and behavior of many other animals, including some of the rarest and most spectacular in the world, especially reptiles and amphibians ("herps" to the cognoscenti). It has been my privilege to accompany him to the springhead habitat of the dwarf amphiuma salamander in the Florida panhandle, and to the steep mudstone ravines of south Alabama, home of the endangered red hills salamander. These experiences rekindled the long-ago excitement I felt when, as a teenager, I roamed similar habitats in this same region in search of snakes and butterflies.

Bruce Means is more than scientific natural historian, however. He is an adventurer of the old school, true to my own dreams. As a young boy I had feasted on the tales of an earlier generation of wildlife jungle explorers and wildlife collectors. I could not imagine a greater calling than that dramatized by Frank ("Bring 'Em Back Alive") Buck, Ivan T. ("Animal Treasures") Sanderson, and the great explorer-naturalist William Beebe, organizer of rainforest expeditions and explorer of the deep sea. Heaven for me would be to join their ranks. Bruce Means has done so, and shares their charisma. As *Stalking the Plumed Serpent* testifies, he is the incarnation of an endangered species.

I am reminded by this book of the time I met Beebe, in 1961 at Simla, his rainforest retreat in Trinidad, when I was a young professor at Harvard and he was in the last year of his long and fruitful life. I said, "Your stories of adventure inspired me and helped draw me to the tropics."

"No, no," he huffed; "I want to be remembered for my scientific contributions, not those stories."

Beebe will be remembered for both, and so will Bruce Means. Means's career, like that of other master naturalists, has been a collage of what he refers to as small experiences of the magnificence of nature. To read his essays and examine his photographs is to understand how much of the living world remains to be discovered, and how exciting the effort will continue to be for those who choose to join him. To press on in such a calling is important for the growth of biology, of which not least will be the deeper understanding of Earth's creatures most in need of saving.

—Edward O. Wilson

PREFACE

THIS BOOK IS ABOUT THE MALIGNED CREATURES OF the earth. I have spent a 40-year professional research career studying snakes, lizards, frogs, salamanders, and other animals that are loathed or feared by most people. For a long time I fended off criticisms like, "Yuk, why are you studying *that* thing?" I was offended when I was called a "snakeman." I call myself an ecologist because I don't like the sniggers and sideways glances I get when I explain what a herpetologist is. Right to the end of her life, even my 88-year-old mother still thought my studies of creepy, crawly things was weird. Well, it's time to set the record straight. I like creepy, crawly animals and I'm worried that people are missing out on the wonderful life stories of these fascinating animals. More than that, I'm worried that, because people are uninformed about the intrinsic value of the creepies, these animals are underappreciated and thus more of them will be lost to us forever by failure to give them the appropriate conservation attention they need and deserve.

My passion for these animals probably derives from my boyhood experiences. I became fascinated with bugs and snakes and things that go bump in the night in the Santa Monica Mountains of southern California where I lived until I was nine years old. When my family moved to Alaska, my interests in herps went on a ten-year hiatus—until I enrolled in college in north Florida. There, in the Florida panhandle, richest place for snakes, turtles, and frogs in the U. S. and Canada, my love for creepy-crawly animals was rekindled and blossomed into a full-fledged life of studying the animals I love.

This book has an ulterior motive. Something profound happened to me along the way while studying snakes, frogs, salamanders, and other animals. Acquisition of knowledge about these creatures has given me a deep appreciation for them. And when you appreciate something and see it threatened, you feel compelled by that appreciation to take action to protect or preserve what you appreciate. That is what popular writing, for me, is all about. It is the best that I can think of to do to protect the animals, plants, and habitats that I love, and that have given me so much pleasure over my life. I believe that other people, likewise, will feel compelled to protect only what they love. Showing the reader some of the splendor of a creature so alien to us as an earthworm or a snake, therefore, is my way of guiding the reader to that love.

While studying herps, I also came to observe and enjoy their habitats, the plant communities they live in, the geology of their geographic ranges, and many other aspects of their natural history. In the chapters that follow, I have tried to capture in text what it really feels like to be out in the field working with these animals. I chose particular instances in which I was immersed in nature, searching for and interacting with herps. I keep detailed field notes and a daily journal, so most of the text is fresh from notes written within hours of the experience. My hope is that the reader will be as excited and fascinated with nature as I was during the particular episode I am recounting.

Herpeto- comes from the Greek word, *herpeton*, for creeping, and -logy comes from the Greek *logos*, to study. Quite broadly, herpetology is the study of creeping, crawling things, and that is the broader use of the word that I intend in this book. More specifically herpetology has come to mean the study of amphibians and reptiles, and many of the chapters in this book are, indeed, about those animals, called herptiles or herps for short. However, other animals creep and crawl, such as earthworms and rats, and I love them, too.

ACKNOWLEDGMENTS

Some of my mentors stimulated me directly or indirectly by their examples. The most memorable were Theresa Thilmony, a traveling lady science teacher by the name of Dr. Grant, Wendell Crouch, Henry M. Stevenson, Robert K. Godfrey, Margaret Y. Menzel, Horace Loftin, Edwin V. Komarek, and Daniel Simberloff. Many friends and colleagues also stimulated in me a love of nature because of their own love and expertise. The most influential of these were Camm Swift, Storrs L. Olson, Larry G. Abele, W. Wilson Baker, Virginia A. Vail, Ellie Whitney, Kenney Krysko, and Jim Eggert. Most of all, my two sons, Harley and Ryan, have grown up to be my colleagues and now have turned the tables on me. From them I now get as much as I give. They have always been my best field companions, and now they are my professional colleagues. I owe a huge debt of thanks to my wife, Kathy Steinheimer, for supporting me in every way, and for companionship in the field. She didn't like my kind of critters at first, but now we have a house full of *her* lizards and tortoises. And my writing has been much improved by the careful editing of Ellie Whitney, my friend and colleague, to whom I am indebted for so much over the past two decades. I also thank my editor, June Cussen, for helping me improve my writing.

To the unbroken chain of reproduction that led from the beginning of life to me . . . not to the individual organisms that never missed a mating, but to the proliferating deoxyribonucleic acid (DNA) that began as pond scum or sea soup and eventually created me, and everything else alive today.

1
THE EASTERN DIAMONDBACK

Gentle Ben of Rattlesnakes

MY HAND RECOILS AS IF I HAVE TOUCHED A HOT SKILLET. I look down and see a ruby-red jewel of blood welling up from the pinprick where a fang pierced the skin on the top of my right index finger. I feel a little sting from the puncture wound. More alarmingly, only seconds after the bite, the tops of my forearms and the backs of both hands begin tingling.

Instantly, I am overwhelmed by the gravity of what I have done to myself. I am all alone in the outdoors with no one to help me. My God, I can't believe it! How could I possibly have put myself in so much danger? Of all people, I should know better. I quell a couple seconds' worth of rage in which I feel like thrashing the poor snake to death. My predicament is grave. After my first bite from an eastern diamondback rattlesnake (*Crotalus adamanteus*) 17 years earlier, my legs collapsed in four minutes. This time I am all alone on a barrier island with no one to assist me. I have to walk back to the kayak, paddle myself across the bay, and drive myself to help.

I put on my backpack and begin walking in a straight line for my kayak. Emotionally, I am a wreck. I want to cry out in anguish for my stupidity. I feel panicky because I know that, against all medical recommendations to lie still so the venom won't be more rapidly pumped through my body, I must exercise vigorously to get off this island and save my life. If I don't, I may be here for days before anyone comes by—long after I am dead.

During lectures I give on snakebite first aid, I stress the importance of getting quickly to medical help. I suggest that victims have other people transport them to the hospital and that they move as little as possible. Somebody invariably asks, "What do you do if you are all by yourself in the boondocks?" As I walk, I think how ironic it is that I am faced with that very situation.

Then I take my own advice. I do what anyone must do in such a circumstance. I decide to steel my mind and body to survive no matter what. I suppress my fear and anxiety and use the most determined force of will I can muster to get myself into the hands of help. I do not run: I walk with purpose. I take a few deep breaths, clear my mind of any negative thoughts, and start repeating in my mind, "I'm gonna do it, I'm gonna do it, I'm gonna do it. . . ."

The walk seems like an eternity, but I reach the kayak exactly ten minutes after the bite, and 735 yards from the snake. My legs and arms tingle strongly, with numbness coming over them, and my legs are now very shaky. My forehead, mouth, and temples also are tingling and going numb. Oddly, my finger is neither swollen nor in pain. In fact, the bite itself is no more distressing than any puncture wound. A sense of despair haunts me because of the long kayak haul ahead, but I fight it off. I drag the kayak out of the bushes and into the water. This requires some effort, and I feel shaky after doing it. Then I walk a 70-yard round trip to fetch the paddle that I hid in the bushes in case someone found my kayak and wanted to steal it. When I return to the kayak, my legs quake and I begin to stumble.

I let myself down into the kayak and begin paddling into the wind and whitecaps. I make regular, strong strokes, and try not to thrash wildly at the water and lose efficiency. The tingling numbness in my hands, arms, legs, and feet increases to a buzzing feeling.

Somewhat dehydrated, I take a drink of water and notice that the roots of my teeth and my tongue also tingle. So far, I have no grogginess or loss of mental acuity. For that I am thankful. My breathing also is not affected by the venom, but I have to keep fighting hard to suppress panic.

Twenty-one minutes after the bite, my kayak noses onto the beach at the end of a sandy road. I do not get a chance to feel relief, however, because I cannot get out of the kayak. When I try to move my legs I get nothing but spastic jerks. I cannot lift myself using my arms on the gunwales. So I roll the kayak to my right and fall sideways into the water. I pull myself out using my arms and crawl onto the dry beach where I try with all my effort to stand up. I must look like a newborn giraffe. My legs are rubber. On the second try I make it to my full height, then crash down on the ground in a twisted jumble. My legs are completely paralyzed. I have no control over them. I'll have to crawl or drag myself over the sand, and at this hour the sand is uncomfortably hot to the touch.

I look at the car 25 yards uphill from the beach. Can I reach it? Can I get up into it? Will I be able to drive? I look down the dirt road leading to help—no way could I ever crawl to the paved road a half-mile away. My clothes are wet with salt water and full of sand.

The crawl to the car is scary. I am so uncoordinated that when I feel sandspurs pricking my palms, I do not try to remove them because I can't pick them from one hand using the other. I fight off visions of dying in the sand and desperate urges to lie down grief-stricken. This is the greatest physical challenge I have ever faced. My heart is racing wildly, just what I need to avoid. I clench my jaws and remember my determination.

I make it to the car. I get the door open and pull myself up into the driver's seat. Now I face another challenge. How do I operate my stick-shift car if I cannot depress the accelerator, brake, or the clutch pedal? My legs are useless, but my arms are still functional, even though numb and buzzing. I use my arms to position my legs and feet, and I push with my arm to help my leg depress the clutch. The car starts, but I have difficulty crossing my arms over one another while turning the steering wheel sharply. I gun the engine and crash through roadside brush. The mile-long drive goes successfully.

When I reach my destination, I clumsily fall out of the driver's seat down onto the pavement, bruising my hands and knees on the knobby granite asphalt. On all fours, I am too wobbly to move across the parking lot, but I discover I can roll. I must have made a strange sight, a grown man rolling through a parking lot among cars, up a low curb, onto a sidewalk, and then to the door of the building. I reach up to the handle, crack the door open, and finally know I am probably going to survive when I hail people who come to help me. My recovery requires 26 units of antivenin and a two-day initial stay in the hospital, but complications from my allergy to the horse serum in which the antivenin was developed require me to make three life-threatening visits to emergency rooms a week later.

If anybody should hate snakes, it should be me. After such a grueling physical and emotional ordeal, one might wonder why I don't loathe venomous snakes. On the contrary, after more than a quarter century doing research on the life history and ecology of the eastern diamondback and other pitvipers, I have great admiration for them. The snake that bit me was only defending itself after I had made a clumsy attempt to pin its head in the sand with a stick too short for the job. In fact, I have discovered that the eastern diamondback is actually a non-aggressive animal that rarely moves or even rattles when approached by humans.

The tendency to lie still and not rattle helps the rattlesnake remain camouflaged. The diamond-shaped color pattern of the eastern diamondback blends very well with the dappled light and shadows of grass stems or dry leaves of its natural habitats. This non-aggressive strategy makes sense in the open pine forests of its native habitat where there are no rocky refugia in which to escape from the enterprising two-legged predator that arrived in the New World about 13,000 years ago. Rattling, which may have evolved to keep Pleistocene megafaunal mammals from trampling the snake, became a distinct liability after the megafauna went extinct about 10,000 years ago. Ancient Amerindians were attracted to any rattling snake as an easy source of food, as rattlesnake remains in Amerindian middens attest.

The gentle nature of the eastern diamondback is further revealed by hundreds of encounters with the snake in which I was never struck in spite of being within striking range (in snake boots, of course). Recently I performed a crude experiment to demonstrate how complacent the eastern diamondback really is. When my field companion found a rattler coiled under a clump of muhley grass, I purposely stepped with my right foot on and off the muhley grass beneath which the snake lay—twice. Then when I attempted to capture it, I was shocked to discover that under my left foot my full 250 pounds had been bearing down on a second snake coiled under an adjacent muhley grass clump only 12 inches away! During the episode, neither snake moved nor rattled. And, most amazingly, I was completely unaware that I was standing on top of the rattler under my left foot.

That the eastern diamondback is loath to strike or bite without provocation is no comfort to most people. Telling people that my radiotelemetry studies reveal that the eastern diamondback does not rattle unless startled or threatened, and that while on woodland hikes you pass by many more rattlesnakes in the field than you realize, does not win over any converts to my rattlesnake fan club. It did not surprise me, then, when the Georgia Game and Fish Commission required a permit to collect or possess any Georgia native snake—except venomous ones! My admonishments have fallen on deaf ears that the eastern diamondback is declining over most of its range and should, at least, have bag limits placed on its taking.

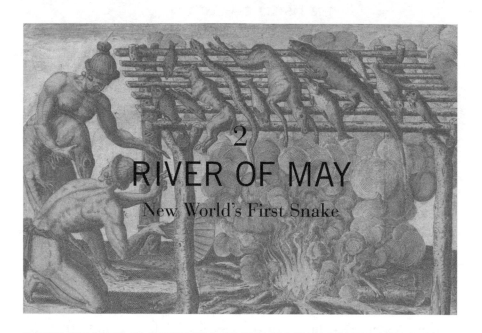

2

RIVER OF MAY

New World's First Snake

CRIES OF MEN IN DISTRESS CREEP INTO JACQUES LEMOYNE'S dreamless sleep. His barely conscious brain, numb with fatigue, seems to be playing tricks on him. Only moments earlier he had collapsed into his hammock after a long night standing watch in torrential rains. When the downpour—the aftermath of a fierce September hurricane— strengthened just after the first light of dawn, his watch commander dismissed all but one sentry at the gate of Fort Caroline, on the banks of the River of May, now called the St. Johns River. Everyone had taken refuge from the weather inside the palm-thatched barracks in the inner courtyard. No one anticipated the horrors about to be visited upon the fort.

Suddenly the terrible screams and groans of men being hacked by sword and pierced by pike awaken him fully. Jacques jumps up from his hammock, still in his wet clothes, and bolts through the door of the barracks. Two Spaniards lunge toward him with swords drawn, but for some unknown reason, do not attack. Jacques runs to arm himself, but the Spaniards already have possession of the fort's cache of arms. He turns and quickly dashes for a cannon-notch in the fort's nine-foot-high walls, where he scrambles over the butchered bodies of five or six of his companions and hurls himself down into the moat. Running like a man who has lost his senses, he races upslope into the protection of a dense hardwood hammock on a high sand ridge (now called St. Johns Bluff) overlooking the fort. Greenbriers and the serrated stems of palm fronds rip at his flesh as he stumbles through a dense patch of saw palmettos.

When he reaches the summit of the sand ridge and seems out of immediate danger, his head clears from the desperation and frenzy of the rush to escape with his life. He was compelled to abandon all his belongings—clothes, footwear, sleeping gear, and worst of all, the precious drawings and paintings over which he had labored so long and hard during the past seventeen months. Praying to the Almighty for guidance, he walks a faint woods trail where he soon meets up with four other bedraggled Frenchmen who have made a similar escape. They sit down and deliberate what to do next.

There are three choices. One man suggests that, rather than take the risk of being eaten by wild beasts or dying of hunger, they should all wait until the next day and surrender to the Spaniards. Another thinks it would be better to make their way to some distant Indian village and await the course of events. Jacques volunteers that they all should make their way to the seashore five and one-half miles distant and try to find the three small vessels that were left behind when Captain Ribault led the French fleet on an attack of the Spanish down the coast at St. Augustine.

The men set off to find the Indians, leaving Jacques behind, but another refugee, a tailor, appears on the scene and agrees to accompany Jacques to the seashore. The two men set out walking through the woods all the rest of the day in a steady rain. At night they press on through a large salt marsh choked with black needlerush, at times pushing through water to their waists . . . and still the rain keeps falling. At daybreak, the exhausted tailor refuses to fight the elements any longer and turns back to surrender to the Spaniards. Jacques, wishing to end the physical ordeal, but not trusting the Spaniards, follows the tailor back to the fort and secretes himself in the woods to observe how the Spaniards will treat his companion.

The tailor falls on his knees before the Spanish soldiers, begging for his life. Jacques watches in horror as they hack the poor tailor to pieces and carry off the dismembered fragments of his body on their spears and pikes. Jacques flees again into the woods.

After about one mile he meets up with two Frenchmen and a maidservant who has been wounded in the breast. Then, while struggling through the salt marshes, they meet Captain Laudonièrre and another man with a sword wound in the neck. Their objective on the far side of a broad salt marsh is a forest they can see on the eastern horizon. The stalks and leaves of black needlerush and sawgrass prick and cut their feet and legs and make them bleed. They are always in water up to their knees, and their misery is increased by the heavy rain. The more they progress, the deeper they wade in the water. At length, when they are convinced they have come to the end of their lives, they arrive at a large river running through the middle of the marsh. Though the stream is not wide, it is very deep and swift. This river adds to their troubles, for few dare to swim across it.

One man retraces their path to the hardwood forest on St. Johns Bluff, cuts a long sapling, and returns with it. Laying the sapling across the water for a handhold, the party makes its way across, one by one, swallowing so much salt water that "We were half-drowned, and our hearts failed us." They move on through the salt marsh toward the forest on the eastern horizon, crossing another large tidal creek in the same manner as the first. Towards nightfall, they enter the woods, where they remain all night in great depression and fear, standing upright with their backs to the trees. Next morning, they emerge from the woods and catch sight of the sea, but before them lies another large salt marsh. Wading through briars and wild roses, they meet up with other desperate refugees. Altogether the desolate party, mostly naked, some wounded and suffering from exposure, now numbers 26.

After more privations in salt marshes and crossing two more large tidal creeks by means of clinging to long saplings, they reach the beach and are in sight of their boats. Too weak from hunger and exhaustion to swim through the surf, they are rescued one at a time by mariners in small dinghies.

Three days earlier when the French fleet sailed out of the mouth of the River of May to confront the Spaniards, Jacques Ribault remained behind in one of the three smaller vessels with sixty solders and crew. They now spend two days taking on board water and food from the other two vessels, sinking them so the Spanish cannot gain from their capture, then depart for France on Thursday, September 25, 1565, in two boats. The ships are soon separated, never to meet again upon the seas. LeMoyne's ship, *Levrière*, reaches the British coast at Swansea Bay. From there LeMoyne travels to London, where he marries, and becomes a servant to Sir Walter Raleigh.

Jacques le Moyne de Morgues had been employed to accompany the French Huguenot expedition to colonize the American continent. His charge was to map the seacoast and harbors, indicate the position of towns, plot the depth and course of the rivers, and portray the dwellings of the natives and anything else in the country worthy of observation. All his efforts, however, were laid to waste by the ruthless Spaniards when they demolished Fort Caroline.

In 1586, 21 years after his escape from the massacre at Fort Caroline, Laudonièrre published his personal narratives on the French colonists in Florida. An English translation mentioned that James Morgues (none other than Jacques LeMoyne) a skillful painter living in Blackfriars in London, had "drawn in lively colors diverse things of chiefest importance" about the French exploits in the New World. Over the two decades since he arrived in England, LeMoyne had made a series of paintings of the Huguenot colony in Florida, depicting scenes and episodes from memory. Not only was LeMoyne an artist and engraver, but since he had become a book publisher in England, it is fair to assume that he had painted the pictures with the idea of engraving and publishing them himself.

Theodore De Bry, a Flemish goldsmith and also an engraver, upon learning of the existence of LeMoyne's pictures, journeyed to London in late 1587 or early 1588 with the intention of purchasing LeMoyne's paintings, but LeMoyne refused to sell. Later in the year LeMoyne died, enabling De Bry to purchase the paintings from his widow. Thus, the first true and artistic scenes from the New World, 42 engravings of Jacques LeMoyne's work, were finally published in 1591—after two and a half decades of personal exploration, privations, escape from near death, loss of his original notes and paintings, and struggle to repaint from memory.

Among these engravings are the first illustrations of some of the practices of the now-extinct Timucuan peoples who lived in the vicinity of Fort Caroline. De Bry's Plate 24 shows Timucuan men smoking animals on a rack over a fire (Fig. 2–1). One of the animals is a large snake with a pattern of diamonds down its back. The tail, dangling in the smoke, does not show a rattle, but no other similarly patterned snake, nor one so large, exists within hundreds of miles of the River of May. This picture is the first published illustration of any New World snake, the eastern diamondback rattlesnake. Largest and most dangerous venomous snake in the U. S. and Canada, it has been part of American history from its beginning.

I pieced together the details of LeMoyne's story from historical documents, especially Laudonièrre's personal narratives, but to get a genuine feel for what LeMoyne had experienced, I visit Fort Caroline National Monument one hot, muggy summer weekend in 1998. On a high, sandy bluff overlooking what's now called the St. Johns River, I sit in the shade near where the French had placed a monument staking their clam to North America. Looking out over the waters I try to paint a mind picture of French sailing vessels at anchor. I climb all over the two-thirds replica of the old fort, located at the base of the bluff in a deep swale, trying to imagine what it must have been like to be awakened from sleep by murderous soldiers and to jump frantically into the salt marsh. I wade through black needlerushes, clamber among the greenbriers and saw palmettos, and creep through what is left of maritime hardwood forests on the ancient dunes, getting my bare arms and legs scratched while doing my best to retrace LeMoyne's path to the safety of the small ships anchored in the mouth of the river.

All of these things give me the proper perspective to try to piece together an authentic portrayal of LeMoyne's perilous escape. Before arriving, I had hoped for some sort of epiphany in which suddenly I might find myself mentally transported back into the past. I want some sort of mystical sensing of the ghosts of history, but something is lacking. My mind just can't conjure up LeMoyne, Laudonièrre, or even the murderous Spaniards. Maybe my difficulty is caused by all that is modern at the scene: a manicured visitor center with National Park officials in uniform wearing smoky-bear hats; diesel-driven barges and motorboats in the river; the noise of the big city of Jacksonville all around me: automobiles, airplanes, and heavy industry. These trappings of modernity must be what are blocking my senses.

Then a strange and wonderful thing happens and I get my revelation. I had traveled half a day from my home base without any expectation of the wild and wooly wilderness upon which the French had made a beachhead. Surrounding Fort Caroline National Monument is a developing subdivision. There are paved roads and streets everywhere. This, after all, is Greater Jacksonville. I linger talking with the rangers until closing time. The afternoon light is turning soft. I say my goodbyes and walk towards my car in the parking lot shaded by large, mossy liveoaks. Just then a car races up and jolts to a stop at the curb.

A lady and her young son blurt out that they have just seen an eastern diamondback rattlesnake crossing a road into the park. "No way!" I think to myself. Had finding an eastern diamondback been on my list, I would never have expected to see one because of the developing suburban environment—and rattlesnakes are just very hard to find. The lady and her son lead us back to where they saw the snake and she tells me that she sat still blocking traffic so the snake could get off the road safely. I am amazed at her altruistic behavior, quite the opposite of what most people would do. I get out of my car and walk in my sandals into a tangle of muscadine vines and blackberry bushes piled on the ground.

I have only taken one step into the mess when I stop myself and think, "This is stupid in sandals. I probably won't ever see the snake, but if it happens to be nearby, I shouldn't be clunking around in this dense groundcover practically bare-footed." Instantly, only one giant step in front of me, I spot the lovely diamonds of an eastern diamondback coiled under the leaves. This is truly a thrill. I never dreamed I'd be viewing a rattlesnake in the vicinity of Fort Caroline, but here I am, staring down at what could be a descendant of the very rattlesnake that LeMoyne figured in his painting. At that moment I have my little epiphany. The rattlesnake, likely to be carrying at least some of the genes that were possessed by the LeMoyne snake, is a living connection to the past. I feel the hairs standing up on the back of my neck and goose bumps rising on the skin of my arms. The great-great-great-great-grandparent of this lovely creature might have been the snake figured on a smoking rack that LeMoyne once viewed hereabouts.

None of the inanimate qualities of the historic park had so inspired me, but this coil of diamonds—these diamonds in the rough—transport me 400 years back in time. All the trials and tribulations of LeMoyne's life leading to his published woodcut and all the human history that has transpired since then come to me in a flash of reflection. Mesmerized by the snake and my thoughts, it occurs to me that many rattlesnake generations, too, have passed since LeMoyne's time. I wonder how many tragedies and difficulties this snake's ancestors have survived in order for this one to be present. I feel very lucky to have seen this snake. I think about the irony of the fact that the French were expelled in 1565, the ancient Timucuans were gone by 1700, the Spaniards by 1825, and yet the eastern diamondback survives here still.

Then I look around me. In every direction I see new homes and lands rapidly being developed. The crush of people, roads, pollution, and loss of habitat from development makes me wonder whether, 20 or 30 years from now when I am gone, this eastern diamondback and his potential descendents will finally be gone forever. I look back down at the snake. It has silently vanished.

3
DIAMONDS IN THE ROUGH
Afternoon Delight

THE LION IS A WILDLIFE ICON THAT WE ALL ASSOCIATE WITH Africa. India has its tiger, Australia the kangaroo. Why shouldn't North America be proud of the world's largest rattlesnake, the eastern diamondback? Here is an account of a single day in my life, a story of the excitement, beauty, and knowledge one can get from this noble animal.

Hot and humid air, hardly stirring. The sun glares down through a cloudless sky, heating my sweaty face. I squint far across the salt marsh toward a line of low vegetation I am struggling for. It marks a long, thin rise of sand fringed by dark-topped wax myrtle shrubs.

My snake boots weigh heavily, dragging through dense glasswort and cordgrass. It's the first time I've worn them in several years. From sitting up in my storage shed, the leather is stiff and unbending as I clunk along. I tugged and strained and stamped fully five minutes getting them on. Success came only when I powdered their insides with cornstarch to reduce friction so my feet would slide in.

Little St. Simons Island is a rattlesnake-lover's paradise. On two previous trips here I established that low sandy beach ridges grown up in muhley grass (*Muhlenbergia capillaris*) support good populations of the marsh rabbit and the cotton rat. In turn, these two important food animals support a healthy population of the eastern diamondback rattlesnake.

Years ago I learned the futility of searching for rattlesnakes during summertime when they are out of their overwintering holes. All day I searched in vain with three other men. We lined up an arm's length apart, all wearing snake boots, and swept through superb rattlesnake groundcover along the borders of cornfields on Tall Timbers Research Station near Tallahassee, Florida. All we ever found was a solitary cottonmouth. That was quite a surprise, for the cottonmouth was half a mile from water—but that's another story.

Then there was the case of my graduate student, who bull-headedly refused to take my advice that searching for the eastern diamondback on foot in summer was a lost cause. Aided by fellow graduate students, all one summer he was singularly unsuccessful. I didn't feel like gloating because his conviction that he could "herp up" rattlesnakes resulted in a failed thesis project. But deep down I was chuckling and saying, "I told you so."

With these thoughts in mind, I groan onward in the midsummer (13 August), midday (11:30 A.M.) heat, not really expecting to find even one of three big rattlers that Joe Taylor told me about this morning. He said he had seen them several times last winter on the two sandy strips I'm heading for, each strip about 250 yards long by 50 yards wide.

I have come to Little St. Simons Island to gather data on habitat utilization by the eastern diamondback rattlesnake in coastal ecosystems. Hopefully, I might also see and photograph courtship and combat behavior, which I believe is initiated in August. After three hot days of chauffeuring me around Little St. Simons Island in the bed of a pickup truck in first gear while I peer into the bushes for snakes, my wife, Kathy, needs a day off. I decide to spend the late morning walking through prime habitat to familiarize myself with it and to take some habitat photographs, but not really expecting to encounter my favorite animal. And yet . . .

I cross dusty salt flats devoid of vegetation, then plow through alternating patches of knee-high cordgrass, saltwort, and glasswort. Teetering along a log placed across a tidal creek as a makeshift bridge, I spot a five-foot alligator just under the surface of the rising water. The gator is bent into a C-shape, facing downstream. The shape is perfect for trapping small fishes between the gator's tail and voracious mouth, as the fishes swim upstream into the "C." I wonder if this is purposeful fishing behavior, and whether it has been reported in the scientific literature. I make a mental note to check.

Fiddler crabs by the hundreds scurry out from underfoot as I trudge along. American egrets scare up from the tidal creek as I pass a bend in it. Four hundred yards from where I left the vehicle I come to a low place between the two sandy rises that form habitat islands in a sea of marsh. The low place is also salt marsh, vegetated with patches of knee- to chest-high, woody, sea oxeye and succulent saltwort. The skinny, fingerlike, sand "islands" appear to be only 25–50 yards wide. Beyond them to the east, about 100 yards across more salt marsh, I can see a long, broad, and continuous sandy ridge paralleling the two "islands."

The sandy habitat islands and the ridges on Little St. Simons Island were thrown up by storms during the past 1500 years in the classic manner by which barrier islands form, accreting seaward as occasional storms pile up barrier ridges paralleling the shore face. The ridges can later grow upward when sand blowing inland from the new shore piles up in dunes. Many long sandy ridges on Little St. Simons Island are relatively low lying, because new barrier ridges were thrown up seaward of them before blowing sand had much of a chance to build up the last ridge with dunes. These low-lying sand ridges, covered with a dense growth of muhley grass, provide excellent habitat for the eastern diamondback rattlesnake.

Each island is fringed by zones of dense woody vegetation. First, the sea oxeye (a daisylike plant, but twiggier) gets taller, rising to about waist height before giving way to eight-feet-high marsh elder. Marsh elder grows in dense, twiggy thickets with hundreds of small diameter caney stems that form a barrier to the easy passage of one's body. Sometimes thick mats of the black needlerush, *Juncus romerianus,* grow in the marsh elder zone and above and below it. Going higher on the ecological transect toward the interior high ground of the sandy ridges, one enters dense-canopied forests of wax myrtle, *Myrica cerifera.*

From outside, the wax myrtle zone appears impenetrable, but inside the phalanx of greenery, I can easily walk upright among the tall stems. The floor of these low forests is a carpet of dark rusty brown, crinkly, dry wax myrtle leaves. Light penetrating the canopy is so rare that little groundcover vegetation grows here. Rattlesnakes would be easy to discover on these bare forest floors, but I doubt they loiter here because no sane rat or rabbit would hang out in the open where they would be vulnerable to all sorts of predators, especially raptors. For that matter, small snakes such as young rattlers would also be vulnerable.

I find the transition to the next habitat very dramatic. The wax myrtle shrubs stop abruptly, and I push blindly through the dense, leafy verdure that grows right to the ground. I burst out into brilliant sun shining on a flat to gently rolling sandy landscape tufted by gray heads of muhley grass.

This grass has long, round, wiry leaves, quite similar to wiregrass—the dominant grass in the longleaf pine forests that are the native habitat of the eastern diamondback on the mainland. Like wiregrass, muhley grass grows in clumps with its long wiry leaves trailing out far away from the base of the clump. Arching over to the ground from the center of the clump, the blades of muhley grass form perfect hideaways underneath. Rats, rabbits—and rattlesnakes—find cozy cover there from overhead enemies, and from the hot sun.

The grass grows densest at the edge of the wax myrtles. Precisely there the hot, dry sand of the high interior of the ridge drops a couple feet in elevation, and I presume, allows the muhley grass better access to moisture in the soil. The combination of drooping wax myrtle branches over dense muhley grass is a microhabitat much frequented by the marsh rabbit and cotton rat, as evidenced by their abundant sign.

Out in the middle of the sandy ridge, the muhley grass grows also, but in a mosaic of patches of variable density from too thick to walk in to bare, open sandy spaces. This is it . . . the highest I can go on the ecological transect. In all directions, there is no other habitat, save going downhill and back through the wax myrtle zone.

I begin walking slowly south down the length of the muhley grass on the sandy "island." The place looks very snakey. My blood is up. The hunt is on. Reason and experience keep telling me I probably will not find a rattlesnake, but the habitat looks so good I get excited anyway. Fresh rabbit pellets lie in tight little bunches everywhere I look—at the base of muhley grass clumps and under the draping grass when I lift it up with my snake stick. I can't explain it, but this place has a "snakes-are-here" feel to it. A cotton rat bolts out of the grass across my boot and startles me.

Thirty yards from the south end of the 250-yard-long "island" I see a break in the verdure where a small wax myrtle tree has fallen onto the muhley grass. I walk slowly forward out of the muhley grass onto the dry leaves under the wax myrtle canopy. I stand still . . . too many hiding places to search while moving. Scanning all the likely nooks and crannies, I glance back over my left shoulder under the downfallen wax myrtle. From the corner of my eye, camouflaged by the criss-crossed twigs and nestled under a pompadour of muhley grass, I see yellow diamonds. They could be dry grass stems lying at angles to each other—but I know these gems.

I get a real rush, same as buck fever. My heart flutters, I inhale deeply. By god! It is a rattlesnake!

I gently part the branches of the downfallen wax myrtle to get a better look. Not eight feet away I see so much snake that my first reaction is "Two snakes!" I put down the five-gallon lard can and snakestick I am carrying, and take off my camera backpack. Fumbling for my camera because I am jittery with excitement, I examine my prizes through my 105 mm macro lens. Wow! I count 14 rattles with no taper. At least one of these babies has about seven years of life recorded in its rattle string. Then my eyes trace the coils and see, to my amazement, that this huge pile of rattlesnake is only one snake. I can't believe it. I look again, and then I shoot off several photos.

Bringing my excitement under control, my demeanor becomes strictly businesslike. I've got to grasp him with my snake clampstick before he spooks and takes off for thick brush where it will be more dangerous for me to try to capture him. Already he breaks his perfectly motionless cryptic behavior and begins to edge into denser briars next to him.

I grab the tongs, get on my hands and knees so I can work under the downed branches, and carefully reach for his neck. My intention is to capture him gently and not to freak him out, but he has a mind of his own and suddenly bolts. I clamp down on his neck and pull him forward toward me. Everything gets wild. He resists violently. I pull him free from vegetation that he tries to wrap around and I stand up, nearly stepping in my open camera bag as I back up. I lose my hold when again he thrashes wildly. He heads for his escape cover and I learn just how big he is when I realize my three-feet long clampstick may not be long enough to work with him safely. If I grasp him below midbody, he seems long enough to nail me on the hand.

A melee ensues. Repeatedly I grasp him and repeatedly he breaks free. You shouldn't use a clamp stick on a big pit viper close to the back of the head for two reasons. First, grabbing the anteriormost one-fourth of any snake makes them attempt to back up. Second, the neck region is very delicate so a heavy-bodied rattlesnake is easily injured if it is held by its neck. My dilemma is to grasp the snake far enough in advance of midbody so I won't get bitten, but far enough below the neck to keep him from trying to pull his head backward.

This is a magnificent snake. He rattles and strikes at me commandingly. I grasp and pull at his body while he attempts to escape fast into the brush I want to keep him from. He knocks my camera into the sand when he rudely crawls over the middle of my open camera bag. I tip over the lard can as I jockey around for advantage. We go round and round, but soon he begins to tire. Now I try to lift him. The snakestick bends and I wonder if it will hold him. This is truly one of the largest rattlesnakes I have dealt with.

I make several attempts to get him into the lard can, but he springs out at every try. Then I realize that I must capture him by hand if I am ever going to bag him. I maneuver him into position several times before I can get a good pin of his head, then I finally have my prize. My god! His head is almost the size of my hand. What a beautiful creature.

I lift his body and place his tail in the lard can, but still he is resisting—and so huge that I have to walk around the lard can to spiral his lower body into the container. I get him coiled in, but now what? He is one big coiled spring daring me to turn loose of his working end, and I know it. I have no choice, I have to try. I flick his head into the can and snap my hand away. It works, I'm not bitten, but he springs out of the can like a jack-in-the-box and all my difficult and dangerous handling is for naught.

All snakes eventually tire out, so I keep trying to lift him into the can using my clampstick on his midbody, deciding that trying repeatedly to get him in my hands is courting an accident unfavorable to my health. After several trials, I tip the lard can on its side, goose the snake into it, and then tip the can upright—and he stays in. Hooray! I sit down in the sand and take a deep breath. I feel like a boxer after a hard round, grateful for a few minutes on the stool.

All alone out here, one on one with such a deadly adversary, I realize what a risk I just took. Had I suffered a bite from this large rattlesnake, I might not have made it the full 500 yards back to the vehicle, including 400 yards of wet and soggy salt marsh. But of course, the risk is a large part of the thrill. I wouldn't feel so elated had I just subdued a black racer or captured a rat snake.

Back at Little St. Simons Island headquarters compound where I am staying, I do a standard workup of my prize. I anesthetize him with inhalant Fluothane®, then take a series of data from an examination of his body. I first verify what I have suspected, that he is indeed a male. Sex can be determined with high accuracy in this species by counting the subcaudal scales. More than 26 and the specimen is a male; fewer than 26, a female. I count 31 for this big guy.

When I lay him out on a table for measuring, I also verify his large size: 5 feet, 8 inches from the tip of his snout to the end of the living tissue on his tail, the black first rattle. He weighs a lunker's 8 lbs, 11 oz.

By the time I get to the task of gently force-feeding him a radio-transmitter on a unique frequency, he's coming around. The workup takes less than five minutes and he's back in the lard can for immediate return to the field.

I'm flying high on the return walk across the wide salt marsh and hardly notice the early afternoon sweltering heat. Gently, I slide him out of the lard can onto the exact spot on which he was originally coiled, and I step back to watch. Like liquid gold, he glides into the briar thicket and disappears, rattling like hell.

I spend the rest of the afternoon investigating the two sandy islands, peering under muhley grass clumps and searching other likely nooks for additional rattlers to monitor by radiotelemetry. At 6:13 P.M., as the shadows lengthen and the marsh mosquitoes carry off my blood by the pint, I discover another male diamondback crawling across the "island" just 30 yards from the first male. The anterior two feet of him lie exposed between muhley grass tufts.

This 5 lb, 9 oz–snake is quite large in his own right. Normally, his capture would "make my day," but his discovery, capture, and release are a mere footnote to earlier events with the leviathan. In marked contrast with the "big guy," the second male is a real gentleman. He allows me to grasp him with my tongs and lift him into the lard can on the first try. He never rattles or becomes aggressive.

The two eastern diamondback rattlesnakes I caught today are among approximately 1,000 captures I have made of this amazing animal. One of these snakes put up a big fight, resisting capture, but the other snake was as placid as a dishrag. Each encounter with a wild diamondback is thrilling because it is also potentially life-threatening, but the real thrill for me comes later, after releasing the snake with a transmitter in it. Then I am able to locate the snake at any time I wish, day or night, to see what it is doing. Radiotelemetry has assisted me in making over 6,000 observations of the eastern diamondback, witnessing many of its life secrets and behavior. Sneaking up on a study animal and discovering it engaged in courtship, swallowing a rabbit, or giving birth, for instance, has given me much more pleasure than the one-time cheap thrill of its capture. When you become as familiar with a species as I have—even a deadly venomous rattlesnake—you empathize with its existence. Without purposely trying, you learn to appreciate the creature's biological complexity. And when you appreciate something, you value it.

Late at night, after writing up my journal notes for the day, I slump down on the bed and click off the lights. Lying under a high ceiling fan in the lovely old Helen House in the headquarters compound, my tired muscles and achy bones begin to relax. A great and memorable day in my life comes to a close as a fine feeling of euphoria sweeps over me. I exult in the privilege I have been given to share a few moments in the lives of two large eastern diamondbacks. I relive in my mind the contrasting behaviors of the two snakes. Then, just as I am dozing off, Kathy punches me awake and complains of the faint musky rattlesnake odor still clinging to my skin. She wants me to get up and wash again. Getting up is the last thing I want to do. Besides, I kind of like the smell.

4
HERPETOPHOBIA
Roundups or Festivals?

ONE COLD FEBRUARY MORNING IN 1978, MY TWO YOUNG SONS, Harley ten and Ryan six years old, and I drive up to the Osierfield, Georgia house of my friend and master naturalist, Milton N. Hopkins Jr. We all pile into his pick-up truck with his teenage son, Bubba, and begin looking for a special place known to Milton and Bubba—a sandy location on the farm that has not been used to grow crops.

When we find it, we all get out and begin searching through the turkey oaks and broomsedge grass for the white, sandy hummocks in front of half-moon-shaped openings in the ground. Harley and Ryan warm to the search. Soon I hear, "I found one!" We all converge on the mouth of a 12-inch-wide tunnel that we soon discover runs underground about 20 feet and declines to about five feet deep at the end. It is the burrow of the gopher tortoise, the only turtle in the eastern US that digs a long burrow in the ground in which it spends much of its life.

Milton brings up a 25-feet-long piece of black, flexible plastic pipe and runs it down the burrow, twisting it gently as he works it down the hole. Periodically he holds the end of the pipe up to his ear and listens. When the pipe is unable to be worked further down, presumably because it has reached the end of the burrow, he listens for a few seconds and then says, "Nope. Nothing here," and we continue our search for burrows. At about the fifth burrow, Milton feels a clunk at the end of the pipe and listens at the end that is in his hand. "This is a tortoise," he says. "Listen and you can hear it breathing, especially if you bump it with the pipe and make it exhale." We all take turns listening and bumping the tortoise. Milton is right. After a bump, the tortoise makes an obvious exhale that you can hear, but the tortoise is not what we came for.

We try several more burrows, and then we hit paydirt. Milton shouts, "Listen. There's a diamondback in this one!" It is not necessary to listen through the pipe because the snake's rattling is a muffled sound that we can hear while squatting next to the hole. "By the way, boys," admonishes Milton, "remember what I told you about watching out around the mouth of the burrows. Rattlers often are coiled under vegetation right next to the burrow. You might get a nasty surprise when you get down on your hands and knees to look or listen down a burrow. Be very careful to make sure there is no rattler within striking distance." We all nod, yes, and then take turns listening to the much louder whirring sound we can hear at the end of the pipe—after keenly searching the ground within ten feet of the burrow entrance.

After we all have a good listen, Bubba hands Milton a plastic milk jug half full of gasoline, and then Milton says, "Now watch this. I'm going to pour just a little gas down this pipe—not too much, only a couple of teaspoonfuls—and then we wait." After the gas is poured into the end of the plastic pipe, Milton holds it to his mouth and blows several times. "The idea is to use just enough gas to blow fumes into the burrow, not to run liquid gasoline out the end of the hose. Too much gas will kill the rattler and no telling what else," he says.

Milton pulls the pipe from the burrow and asks us all to move about fifteen feet to the side of the burrow so the snake won't see us as it attempts to exit from underground. About the time we are getting restless, five minutes later, Milton whispers, "He's coming out. Watch." And when we strain our eyes, we can see a tongue flicking from the side of the burrow. The snake stays there for several minutes, and then Milton says, "Bubba, grab him." Bubba quickly approaches the hole and hooks out the rattlesnake with my snake hook. "And that's how most people harvest eastern diamondbacks in the South," Milton says.

Ryan asks, "When is the tortoise coming out?"

Milton says, "I don't believe there is one in that burrow, but there could be one I didn't hear. As far as we know, the gas doesn't kill the tortoise, but you can imagine if it can kill the rattlesnake, it couldn't be very good for the tortoise. More than that, Ryan," Milton continues, "there are all kinds of other animals that live in the burrow with the gopher tortoise that the gasoline does harm or kill, including many kinds of insects, the gopher frog, lizards, other snakes, and even any mouse or rat that might be down in the burrow."

"What happens if the rattler doesn't come out?" asks Harley. Milton replies, "Then it probably got so overcome with gas fumes that it is stupefied and has to be dug out. Many rattlers die from the gas fumes, sometimes days later after being subjected to it. And what's worse, what do you think the burrow looks like when it is nothing more than a deep trench in the ground? Do you think the tortoise or any of the other animals would use a burrow with no sides and no roof?" asks Milton. The look on both kids' faces tells me they have just realized that digging out the tortoise burrow is probably the worst thing that can happen when using the gasoline technique to evict rattlers.

It is the weekend of the Fitzgerald Rattlesnake Roundup. I take the kids and am glad when they express disgust at what they see. Harley leads us to a screen-wire holding pen in which at least 50 rattlesnakes have crowded into one corner to hide from the sun and seek what they feel is the safest part of the pen. Ryan points to what appears to be a squashed dead snake at the bottom of the pile. A few weeks earlier I had taken them to the Whigham, Georgia, Rattlesnake Roundup. What we see at Fitzgerald is much the same, men scurrying about with wooden boxes or metal garbage cans containing rattlesnakes they have caught and saved up for the prizes for the most brought in or the largest by weight. A skin dealer hoists rattlesnakes from boxes and puts them into screened holding pens for the public to see while a fat man squeezes the yellow venom from each snake on a makeshift table in front of a crowd of onlookers behind a heavy-duty, hog-wire fence. At both roundups rattlers are taken to a cook shack where heads are chopped off and bodies are gutted and skinned, then chopped into fry-sized pieces. Then they are dipped in batter, deep-fat fried, and offered for sale to the curious public as a novelty food.

The boys and I sit down for a hotdog and I ask them what's wrong with roundups. Having spent many hours with their daddy safely observing eastern diamondbacks on my study area, they hold the rattlers in great respect, although they well recognize the dangers of snakebite. Both boys tell me that they don't like the way the rattlers are treated. Then Harley asks me what I think is wrong with roundups, and I am only too glad to have the opportunity to spell it out for them.

I say, "Three things. First, roundups only reinforce people's fear and loathing of rattlesnakes. They capitalize on the sensationalism surrounding the dangers of rattlesnakes to bring in revenues. They make no attempt to educate the public about the interesting natural history of snakes and their rightful place in nature. Second, roundups are an important cause of harmful impacts to the animals associated with the gopher tortoises, either by gassing or by the excavation of the gopher tortoise burrow, as Milton told us about. And third, there is no regulation of snake hunting by roundups or state or federal agencies."

I explain that rattlesnake populations are declining, and so are the populations of the gopher tortoise and the animals associated with it, but nobody is making any attempt to learn if the hunting pressure is excessive. I tell the boys, "We eat animals and use their skins and body parts for clothes and other useful things, so to be honest, killing, eating, and skinning rattlesnakes for profit is no different from raising chickens and cattle for food and profit. However, because early settlers killed animals indiscriminantly, we lost the bison, passenger pigeon, and some other animals from the eastern US. And we almost lost the white-tailed deer, wild turkey, and many of our ducks and geese to unregulated hunting, but we formed state game and fish commissions and the US Fish and Wildlife Service to make rules and regulations about harvesting these animals and now we have them aplenty, and we still can harvest them—within reason—as sustainable resources. That is what we need to do with the eastern diamondback rattlesnake." Almost simultaneously, both kids blurt out, "So why hasn't this been done?"

I hang my head and think a moment. Then it comes to me. "Herpetophobia is the reason," I say, "the fear and dislike of creeping-crawling things. It's all about politics. Deer, quail, and wild turkeys aren't feared by people, but snakes are. If a state legislator tried to promote the protection of venomous snakes, what do you think most people would think about that? Most legislators probably dislike snakes, anyway, but can you imagine how many votes a legislator might get who promoted conservation of animals hated or feared by most of his constituents?" Both kids sit wide-eyed, looking into the crowd. When we leave, they both tell me, "Daddy, I don't want you to take me to anymore roundups."

Over the years, I and my herpetologist colleagues in the Southeast have lobbied roundup officials to stop roundups, or at least to change their thrust from exploitation to environmental education. Our efforts have met with little success, and we are often told that the roundups make little or no impact on the rattlesnake. An example of this denial comes out of the program for Alabama's 37th Opp Roundup Program for 1996: "Despite the annual harvesting, diamondback rattlesnakes elude the searchers and continue to survive in abundance." Ironically, the founder of the Opp Roundup, Mr. J. P. Jones, was quoted in a 1990 *Audubon* magazine article as saying, "We have to drive a hundred miles from here [on real snake hunts]. They a lot scarcer now. When I started we just hunted in the woods around here. You won't get none today."

Words of the Whigham, Georgia, Rattlesnake Roundup hunters and officials give conclusive evidence that roundup activities have accomplished the main goal, causing eastern diamondback populations to decline in southwest Georgia. Whigham's first rattlesnake roundup was held in 1961 and focused on rattlesnakes in the Grady County area. Three years later, the local newspaper, the *Cairo Messenger* of 7 February 1964, reported, "Rattler hunters are saying that in Grady County over areas that have been hunted for the past four years the hunting is not as good as it used to be. It is the opinion of some that a majority of the rattlers caught during this roundup came from adjacent counties."

The rattlesnake population in Grady County had declined so

severely by 1971 that the *Cairo Messenger* of 5 February reported, "The Whigham area has developed a large group of skilled hunters, but they said Monday night that the club seemed to be approaching its goal of reducing the snake population because many hard hours of hunting in this area proved that the rattler is getting scarce. Some of the most skilled hunters said they hunted for days sometimes without seeing a rattler. In view of this development, consideration is being given to expanding to adjacent counties. It has been no secret for some time that more than half of the big ones caught and brought in on roundup day came from Decatur, Thomas, Mitchell, and Gadsden counties."

The Evans County Wildlife Club operates the Claxton Rattlesnake Roundup, about 170 miles northeast of Whigham. In 1976, club member Danny Strickland was quoted in the *Rural Georgia* newspaper: "Only about 9 to 10 percent of those snakes are actually snakes from Evans County. These snakes are coming from all over South Georgia." By 2004, the *Claxton Enterprise* wrote, "While little of the hunting took place in Evans County, snake hunters from surrounding counties and as far as Alabama and Florida helped bring in 348 snakes, 114 more than last year." In all the roundups involving the eastern diamondback, roundup officials acknowledge that rattlesnakes have declined and that hunters have to go ever farther afield to bring in rattlers.

By 2002, after a run of 27 years, the Fitzgerald Rattlesnake Roundup became a Wild Chicken Festival. The change in focus resulted from significant drops in the number of rattlesnakes brought in during the previous two years and in response to concerns expressed by the Georgia Department of Natural Resources about the population decline of the eastern diamondback in Georgia. In spite of coaxing from the Georgia Department of Natural Resources, however, in 2008 two eastern diamondback rattlesnake roundups were still operating in Georgia, in Claxton and Whigham. Also, the roundup in Opp, Alabama, was still operating and had spawned another one held in Andalusia.

An environmentally beneficial and commercially successful solution exists for these roundups. It is the voluntary solution adopted by the only rattlesnake roundup in Florida, which is called the San Antonio Rattlesnake Festival. Originally started in 1967, visionary roundup officials headed by Eddie Hermann decided in 1976 to make snakes the focus of environmental education rather than unbridled exploitation. Instead of races with live gopher tortoises, the festival features mechanical tortoises invented by Eddie that young children operate using pull-strings. Several kids sit on the ground pulling furiously at long strings to bring his or her wooden tortoise across the finish line first. It's great fun and everybody loves it, but animals are not the targets of destruction or abuse. As for the snakes, a few are tastefully displayed with someone standing by to discuss snake biology and answer questions. Moreover, the festival often hires talented presenters to put on educational snake shows. The San Antonio Rattlesnake Festival has been hugely successful in bringing in revenues for the community with a simple change in the philosophy of how it presents itself and in the types of events it features.

Fortunately for the gopher tortoise and the more than 300 species of arthropods and vertebrate animals that use the tortoise's burrow, the states of Georgia in 1983 and Florida in 1978 enacted bans on using gasoline to evict rattlers from burrows. Alabama, however, still has no specific prohibition. The ban would be especially valuable in regulating the impacts on the gopher tortoise burrow ecosystem by rattlesnake hunters who capture rattlers for rattlesnake roundups. Unfortunately, however, enforcement is so difficult and so rare that most of the rattlesnake hunters I have talked with still use it, but commonly make public statements that they don't.

Knowing how awful it is to be envenomated by the eastern diamondback rattlesnake, I stand in horror watching a snake handler at the rattlesnake roundup in Opp, Alabama. With the snake's head—mouth open and fangs bared—restrained in one hand and holding the tail in the other hand, the handler drapes the heavy midbody of a big rattler across the shoulders of a frightened twelve-year-old boy. The handlers—there are several of them—sell Polaroid photographs to spectators seeking a thrill and a trophy of their bravery. The macho handler has no hand free for emergencies. A gaggle of spectators crowd around and an accident could easily result from a slip of the hand, the sudden, violent twisting and thrashing of the snake, or an unwitting spectator not watching where he is walking.

One aspect of human behavior is an oxymoron: we are drawn to things we fear if we can observe them in safe surroundings. That is why action movies packed with blood and guts, murder, high-speed chases, and fistfights are so popular. We don't normally participate in such activities, but it titillates us to experience them vicariously with the actors who do so on screen. It is why television nature films pander to the sensational, such as cheetahs bringing down a gazelle, crocodiles drowning a wildebeest, and any topic featuring fangs, venom, or claws. For a number of years I have tried to find funding for a documentary film about one of the most remote and beautiful wild places left on earth, the tepuis of northeastern South America. But at every inquiry I am asked, what's the hook? What will you find on the summit of one of these breathtaking mesas, a dinosaur? A dangerous giant spider? A killer snake? Never mind that tepuis have thousand-foot cliffs protecting their summits with a dozen thousand-foot-high waterfalls, or that half the animals and plants on tepuis are endemic species found nowhere else. I can come up with only a giant earthworm or several species of pretty frogs new to science, but that is not enough. I need an earthworm that squirts poison or a treefrog with venomous fangs to sell the idea to producers.

The hatred of creeping, crawling things is herpetophobia, and we all know it too well. Herpetophobia usually has negative consequences for herps, as rattlesnake roundups attest. Herpetophilia, on the other hand—the love of creepy-crawly things—is a fast-growing human activity that is much less well known, but may also have negative consequences for herps. They can be loved to death . . . or to near extinction, as we shall see in the next chapter.

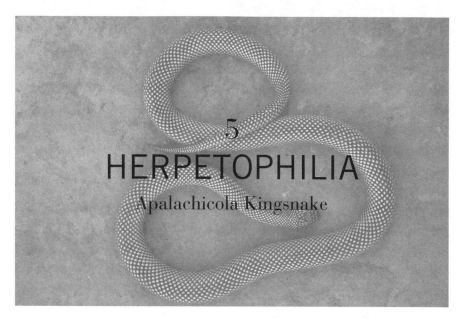

5
HERPETOPHILIA
Apalachicola Kingsnake

PROFESSIONAL HERPETOLOGISTS ARE OFTEN ASKED WHAT events of their young life stimulated their interest in reptiles. You'd never guess that a kid like me, who attended schools in Anchorage, Alaska, from the 4th through 12th grades, would grow up and have a Florida snake named after him. In my Alaska days, the only wildlife I was familiar with was big furry animals such as moose, caribou, Dall sheep, and black, brown, and grizzly bears. When I was 13 and old enough to operate safely a 4-10 shotgun, I hunted smaller game such as snowshoe rabbits, spruce grouse, and an occasional ptarmigan for the family table, and I often fished the cold creeks for dolly varden trout with a large, red salmon egg for bait. But snakes? Forget it. There's not a single one in all of interior Alaska.

For three formative years, however, from the first through the third grades, my family lived in a remote canyon in the Santa Monica Mountains of southern California in the late 1940s. During those idyllic times, I roamed the stony, chaparral-vegetated mountains with little restriction and great gusto, picking up and bringing home in glass jars every scorpion, tarantula, Jerusalem cricket, centipede, lizard, and, occasionally, snake, that I could find. My enthusiasm for creepy-crawly critters was interrupted by Alaska . . . until I chose

30

Florida State University in the Florida panhandle to begin my college education. I wanted to get as far away from the cold and snow and long, dark winters as possible. There, in the middle of more snakes than in any similarly sized area in the United States and Canada (45 species), I rekindled my love of small animals having neither fur nor feathers.

Almost at once, I fell in with a bunch of Floridians who were snake lovers: Rick Blaney, Harry Panzik, and Ron LaBar. Rick had a trailer full of snakes and he and Harry were out snake-hunting every afternoon and on weekends. I sponged up all the knowledge I could about snakes from my buddies, and it wasn't long before I had a bedroom full, too. At one time I had snakes of all kinds stuffed into about 40 cages that I had built from scrap lumber and window glass. And soon, I fancied I was pretty knowledgeable, if not an expert, about the snake fauna of the Florida panhandle.

Then one day in the mid-1960s, I was driving up a lonely road through the Apalachicola National Forest and spotted a snake on the road ahead of me. I came to a screeching halt, jumped out of the car, and was disgusted to find a DOR (dead-on-the-road) snake. But it was unlike any snake I had ever seen. It was patternless, without any bands or stripes, each scale with a wide ring of light yellowish beige pigment surrounding a black center. Lifeless in my hands and about three feet long, it was one of the most beautiful snakes I ever beheld.

Standing there, I strained my brain to remember any information that would help me identify this lovely creature. Nothing came. I took the dead snake home and consulted my field guides. Nothing. Rick, Ron, and Harry had graduated ahead of me and left Tallahassee, so I didn't have them to consult. When I got down to counting scales and examining the details of the morphology closely, it keyed out as a common kingsnake, *Lampropeltis getula.*

The common kingsnake is one of the most wide-ranging snakes in North America, occurring from the Atlantic to the Pacific coasts and from the latitude of southern New Jersey and southwest Oregon to well down into Mexico. Over its large range exist many unique races that have been given subspecies names. There were, in fact, two close matches to my unusual specimen among the many races of the common kingsnake. One was the speckled kingsnake, *L. g. holbrooki*, whose range parallels the Mississippi River and lies mostly west of it. The second race was the south Florida kingsnake, *L. g. brooksi*, whose geographic distribution was confined to the tip of the Florida peninsula. Not knowing whether I had a *holbrooki*, *brooksi*, or something else, I began looking for kingsnakes every time I had a spare moment.

Months passed. Winter came and went. After a couple of years I had a growing number of road-killed specimens collected from all over the Florida panhandle. I began to realize that a unique population of kingsnakes resided in a small area bounded by the Apalachicola River on the west, the Ochlockonee River on the east, and north to south, from Telogia Creek to the seacoast. This is the eastern part of the area known as the Apalachicola Lowlands. In time I learned of a smaller population across the Apalachicola River in lower Gulf County. The blotched kingsnake (*L. g. goini*), named by Wilfred T. Neill and E. Ross Allen on the basis of specimens caught near the town of Wewahitchka across the Apalachicola River from where I was finding my specimens, resembled my specimens in only one character, its wide yellowish crossbands. Otherwise, *"goini"* was a dark brown to black snake that much more resembled the nominate race of the rest of the Florida panhandle, the eastern kingsnake, *L. g. getula*.

I became convinced that I had found a new race of kingsnake. Although many had lightly colored crossbands, the crossbands were all wider and fewer in number than those of the surrounding populations of the eastern kingsnake, as well as many fewer than in *L. g. brooksi*. Moreover, all specimens in the eastern Apalachicola Lowlands had some degree of light pigment in the normally dark brown to black interband scales. Finally, a large percentage of these snakes had their light and dark pigment arranged in longitudinal stripes or were totally patternless, like the first DOR I found.

About the time I began to voice my opinion about this small but unique race of kingsnakes in the Florida panhandle, my old buddy, Rick

Blaney, published his Ph.D. dissertation in 1977. It was an exhaustive study of all the races of the common kingsnake. Rick believed that my Apalachicola Lowlands kingsnakes were possibly intergrades between the south Florida and eastern kingsnakes that had become stranded in the Apalachicola Lowlands by rising sea levels of the past 10,000 years. After some lively discussions about our differences of opinions, I realized that to test our ideas, I was going to have to do an exhaustive study of my own to see whose hypothesis could be refuted.

So I set about gathering data from road kills and live specimens, and I established a captive breeding program to determine what genetics would tell me about the relationships of Florida kingsnakes. During this same time period, the late 1970s and 1980s, captive breeding of snakes was becoming fashionable and the colorful and uniquely patterned kingsnakes of the Apalachicola Lowlands began bringing top dollar ($200 – $300) in the herp pet trade. I soon learned of hordes of snake collectors hunting the Apalachicola Lowlands. Apparently, so many snake-fanciers were enamored of this snake that the demand for live specimens as pets escalated to heights rivaling the demand that is thought to have partially been responsible for the decline of the eastern indigo snake.

Two animal dealers I knew maintained a network of local people who collected snakes for them in and near the Apalachicola Lowlands. One of them, the late Art Meyer, shared some of his breeding stock with me. Over a period of a decade, breeding several generations of kingsnakes and doing the appropriate backcrosses, I discovered that the patternless kingsnakes breed true. That is, they produce only patternless offspring. Likewise, eastern kingsnakes breed true, producing snakes with narrow yellow crossbands on a dark brown to black ground color. Crossing patternless individuals with banded ones produced an array of intermediates between the two parental types. Likewise, crossing broad-banded individuals with broad-banded individuals produced nearly every pattern type from patternless to narrowly banded, indicating their intermediacy between patternless and the narrowly banded *L. g. getula.*

I was convinced. My breeding studies demonstrated that there was a genetically distinct population of kingsnakes in the Apalachicola Lowlands that were not hybrids between eastern and south Florida kingsnakes. Moreover, Kenney Krysko showed that kingsnakes of the southern half of the Florida peninsula were only one race, now called the Florida kingsnake, *L. g. floridana*. These, and snakes with the old *brooksi* patterns, are very different from the patternless and wide-banded population of the Apalachicola Lowlands. The differences are most easily seen in the more numerous and much narrower crossbands of *L. g. floridana* in comparison with fewer, wider crossbands—or striped or patternless—in snakes from the Apalachicola Lowlands.

In the late 1990s, during his exhaustive studies of the kingsnakes of Florida, Kenney Krysko joined me in studying the fascinating population of the Apalachicola Lowlands. We published the results of our morphological study in 2000, and Kenney followed up with additional work on the biochemical genetics of the Florida races, concluding that kingsnakes in the Apalachicola Lowlands are, indeed, a genetically distinct race. In addition to the genetic data that tell us this, there is evidence from biogeography. No less than 15 plants are endemic in the same Apalachicola Lowlands as well as one other race of snakes, the brown-chinned black racer, *Coluber constrictor helvigularis*. Apparently, all these plants and animals were isolated for a time, possibly on a barrier island, and diverged from their mainland ancestors. As a matter of fact, a pair of ancient barrier islands today lies stranded some 30 miles inland from the seacoast right in the middle of the eastern Apalachicola Lowlands.

Lying against the white sands of a barrier island, the cross-banded but generally dark brown eastern kingsnake would stand out like a sore thumb and make for easy pickings by aerial predators such as raptors—or any visually oriented predator. A lightly colored snake without crossbands would more easily be camouflaged on coastal sands, but in addition, a lightly colored snake has another advantage in hot summer coastal environments. It is better able to reflect the heat of the sun than is a dark snake. Thermoregulation in a hot, sunny environment, therefore, may have been at least as important a selective force as camouflage. The lightly colored, patternless snakes probably evolved from a population of the eastern kingsnake that became isolated on a barrier island for a time. After sea levels dropped and the island became stranded inland, patternless genes spread out from the island as patternless kingsnakes began to interbreed with its closest ancestor, *L. g. getula.*

Kenney Krysko honored me in 2006 by naming the new race *Lampropeltis getula meansi.* Its common name is Apalachicola kingsnake. Individuals previously called the blotched kingsnake, *L. g. goini,* are intergrades between the Apalachicola and eastern kingsnakes. Because blotched kingsnakes are intergrades, neither the common nor scientific names are valid and should no longer be used.

Now that *L. g. meansi* is properly recognized as a distinctive race of snakes found in a geographically circumscribed area, I am quite worried about the status of the population. During my 1970s studies of kingsnakes in the Apalachicola Lowlands, I accumulated data on about 85 road-killed and museum-preserved specimens and 17 live kingsnakes that I was responsible for removing from the population. In that same period, I saw about 30 additional live kingsnakes that local dealers removed that I knew about. Also, in the 1970s and early 1980s, I was aware of many more (possibly hundreds) that were collected by snake hunters for personal and commercial gain. Sorrowfully, from 1985 to 2008 only about ten wild-caught Apalachicola kingsnakes have come to my attention and I have spent a similar amount of time each year in this area. Something has caused this population to decline. My first suspicion is that heavy over-collecting is the reason, and there can be no doubt that the population was assailed by enthusiastic snake hunters since the early 1970s. Snake hunting pressure, for commercial purposes and for personal pets, continues to this day. To be fair and properly scientific, I must admit that throughout Florida, many populations of the common kingsnake and its races have declined for no obvious reason.

My most puzzling example comes from Tall Timbers Research Station north of Tallahassee, where I was employed for 15 years and had the snake population under radiotelemetry study from 1976 to 1984. I and my biological research station colleagues caught, marked, and released 24 eastern kingsnakes in that eight-year period on approximately 2,800 acres of the research station. Twenty years later, two bright graduate students from the University of Georgia, Seth Stapleton and Kim Sash, operated big drift fences to capture large snakes on Tall Timbers. They trapped snakes a total of 1,341 times in four years, without capturing or seeing a single eastern kingsnake. Between 1984 when I released my last kingsnake on Tall Timbers and the termination of their studies in 2005, the kingsnake population of Tall Timbers Research Station completely disappeared—for no obvious reason. The research station had experienced no drastic land use changes during that time.

The cause of this decline might be related to a predator eradication program that was ongoing in the late 1990s on adjacent quail hunting plantations. In 2000 the US Fish and Wildlife Service cited plantation managers for setting out fake quail eggs laced with the potent poison Furadan to kill opossums and other predators known to prey on quail eggs. The common kingsnake is a fossorial animal whose diet includes eggs of ground-nesting birds. How far Tall Timbers' kingsnakes might have traveled into the range of poison baits is unknown, as is whether any of the poison eggs might have gotten distributed on Tall Timbers property somehow. It is the only reason I can think of for the otherwise inexplicable decline.

It is no surprise that the fear and hatred of snakes by humans has had many negative consequences for snakes. On the other hand, a rapidly growing phenomenon—the love of snakes for pets, ophidiophilia—may be having its own negative consequences for snakes. Snake collectors fancying a pretty snake to keep in their personal collections may have been responsible for the decline of the Apalachicola kingsnake, as has been argued for the eastern indigo snake. And it grieves me that my studies may have aided and abetted collectors by bringing attention to this special population. It is sad chapter in the history of our society that as of 17 January 2008, the Bush administration has had the worst record in the history of the Endangered Species Act, not having listed any species under the Act in 617 days. This set a new record, surpassing even that of the Reagan administration's 382 days of no species listed. The Bush administration has listed just 58 species compared to 522 by the Clinton administration and 234 by Bush Senior.

The Apalachicola kingsnake, living mostly on publicly owned national and state forest lands in a small region only 30 by 40 miles in size, surely would qualify for listing. My calls for requiring a permit to hunt snakes and other herps on national forest lands in Florida have gone unanswered by the U. S. Forest Service for years. Hating snakes has always been unequivocally harmful for snakes. On the other hand, under certain circumstances, loving snakes may be also bad for them.

6
BLUE INDIGO
Forest Ruler

AT 9:30 ON A LOVELY, CLEAR MORNING IN EARLY FEBRUARY, Dirk Stevenson pulls our vehicle over on the side of a lonely sand road on the Fort Stewart Military Installation about 40 miles west of Savannah, Georgia. We step out into a sandhill environment that is being restored to its natural condition. Originally, back in the 1800s, it was a longleaf pine–wiregrass–turkey oak habitat, but its majestic pines were clear-cut around the turn of the century and the land lay fallow for decades. About 1960, the site was planted to slash pine, a species that does not naturally grow here. Recently, the slash pines and unnaturally large turkey oaks were removed and longleaf pine and wiregrass were replanted.

It is crucial to try to restore the native trees and groundcover wherever possible because the native habitat best supports those animals and plants that evolved in it. In this case, those animals were components of a very rich fauna of specialists that live in, and are dependent upon, longleaf pine forests. They include such species as the red-cockaded woodpecker, southeastern pocket gopher, oldfield mouse, mole skink, Florida pine snake, southern hognose snake, gopher tortoise, flatwoods salamander, striped newt, gopher frog— and the eastern indigo snake (*Drymarchon couperi*), locally called blue indigo snake, that lives here still.

The eastern indigo snake, longest snake in the United States and Canada, is what I have come to see. Dirk, who has been monitoring this northernmost population of the species since 1997, has become one of the leading experts on its biology. Shortly, Natalie Hyslop, a University of Georgia graduate student who is also studying the eastern indigo, drives up and the three of us prepare for a snake hunt.

I have come here to learn what Dirk and Natalie can teach me about the biology of this magnificent snake. I need to round out my understanding of the snakes of the longleaf pine ecosystem. Many of them I have studied myself, but even though I have lived since 1961 in north Florida, the center of the geographic distribution of the eastern indigo, I found only one indigo snake alive there in the wild in four decades. As a result, I have virtually no first-hand knowledge of this important species. Dirk and Natalie have kindly agreed to let me tag along and ask questions during their field work.

For several decades, I have been actively studying snakes and searching for them from the Suwannee to the Escambia River, a huge area about 200 miles by 75 miles in size. Alas, the dearth of indigo snakes in the Florida panhandle is a reflection, not of my poor snake-hunting skills, but of a true dwindling of a marvelous beast that old records indicate was once locally common throughout the region. The decline of the indigo snake in the Florida panhandle is part of the reason, in 1978, the indigo snake became the first snake species listed by the US Fish and Wildlife Service as threatened. Throughout much of its natural range, from southern Mississippi to the Florida Everglades and north to the Savannah River close to where I am now standing, the indigo snake has disappeared.

Dirk and Natalie tell me that the air temperature, sunlight hitting the ground, and time of the morning are perfect for finding indigo snakes emerging from burrows of gopher tortoises (*Gopherus polyphemus*). He and Natalie know where a few adults are overwintering in gopher burrows within a mile of the car, so we set out to find some gopher burrows and see if we can capture an indigo snake or two. Operating under the proper permits, Dirk needs to find snakes as part of his long-term monitoring study and Natalie needs to recapture the fifteen snakes that still have her radiotransmitters in them. She has completed the fieldwork for her Ph.D. studies of the indigo snake and now she needs to remove the expensive transmitters so the snakes can live out their lives free of them.

We begin a meandering walk on the sparsely vegetated sandy soil, looking for the hummocks of excavated sand that mark where gopher tortoises have methodically dumped the dirt from their crescent-shaped burrows over the years. Near each burrow, Natalie has tied a twelve-inch-long piece of blue ribbon on a branch and scribbled on it in magic marker the name and date of occurrence of one of her study snakes. In the past three years, she has followed a total of 32 indigo snakes throughout the seasons. We come to a hole and she says, "Here's where 'Bug' spent the winter last year." Natalie and Dirk have given each of their study snakes special names. "This female may be in this hole now," Natalie says, "but I don't have a transmitter in her, so we won't know if she's here unless we catch her out sunning."

And, she explains, it would be useful to catch her because we could get some more growth and health data from her and, of course, learn whether she does, indeed, return to this burrow in subsequent winters. Dirk walks off alone searching for indigo snakes without transmitters to add to his population database. I tag along behind Natalie, asking questions.

Natalie turns on her receiver and immediately gets some beeps spaced a few seconds apart. "That's Norton," she exclaims and listens intently for the strongest beeps as she slowly aims the directional antenna in different directions. She locks onto the strongest signal and we make our way to a tortoise burrow where Natalie stands 20 feet back from the burrow mouth in the direction that the burrow is aligned. "He's here," she says, pointing to the ground, and the signal beeps loudest when the antenna dips to her feet.

Natalie counts the beeps over a set period of time that she clocks with her wristwatch. The beep rate of a snake's transmitter is temperature dependent, so Natalie can monitor its body temperature at the same time that she is getting its location. No big surprise: the temperature of this snake agrees with ground temperature deep inside the burrow. Natalie drops to her knees, peers into the burrow carefully, then uses a small mirror to reflect sunlight into the burrow. She finds the dry sand inside the burrow to have been smoothed by the belly of the resident indigo snake. He's been up to the opening recently, but she finds no evidence that he has emerged.

An hour or two pass quickly. Natalie and I check most of her telemetered snakes and dozens of tortoise burrows, but we find no indigo snakes out of their borrows this morning. Dirk joins us with the same story. He and Natalie are frustrated because all the weather conditions are perfect for indigo snakes to emerge for a midwinter bask in the sun. There is a good reason for basking, they think. Overwintering in damp tortoise burrows is not healthy for indigo snake skin. As winter progresses, Dirk and Natalie find that the skin of indigo snakes becomes more and more infected with bacterial lesions—soft pustules at first and encrusted ones later. The ultraviolet component of sunlight kills bacteria, as does drying of the skin.

They tell me that indigo snakes move into dry sandhills seeking gopher tortoise burrows in November and spend the four or five winter months underground, finally emerging to begin foraging in April. During this overwintering time they are not inactive, however: it is thought that mating takes place from November to January and males engage in combat behavior. Males are rarely found in burrows together, but Dirk and Natalie once saw the entwined heads and necks of two males protruding from a burrow as the snakes attempted to try to dominate each other.

We move to the last tortoise burrow in this part of Natalie's study area looking for a snake named Palmetto. They have been saving this stop for last in hopes that I might see this really large male out sunning. It is not out, but the radio signal tells us that Palmetto is, indeed, underground in this burrow. Although the burrow entrance is clogged with dry turkey oak leaves, a single, small hole in the leaves is a telltale sign that a snake has been coming and going and Palmetto was in this very same burrow last winter at this same time. Dirk's and Natalie's data reveal that each indigo snake usually returns to stay in the same tortoise burrow every winter. Such site fidelity is amazing, considering how far indigo snakes wander during the warm months. We speculate on just how a snake, with its chin only an inch off the ground, can see out of the brush and groundcover, through countless boles of trees, and over broken terrain to find its way home. Do they have a memory for landmarks? Do they find their way by smell? No one knows.

I learn that Palmetto is a very special snake. Dirk first caught him a third of a mile away in 2000 and then Palmetto became Natalie's very first radiotelemetered study snake. I detect a little nostalgia in Natalie's eyes as she stands contemplating that when she catches Palmetto and removes his transmitter she will forever lose touch with one of her favorite animals—one whose life was entwined with hers for three years. All afternoon we search for other snakes but find none, in spite of good weather. We only see what could be a few fresh crawl tracks inside the mouths of burrows and some weak tracks outside of others.

The next morning weather conditions are good again and we begin searching at about 9:30. We check fifteen or twenty burrows without finding any snakes outside of burrows, and then we approach an area where the signals indicate that two of Natalie's study snakes are close together. We come to three large tortoise burrows spaced about 75 feet apart and Natalie points to the middle one. She swings the antenna back and forth until, like a water-witching stick, the antenna gives off its strongest signal over the ground about 15 feet from the burrow entrance. This means we are standing on top of the snake, which is probably at least five feet deep underfoot. "That's Shadow," Natalie says. "Let's see where Pretty Girl is," and she turns her receiver to the unique frequency on which Pretty Girl's signal broadcasts. Immediately, the signal is loudest in exactly the same spot. "This is interesting," says Natalie, "because two adult females are in the same hole together. I haven't recorded many of these instances. More often, I find a male in the burrow with one female, but rarely two females together."

In addition, something about this burrow must be particularly attractive to indigo snakes because she has recorded four different snakes in this hole at different times, including a male and female together in her first year of the study. Whatever attracts indigo snakes to this particular one of three large, adjacent burrows is not obvious to us.

As the morning progresses, the temperature drops, clouds move in, and a cold drizzle begins to fall. Both Natalie and Dirk affirm that our chances of finding indigo snakes have declined almost to zero. They rarely ever find one out in cold, rainy weather in winter, and what's more, the wind is now gusting strongly.

We are on the verge of aborting the day's efforts, when Natalie mentions that she would like to check one more part of her study area to see if the last of her radiotelemetered animals are in burrows there. Fieldwork is so much more interesting than office work—even in the drizzling rain—so we decide to have a look. We drive onto private property adjacent to Fort Stewart and find ourselves on a sand ridge paralleling the Canoochee River. The sand ridge long ago was cleared of its longleaf pine trees and replanted to other pines, and it has lost much of its native groundcover. The tree canopy has not closed, however, and gopher tortoise burrows still are abundant.

In the cold, drizzling rain and gusty wind, Natalie alights from the vehicle, holds the antenna over her head, and turns it in different directions to listen for the signals of two of her snakes. Deep down, the three of us know that the chances of finding an indigo snake under these conditions are slim, but we persevere. When Natalie gets a directional fix, we drive closer, to a stand of replanted longleaf pines with a thick growth of grasses. Natalie swings the antenna and mentions that the signal doesn't sound normal. Normal would be regularly occurring beeps with a constant volume in a fixed direction. This signal seems to wax and wane in intensity, and seems to change direction, slightly. We walk generally towards the signal and suddenly Natalie shouts, "Here he is! He's out in the open!"

I am 30 feet away and have missed seeing the snake on the ground before Natalie picks him up. I run up and am presented with Boyl, a beautiful, six-foot-long male in prime condition. He is bright red and cream under his chin and lower lips, and I locate weak keels on the top of his middorsal scales at midbody, a sexually dimorphic trait that only the males possess. All the scales in females are smooth.

There's something magical about holding a large, black indigo snake in your hands. To begin with, their size is impressive. Dirk has weighed three large males that tipped the scales between nine and ten pounds, and up to seven and a half feet in length. Then, too, in your hands an indigo snake is not a supple constrictor but is lithe and hard-bodied like a slightly flexible steel rod, bending a few degrees from the horizontal at the ends, and in continuous motion, trying to crawl out of your grip. And the snake's defensive behaviors can be frightening to the uninitiated snake handler: when annoyed, an indigo snake breathes in noisy huffs and spreads its neck vertically to appear larger, displaying it sideways towards you.

When frightened, indigo snakes may also make biting feints, which the handler is well advised not to ignore. Indigo snakes rarely bite humans, but when they do connect, they inflict serious pain. However, if a wild indigo snake is handled gently, it soon calms down and busies itself trying to crawl out of one's hands. If continuously rough-handled, however, it employs one additional defense: it secretes a thick, disgusting-smelling, tannish liquid from glands at the base of its tail, and rubs it all over you. The function of this nasty-smelling musk is to cause the snake's antagonist to be repulsed and loose its grip so that the snake can crawl away.

Because Boyl is unexpectedly out in this inclement weather, we wonder aloud if the last male of the day, Sunrise, may also be out wandering on top of the ground. The signal is nearby, so we carry Boyl with us and close in on the second signal. Natalie invites me to walk ahead of her toward the signal so I may have the thrill of discovering an indigo snake on my own. As we approach ground zero, Natalie is again having some difficulty getting a firm location and I step up on a mound and search the ground between us. Suddenly, in the brush off to the right, I see a long, black image that is either a big stick or an indigo snake. I stare hard until I see movement. "Eureka! This is it. It is alive," I think, and then I shout my discovery at the top of my lungs and point to the brush: "There it is, I found it!"

We run around the thicket and head off the snake. I take two quick photographs but, when it reverses its direction and attempts to scoot away, I pick it up gently. This snake is also six feet long, and a bit more robust than Boyl. It has an intensely black head with much less red under its chin. I notice that Natalie has a funny look on her face and I look down at the midbody scales to find the weak keels. There aren't any. Simultaneously, Natalie and I shout "This is not Sunrise. It's a female!" Natalie hears no beeps when holding the antenna against the snake. She quickly locates Sunrise underground in a camouflaged hole nearby that is difficult to see. She and Dirk are pleased that we have found an entirely new study snake. And I am standing with the unnamed beauty in my arms and a great big grin on my face.

Natalie will take both of these fabulous snakes to Saint Catherine's Island tomorrow morning where Terry Norton, a veterinarian with the Wildlife Conservation Society who specializes in amphibian and reptile diseases, will remove the transmitter from Boyl and give our new female a health checkup. Next day Natalie will release both snakes back into the environment exactly where we found them. Eventually, one or both snakes may be recaptured by Dirk, who will continue to monitor the indigo snake population on Fort Stewart as part of his endangered species duties.

While I am photographing the new indigo snake, Natalie asks, "What shall we name her?" My suggestion, "Brucie," is quickly rejected, then I get an idea. I blurt out, "Since we caught her in inclement weather, how about 'Clementine?'" I leave Fort Stewart without knowing if my suggestion is accepted, but in my heart, this black beauty will always be "my darlin' Clementine."

My time with Dirk and Natalie has given me some valuable insights about my own study snake, the eastern diamondback rattlesnake, and I think I understand why the eastern indigo snake is a threatened species and the rattlesnake is not—yet. Both snakes are diurnal, but there is a profound difference in what each species does at night.

The eastern diamondback is a classic, sit-and-wait, ambush

predator that spends most of its year (March to November) lying on the surface of the ground, day *and* night, awaiting the passage of prey. Most of its movements are confined to daylight hours, but there is evidence that the diamondback occasionally envenomates, tracks, and ingests prey over short distances at night. In contrast, the indigo snake usually retires underground at night at all times of the year, often in the burrow of a gopher tortoise. In some parts of peninsular Florida where tortoise burrows are in short supply, a roothole, crabhole, armadillo burrow, or other underground refuge is used. Physiological evidence suggests that indigo snakes are very sensitive to dehydration, so an overnight rest in humid soil probably assists indigo snakes in maintaining their body moisture.

Spending nights underground may provide indigo snakes another benefit that is not necessary for rattlesnakes: avoiding predation. Heat-sensitive pits enable rattlesnakes to detect warm-blooded predators at night, and their fang-and-venom apparatus can be used as a powerful defense. The eastern indigo snake, on the other hand, is neither so capable of perceiving an attacker at night nor able to defend itself with such a formidable weapon.

After talking with Dirk and Natalie, I get the strong feeling that differences in the spatial biology of the eastern indigo snake and eastern diamondback may explain why one is a threatened species and the other is not. For starters, the eastern indigo snake has the largest annual range documented for any North American snake. In logged-over areas and hardwood hammocks in Levy County, Florida, Paul Moler found that in warm months adult males utilized activity areas of 47 to 510 acres. In central Florida sandhill habitat, Becky Smith and others found over a five-year period that males utilized upwards of 750 acres and females up to 375 acres. And finally, in Natalie Hyslop's northernmost population at Fort Stewart, Georgia, some males had an annual range of approximately 1,000 acres and some individuals made occasional long-distance moves of between one and three miles.

The eastern diamondback, on the other hand, can maintain a viable population in areas as small as 30 acres. One such breeding population that I studied on the tip of Alligator Peninsula in Franklin County, Florida, consisted of stunted animals because of a limited food supply. Probably every rattlesnake there had the same annual range over every square inch of the 30-acre site. When food is plentiful, the eastern diamondback can maintain dense populations of normal-sized animals. Ross Allen found 281 diamondbacks on Blount Island near the mouth of the St. Johns River in Florida. These snakes were not stunted and yet had only 600 acres of suitable habitat in which to survive; that's a remarkably high density of about one snake per two acres. In shortleaf/loblolly pine oldfield successional habitat (which has replaced longleaf pine forest on clayhills throughout most of the range of the eastern diamondback) in Leon County, Florida, I found the largest annual ranges for males to run about 500 acres and for females about 200 acres. I also learned that some annual ranges overlapped almost completely. And on Tall Timbers Research Station north of Tallahassee, Florida, over an eight-year period, I marked and released 124 diamondbacks on about 1200 acres. No doubt there were more snakes that I didn't find, but if half of these were alive at any given time, the density would have been about one snake per 20 acres. Walter Timmerman calculated annual ranges in native sandhill habitat in north central Florida to be about 208 acres for males and 115 acres for females—at an estimated density of about one snake per 12.5 acres. For the eastern diamondback, therefore, home ranges and density can vary substantially according to food supply and habitat patch size, but this may not be the case for the eastern indigo snake.

Diet may be the major reason why the eastern indigo snake cannot maintain high densities in small areas, except while overwintering. The eastern diamondback is a specialist that feeds exclusively on warm-blooded prey. It does not eat snakes and has never been implicated in cannibalism of its own young. The eastern indigo snake, on the other hand, eats anything that it can overpower, including cold-blooded and warm-blooded vertebrates. The list of recorded prey includes beetles, slugs, frogs, rats, birds, lizards, small turtles (including the gopher tortoise), and snakes of all kinds, including coral snakes, pygmy rattlesnakes, timber rattlesnakes, and especially eastern diamondbacks. Larger individuals also are known to cannibalize smaller individuals and their own young, which is probably why young indigo snakes less than about four feet long are rarely, if ever, found in burrows or habitats where adults are present. Cannibalism of juveniles and agonistic behaviors among adults may combine to keep indigo snake densities from ever reaching the high levels found in some eastern diamondback rattlesnake populations.

It is probably because indigo snake populations can never be so dense nor home ranges so small as in the eastern diamondback that the eastern indigo snake is rare or absent on Atlantic and Gulf coastal barrier islands. The eastern diamondback occupies at least 61 barrier islands from Hatteras Island in North Carolina south to Key West in Florida, and west to Dauphin Island in Mobile Bay, but the eastern indigo snake has been recorded on only four or five of the largest barrier islands in Florida, such as the 140,000-acre Merritt Island off the east coast of Florida, and seven of the Florida Keys, which are not barrier islands but highland remnants that were once connected to the Florida peninsula. Moreover, attempts to introduce the eastern indigo snake onto the relatively large (12,358 acres) St. Vincent Island in the Gulf of Mexico have failed. The species was never recorded as naturally occurring on St. Vincent Island and probably is unable to sustain a population there. Further attempts at introducing the species on St. Vincent Island should not be undertaken. Its presence there would be as alien as if it were Australia's brown tree snake.

If we assume that the average eastern indigo snake population tolerates a density of only five adults per 500 acres, then at least 5,000 acres are required to maintain the minimum viable population of 50 individuals, 25 females and 25 males. In comparison, under rare and special circumstances, the eastern diamondback rattlesnake can maintain a minimum viable population of about 50 snakes on an area as small as 30 acres (Alligator Peninsula), although stunted by poor food supply. This equates to an unusually high density of about two snakes per acre. On another island where food supply was dense, predators were absent, and adult size was not attenuated (Blount Island), a density of about one snake per two acres was attained. The

600 acres of suitable habitat on Blount Island, therefore, sustained more than five minimum viable populations of the eastern diamondback.

With small population densities and large home ranges, the eastern indigo snake is vulnerable to mortality from habitat fragmentation by humans. Very few prime habitat patches of more than 5,000 acres remain as private lands throughout the range of the indigo snake. Good habitat is almost all broken up by roads and highways that inflict a great deal of mortality on the indigo snake. Their large size, black color, and high mobility also make indigo snakes easier to see than the cryptic eastern diamondback, which tends to lie still and rely on its camouflage to go undetected. These characteristics, together with the snake's great appeal as a pet, are all reasons that the eastern indigo snake has declined.

The eastern indigo snake is one of a complex of races or species that range widely throughout Central and South America. Genetic studies are required to work out the exact relationships of all the forms in the genus *Drymarchon*, but the closest relative of the eastern indigo snake is thought to be the Texas indigo snake, which occurs on the other side of a 500-mile-wide gap to the southwest. One could argue that indigo snakes are essentially tropical snakes and that is why the eastern indigo is vulnerable to dehydration. Its need to retire to humid burrows of the gopher tortoise in winter and at night may explain why, in Georgia and north Florida, its association with the gopher tortoise is so strong. The climate of the Florida peninsula becomes warmer and more humid—almost tropical—towards its southern end, and in southern Florida the eastern indigo snake is not so exclusively linked with the gopher tortoise. There it is found along canals, streams, marshes, hardwood hammocks, and even in mangrove thickets.

Sadly, along with so many other vertebrate animals whose principal natural habitat was the longleaf pine ecosystem, the eastern indigo snake is probably well on its way to extinction. This is true because so many of the natural habitats in which indigo snakes evolved, and to which they are best adapted, have already disappeared or are still declining. Longleaf pine ecosystems that once covered sixty percent of the landscape of the Coastal Plain are now reduced to less than two percent of their original extent. The gopher tortoise is declining because its sandhills habitat is prime real estate for development. Wetlands that are important foraging habitats for the eastern indigo snake have declined by at least fifty percent because of drainage and filling to make way for development projects or have become polluted from stormwater runoff, sedimentation, logging, and impoundment. What is left as suitable habitat is becoming ever more fragmented into acreages too small to support viable populations, or too criss-crossed by roads to allow individuals to roam freely and safely.

The father of American herpetology, James Edward Holbrook, must have been as impressed with an indigo snake in 1842 as I was when holding Clementine in 2005. Holbrook was the first scientist to apply a scientific name to the eastern indigo snake. He named it in honor of J. H. Couper, a friend and colleague who brought Holbrook the first specimen from the dry pine hills south of the Altamaha River in Wayne County, Georgia. The genus name was coined a year later by Austrian herpetologist Leopold Fitzinger. *Drymarchon* comes from the Greek words *drymos*, meaning forest, and *archon*, meaning ruler. Unfortunately, the forests this ruler needs are declining in quantity, quality, and patch size. Not only the indigo snake but also other animals that it depends upon for shelter, the gopher tortoise, and for food—frogs and snakes—are declining as well.

As the human population continues to burgeon in Florida and Georgia, indigo snake populations will disappear from private lands and remain only on publicly owned lands. In Georgia, only two publicly owned lands are likely to sustain viable populations: Fort Stewart and the Okefenokee National Wildlife Refuge. The last population of any consequence in the Florida panhandle is on the 464,000-acre Eglin Air Force Base, but the gopher tortoise is not common there, nor is the indigo snake. In peninsular Florida, publicly owned lands that may support indigo snake populations are Big Cypress Preserve, Everglades National Park, Merritt Island National Wildlife Refuge, Ocala National Forest, Withlacoochee State Forest, and several large state parks.

Even on publicly owned lands, however, native animals are not necessarily secure. Native vegetation required by the indigo snake needs frequent fire, but natural, lightning-ignited fires are normally extinguished and prescribed burning is never conducted on the frequency and rarely in the season needed to restore and maintain native vegetation in its optimal condition. Also, publicly owned lands were mostly created for purposes other than preserving native animals and plants, and they are subject to the vicissitudes of changing politics.

I consider myself very fortunate to have been a guest in the field with Dirk, Natalie, and the eastern indigo snakes they have been studying. It bothers me that the many millions of people in Florida and Georgia won't have the thrilling opportunity I had to see and hold a splendid snake like Clementine, even now while some populations still remain, because the species is already federally threatened. There is little chance, therefore, that people can have an experience with an indigo snake that might change the public's disaffection with snakes in general. I can only hope, for the sake of the eastern indigo snake, that populations on publicly owned lands will survive into the far future and that the minority of people who appreciate snakes might have some opportunities to see them in the wild.

7
PHAEOGNATHUS
Secrets in the Red Hills

IT IS A PITCH-BLACK, MOONLESS NIGHT. I FORCE MY BODY
through a roadside tangle of brush, and follow my flashlight over
undulating ground. The light weaves and dodges among the boles of
lofty magnolias, beeches, tuliptrees, laurel oaks, hickories, and loblolly
pines. I come to a steep slope, follow its toe for a short distance, then
turn into a ravine where a tiny brook tumbles and splashes downhill
over logs, roots, and some light gray, soft, siltstone boulders. Brown,
tan, and yellowish leaves carpet the steep ravine sidewalls ten feet
on either side of me. Tufts of moss form islands of green in the sea of
brown leaf litter. In places, bare, light gray soil is exposed, especially
where slopes are steepest. It's the bare soil that I begin to search,
intently.

My eyes focus on a world of tiny creatures. The six-inch circle
of my flashlight beam reveals a long-legged camel cricket hanging
upside down under an exposed root. A black ground beetle scurries for
cover under a leathery magnolia leaf. An orange centipede nervously
undulates into view, its legs rippling along its sides like waves on water.
Mesmerized by the miniature dramas I see in the circle of bright light,
I forget that I am part of the big, black void surrounding me at the
larger scale of my body.

Suddenly, I am startled half out of my wits by the loud crashing of cloven feet in dry, crackly leaf litter. I rise to my full height, yell loudly in the deepest, most threatening voice I can muster, and toss sticks and clay chunks in the direction of a family of feral hogs, making them run away amidst much snorting and grunting. After my heart stops pounding and I regain my composure, I resume my search of the ravine sidewalls.

Looking ahead about 30 feet, I spot the bright, twinkling eyeshine of what I believe is a spider. Normally, when I approach this kind of eyeshine, I find that the jewel-like reflections belong to one of many species of terrestrial wolf spiders. This time, I discover a rarity—a primitive trap-door spider sitting at the mouth of its burrow with trap door held open. This is a sight worthy of a photograph, but before I can get set up, the spider is spooked by my presence and slams shut her door. I look away for a second, and when I look back, I find that the top of the door is so well camouflaged that I can't locate it again.

I look up the ravine valley searching for more eyeshines. The retinas of vertebrate animals reflect light almost straight back along the incident beam, so the best method of seeing the reflected eyeshine is to place your flashlight as close to your own eyes as possible and look along the beam. The angle of reflection widens at close range, so one is more likely to see eyeshines at a distance rather than up close.

Next I see the dull, white reflection of a pair of amphibian eyes, which is my real purpose for coming to this remote ravine tonight. I steal forward, trying not to frighten the owner, and find a beautiful bronze frog (*Rana clamitans*) lurking on the steep bank waiting to snap up passing insects. I photograph the frog, but it is not the object of my visit here.

I ease along quietly, taking small steps and scrutinizing the ravine slopes for tiny animal life. I come to a fork in the ravine, stop, and search the sidewalls carefully. Finally, out of the corner of my eye, I find my prize. A head about the size of my thumb protrudes from under an exposed root on a nearly vertical slope. Then I see another head, about three feet above the first one, just inside a tiny tunnel in the bank, peering out but not exposed.

I don't wish to disturb the silence of the night, but in my heart I want to yell, "Hooray!" My prize is the Alabama red hills salamander, *Phaeognathus hubrichti.* It is a member of the world's largest family of salamanders, the lungless Plethodontidae, and it is the longest plethodontid in the United States and Canada (up to ten inches long). Thirty years ago, before the red hills salamander was federally listed as a threatened species, I found my first phaeogs, as I call them, but in those days I neglected to take any photographs. Since dusky salamanders of the subfamily Desmognathinae—to which the red hills salamander belongs—have been one of my lifelong research interests, it is important that I obtain images of this rare species.

The first individual, a large male, backs into its burrow and disappears. I never see him again all night. The second salamander freezes in my bright light. I take a small twig and "twiddle" the tip of it on the slope about two inches in front of the salamander's snout, crudely simulating the movements of a small creature. Immediately she perks up and creeps forward to investigate. At first her head comes only an inch out of the burrow and then she quickly backs into safety. She repeats this several times, but with patience and repeated wriggling of my fake insect, I get her to come forward almost the full length of her body. She is a beautiful, elongate, dark purplish-brown salamander, almost the maximum ten inches long. I know she is a female because, through the sides of her body, I can see enlarged white eggs that indicate she will soon be a mother.

All night I enjoy photographing phaeogs and other creatures in this and nearby lovely ravines. I find three of the seven species of trap-door spiders that live here, the bigger species of which probably prey on little phaeogs. Spiders of many kinds abound here, including large wolf spiders that probably also prey on baby salamanders. No doubt, though, adult salamanders dine on spiders. I spy the legs of a large centipede rippling along the sides of its blue body. Its venomous fangs are poised alongside its head, ready to clamp down on some unsuspecting, soft-bodied invertebrate.

Then I find a really scary monster. Through the lens of my camera I see the beady, red, glowing eyes of a large crayfish sitting in the mouth of its vertical burrow in the bank. I imagine the terror of being grabbed and crunched in its massive claws, and then dragged down the dark burrow to be devoured, piecemeal, deep in its underground chamber of horrors. Before I walk out of the ravine, I look up at the forest to bring myself back into the realm of my own much safer existence, and leave behind me the many dangers of being small.

Serendipity is well known to operate in the making of scientific discoveries. Lighting problems ruined all the photographs I took that night. And so, a month later, I return to the south Alabama ravine. Neither on the earlier trip nor on this one was I thinking about doing research on the biology of the red hills salamander, but I am keenly aware that many aspects of the life history and ecology of this unique, burrowing species are unknown. I find the gravid female again, peering out of the same burrow. She lurches out of it to eat my fake twig insect and I can see that she is plumper than before. She quickly habituates to my flashlight and camera flashes, showing an amazing lack of fear. Then an idea comes to me. If she stays in this burrow and lays her eggs in it, maybe I can dig them out and make a contribution to science, since we know nothing about the eggs, hatchlings, larvae, or metamorphs of this species.

That night I drive back to my home base in Tallahassee with great excitement. Other biologists, years before, excavated many burrows but found none of the young life stages. Next morning, I apply to the US Fish and Wildlife Service for a permit to excavate the female and study her eggs if I find them. On my next visit, when she is not present at her burrow mouth, my excitement goes off the scale in anticipation of finding her and her eggs. I excavate the bank slowly and carefully, but I am horrified when I find the still-gravid female looped in angular cracks in the siltstone about 12 inches straight back from the mouth of her burrow. I may have ruined her habitat. She now is extremely plump and I can easily count nine large ova visible through her abdominal wall. I place her in the cracks in which I found her, and carefully refill the cavity with siltstone and dirt. I worry that the trauma of excavating her, plus the destruction of the burrow that she has so faithfully used, will interrupt my plans for discovering her and her eggs.

I wait five weeks and once again carefully dig into the bank. This time I am not so expectant because I imagine that she has moved far underground away from the site where I destroyed her old burrow. Voila! My surprise is all the sweeter when I find her and a clutch of six large eggs containing well-developed embryos. She only moved into undisturbed sediments about ten inches to the right of where I found her five weeks ago, and is located at about the same distance deep in the ravine sidewall. I find two large carabid beetles in the cracks near her and surmise that they may have eaten the three missing eggs. I marvel at my good luck. Not only did I find her and discover her eggs, but it is ironic that had my first photographs turned out OK, I would not have returned to the ravine to get replacement photos, and the idea that I might find eggs would not have occurred to me.

The red hills salamander lives in a few ravines in one small area far away from the center of diversity of the plethodontid salamanders in the southern Appalachian Mountains. That it occurs so disjunctly in southern Alabama is explained by the curious siltstone and claystone boulders in the stream bottoms. The boulders are hard, but I can scratch them with my fingernail. They have eroded out of the steep ravine sidewalls that are made up of the Tallahatta and Hatchetigbee formations, ancient marine deposits of diatomites and siliceous mudstones. These are moderately to extremely hard clays that typically display blocky, conchoidal fracturing, which creates a labyrinth of subterranean cracks and fissures. These two formations are found only in a narrow east-west band across the southern one-third of Alabama. It's among these cracks and fissures, between the blocks of the mudstones, that the red hills salamander lives out its life.

Laid down in waters of the middle Eocene ocean some 40 to 50 million years ago, these mudstone ravines have been eroded by rainwater ever since the ocean receded from central Alabama. Today, these ravines are part of a highly relieved landform with elevations up to 600 feet called the Alabama Red Hills physiographic region. The red hills salamander probably evolved in the ravines during dry times when little water flowed in the streams. Since water is needed for larval development, the ancestral salamander sought refuge from the aridity by living in the cracks in the mudstones. There it became elongated by the addition of seven extra trunk vertebrae and evolving stubby legs and a long, prehensile tail.

The tail with its strong muscles leverages phaeogs back into their burrows. An early collecting technique was to tempt a salamander to swallow a cricket tethered on a fishhook at the end of fine monofilament fishing line. The salamander, with its prehensile tail, is so strong, however, that even if hooked, it can't be pulled from its burrow. One has to tie off the line and dig out the salamander. This technique destroys the burrow and, of course, injures the salamander.

Becoming free of larval life is one of the ways amphibians adapt to aridity. Many plethodontid salamanders and frogs have achieved this by hatching as wholly metamorphosed individuals in a process called direct development. Whatever larval morphology they pass through takes place in the egg during embryonic life. Larvae of the red hills salamander have never been found, so it was long suspected that the species might have direct development. My permit enabled me to take the eggs to my laboratory and observe what happens in the early life history of the species.

The hatchlings did possess external gills, but they were resorbed within ten days and the young were completely metamorphosed at that time. This is verification, then, that the red hills salamander undergoes direct development. We still don't know how long it takes hatchlings to grow to sexual maturity, but it has been estimated at six years. Apparently, individuals can live very long lives. A female alive in 2003 in the Cincinnati Zoo was a full-grown adult when collected in 1978, so she had reached at least 30 years of age. From preserved museum specimens we know that a female lays only four to nine eggs, so the reproductive output is low. This is not surprising in a long-lived creature in which adult mortality probably is also low.

Red hills salamanders are rarely found outside their burrows. The main activity of these animals is sitting in the burrow mouth awaiting passing prey. That makes it all the more improbable that, in 1960, malacologist Leslie Hubricht found a red hills salamander, the first one reported, when he stopped his auto by an interesting woodland looking for land snails. He picked up a handful of magnolia leaves and discovered the strange-looking salamander underneath. Hubricht's friend, Richard Highton of the University of Maryland, formally named the species and erected a new genus for it, thus sparking a stampede of herpetologists seeking to learn more about the biology of this strange creature, just new to science.

Three years and many field trips passed before another specimen was found. Then a field team from Ohio State University discovered that the red hills salamander lived in burrows and could be found only late at night. In hundreds of man-hours afield since then, only three or four other instances have been recorded of red hills salamanders out of their burrows. The species is so restricted in its geographical range, and so secretive, that had Hubricht not found that first one, it probably would still be unknown today. It is the only terrestrial vertebrate species found exclusively in Alabama. In 2000, the state legislature formally designated the red hills salamander as the State Amphibian of Alabama.

Lots of other animals live in the cracks and fissures of the Alabama Red Hills mudstones. Other plethodontid salamanders, such as the long-tailed and slimy salamanders, occasionally are seen peering out of similar burrow mouths. Insects and other invertebrates crawl into the burrows and become easy fare for salamanders. I once held an earthworm by one end and dangled the other into the burrow mouth of a phaeog with the result that the worm was grabbed and yanked from my fingers. The red hills salamander's complete diet consists of beetles, ants, cockroaches, bugs, spiders, millipedes, earthworms, and, ironically, the animals that led to the discovery of the red hills salamander—land snails. One study found that 20 percent of the salamander's diet consisted of tiny snails that live in the leaf litter of ravine slopes, the very snails in the very litter that Leslie Hubricht had a hunch might prove interesting.

Seven months after releasing the hatchlings on the slope where their mother still lives, I return to take some more pictures. There, just two feet from where I found the eggs, I spot one of the babies. Having survived a cold winter, it is peeking out of its own tiny burrow and is not much larger than when I released it. In contrast to several shy adults that I spend two hours trying to photograph, it remains visible the whole time, very much as its mother had done. Another idea creeps into my mind. Dare I hope to follow its growth over several years? Truth be told, what I really want is an excuse to return to these hidden ravines and spend some more time enjoying their wondrous, miniature secrets.

You might think that being squirreled away in deep ravines in rural Alabama is a safe way to avoid the impacts of modern man. Not so. Discovered only in 1960, the red hills salamander was listed by the US Fish and Wildlife Service as threatened just sixteen years later in 1976. Unfortunately, in the quarter century that has passed since then, the status of the red hills salamander remains unimproved.

Since World War II, the native environments of the South have undergone wholesale transformation. Virginal native forests of longleaf pine are now replaced with closely planted slash and loblolly pines, and old-growth hardwood forests, such as those on red hills slopes, have been clearcut for commercial profits. In 1976 the amount of suitable red hills salamander habitat remaining was estimated at 54,900 acres, but 3,000 of these acres were severely degraded by selective timber cutting. Moreover, at least 3,670 acres of forest that almost certainly supported salamander populations had been destroyed in the previous decade. I don't know how much has been lost since then.

Humidity is believed to be an important factor in local survival because, in clearcut habitats where the red hills salamander once was common, no salamanders are found. Logging the steep slopes favored by the salamander removes the canopy that holds humidity in the ravines, and full sunlight on the forest floor dries out the soil.

Almost always, the highest burrow densities are found on slopes steeper than about 30 degrees, and usually in old-growth forests. As much as 40 percent of the known habitat is owned or leased by commercial timber companies, many of which have entered into agreements with the US Fish and Wildlife Service that, theoretically, benefit the salamander as well as the private landowner. The landowner develops a Habitat Conservation Plan in which he agrees that what are believed to be optimum habitats (slopes of greater than 20 to 30 degrees) will be completely protected. An Incidental Take Permit may be issued by the US Fish and Wildlife Service for selective cutting on such slopes and clearcut logging or any type of activity on marginal habitats of less than 20 degree slopes. What is not known, however, is whether other ecological factors besides burrow density are important variables that make up optimal habitat. The red hills salamander is like so many of the earth's other small, cold-blooded animals: much remains to be learned about them.

The red hills salamander is not a snake and poses no threats to human life or limb. It lives on steep slopes in the far south of rural Alabama on less than 50,000 acres of non-developable land. And yet, even with federal protection under the Endangered Species Act, it has declined. However, were it not for its protection under the Endangered Species Act, I have no doubt that it would be nearly extinct by now, steep slopes notwithstanding. To log the relatively valueless hardwood timber off these slopes and replant them to pine plantations would eliminate not just the red hills salamander, but a wealth of other small and amazing creatures, plant and animal, that make these ravine habitats so wonderful. If we save the red hills salamander now, the beauty of its fragile habitats will be available for people to enjoy in the future. The rare beech-magnolia forests of the South are worth a visit, night or day. It's up to naturalists like me, however, to teach people to enjoy the ambience of a night-time walk in such ravines, and that a world of special beauty awaits anyone interested in exploring the unfamiliar.

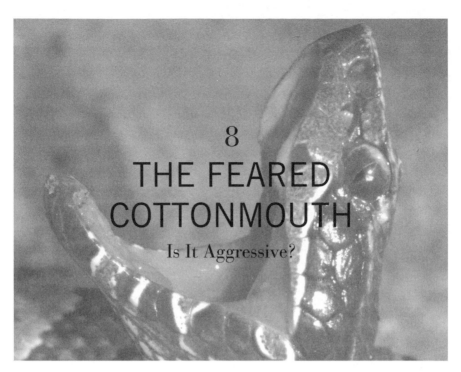

8

THE FEARED COTTONMOUTH

Is It Aggressive?

FOR FORTY YEARS I HAVE ASKED THE QUESTION OF Southerners, "Which snake do you fear most?" Farmers, hunters, fishermen, and just about everybody who lives in the southeastern Unites States nearly always respond vigorously, "The cottonmouth." Until recently, the answer has always puzzled me because the eastern diamondback and timber rattlesnakes possess much more dangerously toxic venom by far—venom that does, in fact, kill people. Cottonmouth bites, while damaging to tissues, almost never kill anybody. Then, when I ask people why they fear the cottonmouth so, they almost unanimously answer, "Because it is aggressive," or, "It chases you."

I have encountered the cottonmouth (also called water moccasin, *Agkistrodon piscivorus*) widely throughout its range in the southeastern states. I have implanted radio transmitters in cottonmouth stomachs and followed snakes all year round. David Cook, my colleague and one-time graduate student, had 335 encounters with cottonmouths in 500 man-hours of field work on the same research tract where I was following cottonmouths by means of radiotelemetry. In hundreds of encounters over the years, neither of us ever experienced any behavior that was overtly aggressive.

It's true that the cottonmouth will strike at you suddenly from a coiled position. This serves to keep you at a distance that is safe for the cottonmouth, and I suppose one could call this aggressive behavior. But when people tell me they have been chased by a cottonmouth, I listen carefully, then write it off as fiction. Wives' tales are so common in snake lore that it is wise to be ultraconservative in accepting secondhand stories. On principle, "I have to see it to believe it."

The cottonmouth has a repertoire of defensive behaviors that helps it avoid injury or death from would-be attackers. Envenomation is the ultimate penalty of getting too close to a cottonmouth, but I wouldn't call biting or striking to fend off an attacker aggressive behavior. Neither would I call aggression the mouth-gaping behavior that gives the cottonmouth its name. A cottonmouth that is uncomfortable with the proximity of a threatening human or other animal will throw its head back and open its mouth, baring the white lining of its buccal cavity. (A white lining is common to most snakes, but is rarely seen in any but the mouth-gaping cottonmouth.) Many animals, especially large ungulates, need this visual cue to pinpoint the location of the cottonmouth and thus avoid stepping on it.

Likewise, I wouldn't call it aggression when a cornered cottonmouth vibrates its tail. This nervous reaction simply serves to give auditory notice of the snake's presence. Cottonmouths also are known to flatten their bodies to give the impression that they are larger than they really are. This is a standard snake bluff, common among harmless as well as venomous species, but it is not aggression.

Considering that I have many years of experience, that no scientific literature documents overt cottonmouth aggression, and that I have heard no credible accounts of being chased by a cottonmouth from my herpetologist colleagues, I lived for years confident in my own dogma that cottonmouths never chase people.

Wrong! One warm May afternoon I had to eat my words. At 6 P.M. while leading a field class of fifteen people down a wide, sandy road east of Sumatra, Florida, I spotted a three-and-a-half-foot-long female cottonmouth stretched out in the characteristic frozen posture of a snake caught in the open. Earlier in the day I told the class, "The cottonmouth does *not* chase people." We all piled out of the van and freaked the poor snake into coiling up. When I approached closely, it struck suddenly and made me and my entourage jump back, just as the behavior is designed to do. Frightened, the dark brown cottonmouth began vibrating its tail. It coiled up, flattened its body, threw its head back, and opened its mouth to display the white lining. I was standing between the cottonmouth and the swamp from which it had come. The van and the students formed a crowd on the other side of the snake blocking that side of the road.

Then an amazing thing happened. The cottonmouth raised the forward one-third of its body off the ground and crawled as fast as it could in this posture right at me! I was forced to back up at least ten feet. I noticed that the neck and head were tilted a little sideways toward me and flattened, cobralike, to appear larger. I shouted at the students, "Look, the cottonmouth is charging me! Take a picture, take a picture." I had only a few furious moments to observe the new behavior, to eat crow for all those people whose own similar observations I had pooh-poohed, and to relish my good fortune—for in the next few seconds I made a momentous discovery. While the cottonmouth was "chasing" me, I stepped to one side, away from the trajectory the snake seemed to be taking, and noticed that the snake did not turn and follow me. It simply kept up its "cobra crawl" in the direction it had been going, which was the shortest distance necessary for it to reach safety. This observation is quite telling. The cottonmouth was using bluffing behavior to make safe passage to where it wanted to go. The snake clearly was not intent on making me a target of its movement. In this respect I was not truly chased, although at the time I sure felt like it. I just happened to be the live impediment that needed to be frightened sufficiently to allow the snake to make good its escape.

I believe the "cobra crawling" behavior I saw in the cottonmouth was bluffing behavior, although I did not stand my ground to see what would happen when it reached me. Webster defines aggression as "a forceful action or procedure, especially when intended to dominate or master"; and "hostile, injurious, or destructive behavior, especially when caused by frustration." On the first count, I readily admit that I was mastered by forceful action. The cottonmouth, therefore, could be considered aggressive by this definition. On the second count, the answer depends, I suppose, upon what the cottonmouth would do if the target of its bluff failed to move. I determined to find out.

Over the next several summers my wife and I stimulated more than twenty other cottonmouths to display this same behavior, and we filmed it. We discovered that some other snakes besides the cottonmouth do the same thing. The behavior is a type of bluff, designed to ward off dangerous predators while enabling the snake to escape. I call the behavior, "shammed aggression during blocked flight."

Our experimental design was as follows. When we found a wild snake moving across a road, I jumped out of the vehicle and ran to block its movement by standing in front of the snake. Usually, a cottonmouth would coil up, vibrate its tail, flatten its body, and open its mouth to display the white lining. Some cottonmouths remained in this posture for 10 to 20 minutes, but others broke into shammed aggression sooner. I discovered that if I used a snake hook or a handy stick to flip the coiled snake on its back, it straightened out when it righted itself, and as often as not, began to flee. It was during these attempts to escape to the safety of the road shoulder that each snake rose up like a cobra, spread its jaws, sometimes struck viciously, and advanced directly towards me. Of course, I reacted just as any dog, raccoon, or other snake predator would do: I backed up rapidly or jumped to the side to get out of the way of the snake. If I backed up in front of the snake, it continued advancing and bluffing; if I jumped to one side, it paid me no more attention. In no instance when I stepped aside, did any of the fleeing cottonmouths change direction and move toward me. They simply continued straight in their intended direction. Even more intriguing is what they did if I did not move aside. In twelve episodes, the snakes simply crawled over my boot or between my legs. None of the snakes attempted to bite me.

When I stood my ground in front of an advancing snake, I did not move my legs. Possibly, had I been stamping my feet or walking in place, the frightened snakes might have tried to bite me. Furthermore, had I been bare-legged, the heat from my legs might have triggered a bite. But I wasn't up to that experiment.

I now understand why the cottonmouth is so feared. Any person, not realizing he is standing in the cottonmouth's path to safety, would interpret the snake's aggressive bluffing as an attack. This conclusion would be especially likely if the person were backing up and the snake continued advancing. Who would believe that he was not being chased by the snake? And imagine the panic one would feel in a canoe with a cottonmouth doing the upright cobra-crawl as it advanced, determined to escape out the end of the boat where you were sitting?

The cottonmouth is arguably the most successful snake in the North America. It has a huge range with three recognized geographic races. The eastern race extends from Virginia to central Georgia. The Florida race occurs in Florida and south Georgia. The western race, with the largest distribution, ranges from the Florida panhandle to central Texas and north to the southern parts of Indiana, Illinois, and Missouri. Adults and juveniles of the western race are smaller and much darker than the other two races, the markings of the head are less distinct, and the crown and snout are darker brown or black. Intergradation is common in zones of contact. The cottonmouth can be distinguished from the many water snakes that superficially resemble it by facial pits, a single anal plate, and a single row of scales under most of its tail.

The young are strongly patterned with dark brown crossbands on a paler brown color, but with age the pattern usually fades so that the adults are uniformly olive or dark brown to almost black. Some hint of the juvenile pattern usually remains on adults, however. The young have yellowish or greenish tail tips that are used to lure frogs and lizards, but this, too, fades with age. Probably the best character to distinguish the cottonmouth from its cousin, the copperhead, is a bold, chocolate, raccoon mask through the eye.

A large adult cottonmouth is impressive in size. It is a stout-bodied snake with a head considerably wider than the neck. The eastern and

Florida races attain maximum lengths of six feet, with the greatest known length at 74.5 inches. One 72-inch cottonmouth weighed ten pounds, two ounces and was as large in diameter as a man's arm.

It is the only semi-aquatic member of the genus *Agkistrodon* (which totals ten species: three in North America and the rest in eastern Asia). Cottonmouths prefer aquatic and wetland habitats such as swamps, vegetated margins of lakes and ponds, and river floodplains, although during my radiotelemetry work I found them living on land up to a mile from water. The preferred habitat is swamps, fresh- and brackish-water marshes, watercourses, bayous, shores of lakes and ponds, and a wide variety of other wetland habitats, including small, rocky-bottomed, clear streams in Arkansas and Missouri.

The cottonmouth has crossed salt water to some barrier islands off the Gulf and Atlantic seashores. On barrier islands it can be abundant in dune and beach areas, in pine woods, and around fresh and salt water, and it is often found in supratidal marshes. It can live without a constant source of fresh water: a population on Seahorse Key in the Gulf of Mexico off the mouth of the Suwannee River had no access to standing freshwater but these snakes drank raindrops off vegetation and from their own skin during a rain. For food, snakes ate refuse falling from nests of a heron rookery. Some individuals were congenitally blind, but survived to adulthood because of the abundance of easy food under the rookery and the absence of predators. On islands where the eastern diamondback rattlesnake flourishes, however, one rarely finds the cottonmouth.

Sexual activity begins in the spring when males search for females, but mating may take place at any time of the year. In 1939 the famous Florida herpetologist, Archie Carr, and his wife, Marjorie, published what they thought was the first record of breeding behavior in the cottonmouth, only to find out later that what they had witnessed was combat behavior between males. The combat begins with one snake crawling over the other. Then they rear into the air, weaving and twisting themselves around each other. They press themselves together so hard that when they slip, their bodies are flung apart. This aerial twisting and twining may go on for an hour or more. Eventually, one snake considers itself dominated by the other and crawls off with the dominant male in pursuit.

Females reach maturity at three years of age and have clutches of six to eight live young in August and September, and every two years thereafter. There is some evidence that adult females in warmer parts of their range might give birth annually. Size at birth ranges from eight to 14 inches. Young snakes shed their skin for the first time about ten days after birth.

The cottonmouth's great success is largely due to its unrestricted diet of animal food, and occasionally carrion. Young snakes eat frogs and sometimes insects and other invertebrates. Later, they eat fish and a plethora of vertebrate animals. Among recorded species are catfishes, sunfishes, pickerel, bullfrogs, treefrogs, spadefoot toads, salamanders, small turtles, all kinds of watersnakes including other cottonmouths (cannibalism), lizards, birds and bird eggs, shrews, moles, mice, rats, squirrels, and rabbits. In one instance, a cottonmouth regurgitated a canebrake rattlesnake with seven rattles. Given a choice, however, fishes are the preferred food. Many a hapless fisherman has discovered, dangling from his fish stringer, a cottonmouth that had swallowed one of the fishes hooked there.

Cottonmouths are preyed upon by hawks, owls, and large wading birds such as herons, egrets, and ibises. Snapping turtles, alligators, and snake-eating snakes are also their enemies. One observer saw a 42-inch common kingsnake kill and eat a 34-inch-long cottonmouth. The cottonmouth exhibits a "body bridging" defense against kingsnakes, which consists of arching the back and flapping the kingsnake with a loop of its body. Obviously this behavior is not 100 percent successful.

Another defensive behavior is to eject a pungent musk in thin jets up to five feet from a pair of glands at the base of the tail. Any large animal that stepped on a cottonmouth and got bitten and sprayed with musk would no doubt avoid that smell in the future. The repulsive odor has been likened to rancid peanuts. I believe that the musk is only released when the snake is physically attacked, stepped on, or is greatly frightened. Some claim they can smell a cottonmouth in the field, but every time I have experienced such an odor out of doors, I was unable to find a cottonmouth nearby. I believe similar odors are produced by certain plants when crushed underfoot. Snakes, generally, cannot afford to be smelly because their predators would have an easy time tracking and finding them. Cottonmouths that I have kept in cages indoors for years do not produce smelly odors unless frightened or roughly handled.

The cottonmouth rests, crawls, and swims with its head raised at a 45-degree angle. It has good vision and can detect movement at least 50 feet away. When swimming along the water's surface, it holds its head high, but when frightened, it dives into the water and burrows in the submerged vegetation or bottom sediments. It is most active on warm nights in hot weather, but basks in the sun during cooler months, usually early in the day and occasionally low in tree branches over the water. It uses its prehensile tail when descending.

Principal overwintering refuges are stumpholes of trees blown over by strong winds, palmetto patches, deep accumulations of leaf litter around the bases of trees, interiors of hollow logs, and stump holes of rotted cabbage palms. In the southern portion of its range, the cottonmouth overwinters underground mainly in stumpholes or abandoned burrows of the gopher tortoise. Further north, in southern Illinois, large numbers are found in association with rattlesnakes, copperheads, and other snakes nestled in cracks between the ledges of limestone and sandstone hills and along bluffs overlooking large swamps. An aggregation of 40 snakes was found in northeastern Oklahoma where a bluff rises 150 feet above a floodplain. In a southern Louisiana floodplain, 112 cottonmouths were counted hibernating under logs and piles of drift.

On occasion, the cottonmouth can be even more numerous. In a low-lying area surrounding a pond in northeastern Kentucky, a population exceeding 300 cottonmouths per acre was reported . One of the snake's most famous habits is cleaning up dying fish and amphibian larvae from drying ponds. I once counted eight cottonmouths ranging in size from 12 inches to full-grown adults nosing around in a drying depression full of stranded pygmy sunfishes.

Of course, the cottonmouth's most dangerous enemy is man. Following a study of the dense population on Seahorse Key, it was reported that more than 400 specimens were removed for commercial purposes. This is the kind of outrageous abuse of wildlife for which there is no excuse. People wishing to capitalize on selling venom almost wiped out the interesting and unique population for the sake of a few dollars.

Habitat alteration, fragmentation, and outright loss are the principal impacts on the species. For instance, the Everglades, once a large wildlife sanctuary, has been severely altered by various drainage projects and agriculture. Less than 50 percent of the original Everglades now remains and the cottonmouth survives there in greatly reduced numbers. Ultimately, as the human population grows, the cottonmouth will find its best hopes for survival on publicly owned lands and wetlands that are not readily accessible to humans and vandals, such as the 300,000-acre Okefenokee Swamp National Wildlife Refuge.

One may ask why we should care about a snake that is loathed by so many people throughout its range? My answer to that question is always "Well, what makes *us* so special?" Snakes and humans are fellow earthlings who have evolved on this planet through similar evolutionary processes. Snake lives are blueprinted by DNA molecules just as ours are. They are a life form on this planet with their own unique history, and that gives them, I think, the same "rights" to be here as ourselves. In their distinctive tubelike morphology, fang and venom apparatus, and unique behaviors, I find cottonmouths fascinating and interesting. I am even unashamed to say that I really like them.

I suspect that most people, had they my many experiences with the cottonmouth and insights into their lives and behavior, would also come to appreciate the cottonmouth for what it really is: one of earth's many amazing species, well adapted for what it does to survive, and worthy of our admiration as a fellow earthling.

9
COTTON RAT
Base of the Food Web

A LOW, SCURRYING NOISE, A FURTIVE MOVEMENT GLIMPSED from the corner of the eye—this tenses the muscles and chills the blood of every self-respecting Southerner at blackberry pickin' time. For generations it has been handed down that rattlesnakes lurk in every blackberry patch—and indeed, they do, but not for the purpose of doing fanged mischief to unsuspecting fingers and toes. Snakes and mega-predators of all kinds find one of their favorite foods in blackberry patches, too—not blackberries, but grizzled balls of fur known as the cotton rat, *Sigmodon hispidus*.

Probably no animal is more important to the vertebrate food webs of Southern pineland habitats than this tennis-ball-to-softball–sized rodent. There are two reasons for this. More often than not, the open, terrestrial habitats of the South contain more cotton rat biomass than that of any other rodent, rabbit, or bird. Second, there are also more individuals per unit area than any other prey animal. This latter fact seemed incredible to me when I first learned of it, because the cotton rat is considerably larger than many of the other small vertebrate prey species that live in the same habitats. One normally associates large size with reduced numbers. For instance, an acre hardly is adequate even as a pen for a single elephant, but can support a breeding population of dozens of mice. The cotton rat seems to be a crude exception to this rule. Why?

The answer may have a lot to do with the remarkable reproductive characteristics of this short-eared fur ball. Foremost among these is quick time to maturity. A newborn pinky can deliver her own first litter in 67 days! The number of young is respectable for a rodent, up to 12, but usually five to seven. Most impressively, the young are weaned and ready to fend for themselves in five to seven days! This no doubt facilitates the mature female's devotion to reproduction, for she comes into estrus again immediately after giving birth to a litter, an unusual trait for any mammal. The gestation period is 27 days; newborns open their eyes in two days and can be ready to conceive as early as 40 days old. Cotton rats may well be the ultimate baby machines.

Theoretically, in the first year of her life, a newborn pinky female cotton rat can spawn at least 72 sons and daughters, 594 grandchildren, 7,182 great grandchildren, 46,000+ great-great-grandchildren, 93,000+ great-great-great-grandchildren—totaling well over 150,000 descendants! Realistically, however, seasonal hormonal cycles, seasonal food supply, territoriality, and predation all interact to inhibit or destroy her productivity, so that the number of her surviving offspring equals only one. This happens under the unrealistic assumption of a stable cotton rat population. In nature, cotton rat numbers usually fluctuate over two or three orders of magnitude from season to season and from year to year. Their remarkable reproductive capacity, however, insures that cotton rats will be back when conditions are favorable.

Every talon, fang, and claw seems sharpened for a cotton rat feast. The list of likely and known predators includes the Virginia opossum, raccoon, bobcat, mink, long-tailed weasel, striped skunk, otter, black bear, locally extinct mammals such as the coyote, red wolf, and gray wolf . . . and those interloper foreigners, the dog and cat. But that's not all. Next are the red-tailed hawk, red-shouldered hawk, marsh hawk, Cooper's hawk, sharp-shinned hawk, kestrel, merlin, barn owl, barred owl, great horned owl, screech owl, cattle egret, wood stork, coachwhip, black racer, gray rat snake, red rat snake, common kingsnake, indigo snake, pine snake, cottonmouth, timber rattlesnake, and eastern diamondback rattlesnake. I'm sure I've left out half a dozen other species.

My appreciation for the importance of the cotton rat, one of the few animals that are active day and night, developed through a long-term study I conducted on the eastern diamondback rattlesnake from 1976 to 1984. The scant scientific literature on this snake led me to believe that the eastern cottontail rabbit was the rattlesnake's main fare. To my surprise the approximate 800 stomachs I examined were stuffed about 50 percent with the cotton rat. Moreover, through radio-tracking studies, I soon became aware that the eastern diamondback, in its sneaky way, specifically hunts the cotton rat.

As the rattler glides over the ground, it tongue-flicks the substrate for chemical "tracks" left by many animals. The cotton rat has a habit of moving from point to point over well-traveled trails it makes. When *eau de cotton rat* is daintily picked up by the tongue tips, rattlers position themselves along cotton rat trails or follow such trails to burrow entrances. There they cock themselves into a striking coil and begin an ambush vigil. Day or night, when the infrared signals emanating from the warm body of a cotton rat fire off the nerve endings in the snake's heat-sensitive facial pits, the rattler aims a swift, stabbing blow at the warm blob, injects the lethal liquor, and quickly retracts its vulnerable head from sharp-toothed rodent retaliation.

Cotton rats require proportionately more venom to be disabled than some other rodents, probably reflecting the long time they have been served up for rattlesnake food. The offspring of those cotton rats whose immune systems were slightly better at neutralizing snake venoms were favored over the generations. Rattlesnake offspring, on the other hand, whose venoms were slightly more toxic to cotton rats, also may have been favored and thus by means of this co-evolutionary seesaw, cotton rats may have been at least partially responsible for the high toxicity of rattlesnake venom.

Nevertheless, what happens to a cotton rat that has received a lethal dose? Amidst a lot of squeaking and initial flight response, the cotton rat's locomotor functions are severely impaired. Almost immediately, nerve impulses are blocked and the rodent's muscles are paralyzed. This is probably the venom's first and most important purpose, to immobilize the prey animal before it can run off so far it can't be found. Shortly, up to 10 to 20 minutes later, the rodent dies from shock and suffocation as its breathing is also impaired by muscle paralysis.

The genus name, *Sigmodon*, refers to the S-shaped pattern made by the cusps of each cotton rat cheek tooth. These grind roots, shoots, and leaves of the plants that make up the main fare of the cotton rat. I was flabbergasted the first time I found the large intestine of a rattlesnake packed with finely masticated plant material. It just couldn't be possible that this rattlesnake was bereft of good rattlesnake sense and had opted for a vegetarian diet—could it? The bones of two adult cotton rats in the stomach brought me sheepishly back to my own senses. But cotton rats, like many other herbivores, will not pass up an easy protein meal. Thus Herbert Stoddard found that quail eggs (and the eggs of other ground-nesting animals) are often eaten by the cotton rat, and George Lowery suspected cotton rat foul play at partly eaten trap catches.

A great way to learn firsthand about the cotton rat is to visit the site of a controlled or prescribed burn after the fire. Here the exposed runways show up clearly as well-trodden paths leading from burrows usually excavated under the base of small woody plants like blackberry, American beautyberry, sumac, and others. The paths radiate from such burrow systems like spokes on a wheel, leading to other burrows, but more often than not, to curious nests of clipped plant parts built on top of the ground. These have been shown to provide protection from extremes of the climate, but probably also shelter the cotton rat from predation.

Immediately after March burns, I have seen lots of cotton rats down in the burrows of the gopher tortoise, apparently taking refuge there after the groundcover they normally hide in had been razed. The depths of these dark tunnels, however, often are haunted by scaly denizens no less murderous than the feathered arrows the rats wished to avoid when exposed to aerial predation on the surface of the ground. Many times I witnessed two, three, and once, four little wide-eyed faces huddled side by side and peering outward from the dark, half-moon tortoise tunnels just back from the overhanging ceiling. Rather than run a few feet farther down the burrow, often they would take their chances and bolt for some distant retreat over the bare and blackened ground at my arrival. Apparently they were more willing to brave the unknown perils of the clumsy tree-sized monster than to face certain death at gleaming fang-point or suffocating coil.

I can't imagine another animal so important to Southern vertebrate food webs. As a generalist herbivore, it forms the base of the consumer food pyramid. Its impacts upon vegetation, on one hand, can be severe and measured in crop losses, but its contribution to wildlife is equally measurable in numbers of hawks, owls, snakes, foxes, weasels, skunks, and other mammals that grace the Southern scene.

With such vital connections to other life, who can deny that this rat is an important contributor to the ecological health of the habitats it lives in? This is a *rat*—one of the creatures most loathed by humans. Cuter rats such as the guinea pig are endearing children's pets, but if guinea pigs were called guinea rats, more truly descriptive of what they really are, they probably wouldn't be so popular. During the Inca civilization in ancient Peru, the guinea pig was a delicacy served only to the royal family. Even today it is a prized entrée on the menu of Peruvian restaurants. Although the cotton rat is not an amphibian or reptile, I include it as another example of human cultural biases against life forms about which humans have little detailed knowledge. Few people realize that its value to the verterbrate food webs of Southern ecosystems is so important.

10
ALLIGATOR SNAPPING TURTLE
Leviathan of Southern Rivers

ON A HUMID MIDSUMMER NIGHT IN 1974, ON THE UPPER
Ochlockonee River, I am whiling away some time in the sand around a
campfire awaiting a trotline check. Lightning flickers on the bottoms
of overhead clouds, illuminating my fishing buddy, Jimmy Atkinson,
and my six-year-old son, Harley. It is little Harley's first night running
trotlines and I hope it will be a classic Southern out-of-doors experience
with his dad that he will always remember.

Earlier, we had stretched several nylon cords across the river with
25 fishhooks suspended from each one on short lines. The hooks were
baited with chicken guts and the middle of each trotline was weighted
down with a brick.

Leaving Harley on the bank with a flashlight, Jimmy and I wade
into the river and retrieve a couple of nice channel catfishes from
our first two trotlines. Harley's excitement at seeing the fishes warms
me. When we reach the third trotline, our excitement ratchets up a
notch or two. Farther out, near the middle of the river, the line is
bouncing up and down in the water in such a way that it is obvious
something very big is tugging at it. Jimmy and I jump into the river
and begin wading toward the source of the disturbance. The current
is moderately strong and the river chest deep, so we move on the

upstream side of the trotline, pushing against it for balance. When we reach the hook on which the mystery animal is impaled, the creature is so heavy that we can't raise the trotline high enough to bring it the surface where we can identify it.

Thinking that any animal that is hooked in the mouth can't bite my hand, I hold the trotline in my right hand and reach far downstream with my left hand to feel the animal's rear parts. I figure I will be able to identify it by feeling its legs, fur, or fins. Suddenly, my left foot feels like it is smashed with a sledgehammer. The notion that a heavy log has fallen on my foot flashes through my mind, but quickly the pressure disappears. Then, just as suddenly, unbearable pain clamps down on my left hand—and holds on. The force of whatever has got hold of my hand is so great that I believe it is breaking my bones. I cry out in great pain and pull back my arm.

The ghostly white head of a monstrous alligator snapping turtle surfaces with my hand tightly clamped in its maw. My hand hurts even worse when I pull against the turtle's hold, so I abandon any idea of trying to forcefully yank my hand out of its crushing jaws. Instead, I give it some slack and feel it quickly release the pressure in order to get a better grip, but then it chomps down again even harder. The pain is excruciating. I resolve that the next time it tries to improve its hold, I will pull my hand from its mouth no matter what. After an eternity of waiting, its grip loosens once again and I yank my bleeding hand free.

Jimmy cuts the trotline and we maneuver the turtle to the far bank in order to work with it in shallow water. There I can see that it is hooked on its left side, and that its head is free to bite hand or foot or whatever else it chooses in its anger.

My poor hand bleeds from cuts inflicted by the sharp sides of the turtle's jaws and I can't open my fingers without additional pain. I fully expect to see broken carpal bones exposed through my skin, but fortunately, my fist was clenched when bitten, so that the larger mass of the bones and muscles of my hand gave me some protection from the full force of the turtle's jaws. I am lucky, too, that the turtle had been suspended in midwater from the trotline and so was unable to leverage its massive body against the streambed while pulling on my hand. Years later you can still see the scars on both sides of my closed fist.

Young Harley hears my shouts of agony and the commotion across the river. When I wade back to him, he is relieved that I am safe, but frightened by the story and my bloody hand. I try to convince him that wading in the river is not dangerous, that monster turtles are not lurking in muddy waters to bite him unless he is so foolish as to offer his hand to an unseen critter thrashing about on a trotline.

In later years during SCUBA dives, however, I think about the painful trotline experience and I'm not so sure I believe my own arguments to allay Harley's fears. Cold water seeps under the neck of my wetsuit, runs down my back, and gives me a chill as I descend into the inky red-black waters of the Aucilla River. I blow gently against my pinched nose to equalize the pressure that is building on my eardrums. A strange, silent world envelops me and my vision goes pitch black. I hold an arm out in front of me to protect my face, and I spread my legs for a landing. Down I go in a slow-motion free fall. In the black water I feel weightless, but water flowing upward through my hands and around my head tells me I am falling. My sensory world now is altogether tactile.

I wait to feel the cold ooze of finely decayed organic mud of the river bottom, but suddenly, my left leg bumps into a large log. Then my right leg and arms hit other logs and I come to a halt. All around me I can feel branches of submerged trees. I haven't yet reached the bed of the river, so I pull myself among the tree trunks and branches, searching for a way to squeeze past and get underneath this tangle of wood. When I reach the bed of the river, I lie belly down with my arms outstretched in front of me. I can't use a light since the cold organic ooze that coats everything billows up and reduces visibility to zero. Instead, I use my arms and hands like a pair of insect antennae to carefully feel my way along the river bed while engaged in finding megafaunal fossils lying there. I work without underwater lights using touch alone to guide me and to feel for ancient bones. As I grope forward and sideways feeling my way along the river bed, I constantly worry about running my hand into the open maw of another giant alligator snapping turtle and having my fingers shortened by a powerful chomp. Over the years during dives in black or muddy waters, my fears haunt me. Harley grows up and becomes an avid river diver himself, but we still remember that trotline encounter vividly.

Then, thirty years later, the two of us have a second encounter, but under more favorable circumstances. By this time, Harley has more experience with alligator snappers than me; he has been diving in the Apalachicola River with his brother, Ryan, for several years and they have had many uneventful encounters with alligator snappers. Also, by this time, we are using high-powered dive lights and I am no longer groping along in the dark.

I receive a call from a television production company that wants to film a large alligator snapper in the wild, so I invite Harley to help me catch one under water. This will be my chance to test my long-held apprehensions about what a large alligator snapper might do to me in an underwater, face-to-face encounter. In the past, I was my son, Harley's, protector; this time it will be Harley's boat and expertise that I will depend upon.

We launch Harley's boat and drive it upstream to an outside bend where trees have fallen into the river. Getting a wetsuit onto my 63-year-old frame is a bit of a squeeze, but with Harley's assistance, I get the belly zipped up. The water is quite chilly, about 64 degrees Fahrenheit, and I am wearing a hood to keep my head warm. I experience trouble with buoyancy, but using lots of lead weights, I eventually settle down onto the bed of the river where the steeply inclined bank gives way to the flat river bottom. Whereas in years past I had groped around in black waters without any light, on this dive I hold a strong dive light in my right hand. Still, the light doesn't penetrate more than about 30 inches into the muddy water.

After about two hours of staring at tan clay riverbed sediments in murky waters and picking my way among logs and unforgiving branches, I am about to give up, thinking that we are looking in unproductive habitat. Harley passes forward of me on my right side, then, only a few seconds after his fins dim out of sight in the murk, the encounter happens. I have no time to think. Suddenly, in the beam of my dive light no more than 30 inches away, I see a huge head coming straight for me. Being right-handed and holding my dive light in that hand, I am not positioned for grabbing the carapace behind that menacing head, the only safe place out of reach of its jaws. Instinctively, I make a lunge for the carapace with my left hand, but the turtle deflects its path and angles off quickly to my right. If I am to capture this beast, I must give it my all. I turn right and kick hard with my legs and propel myself over the turtle. The dive light drops from my hand as I grasp the turtle's carapace behind its head with my right hand, and then I grab the rear of the carapace with my left hand. And now I find myself under water and unable to see clearly, my light dangling from my wrist on a lanyard—but I have the turtle firmly grasped and I am not going to turn it loose.

The snapper churns its strong legs, struggling to get into deeper water and carrying me along with it. I am in a dilemma. In order to surface with my prize, I need to use one of my hands to inflate my buoyancy compensator, but that is out of the question. So, keeping the turtle's foreparts pointing away from my body, I begin kicking my legs as vigorously as I can, trying to pull the beast with me to the surface of the river. Twenty hard-won feet later, I surface huffing like a locomotive, only to find myself in the middle of the wide river in a strong current. The boat is a quarter of a mile downstream, too far to try to reach with a mad snapper lunging left and right, all four legs flailing with heavily nailed feet, so I roll over on my back and kick as hard as I can for the shore, thinking that when I reach shallow water I will be able to haul myself and the snapper up onto the beach. When I reach the shore I am exhausted, and I get another nasty surprise: the shore is a 30-foot-high vertical bank.

By now I am so tired that I contemplate releasing the snapper, but then I spy a shrub growing five feet above the waterline. Using my belly to press the snapper into the soft clay bank, and clamping down tightly on the front of its carapace with my right hand, I lunge for the shrub with my left hand, clutch a scraggly stem in my fingers, and am mightily relieved that it does not give way. There I hang for what seems like eternity. Eventually, Harley surfaces to see what has happened to his diving buddy and hears my loud calls for help.

The big male is so large that it just fits, unable to turn around, in my bathtub at home. In the next few days it gives me an unexpected surprise. Its feces are comprised entirely of dozens of shells of quarter-sized clams. This is no ordinary clam, however, but the Asian clam (*Corbicula fluminea*), an alien species that has invaded Southern rivers, often paving the river bottom with its live and dead shells, to the detriment of native clams and the natural river ecosystem. I would never have guessed that this giant turtle, with a head the size of a five-gallon bucket, would ever be able to find and pick up such small clams the size of a quarter. It is ironic, however, that this giant native American species is capitalizing on the introduced foreigner.

Over the next two weeks, we film the 85-pound leviathan for the documentary and display it as the featured animal in a wildlife festival. Then we release him and today that great reptile once again crawls the bottom of the Apalachicola River, hopefully unfazed by his encounter with me, and probably searching for tiny Asian clams and luring fish with his wormlike tongue.

As for me, I no longer worry about getting my hand crunched under water in the mouth of another monster snapper thanks to the knowledge I have gained from experience, observations, and from others who have worked with this wonderful turtle. I have come to realize that a large alligator snapping turtle can sense the presence of a scuba diver under water. The turtle will most likely run away, posing no danger at all to the diver, even in dark water. Like so many maligned animals that are perceived as a threat to humans, the truth is often obscured by ignorance.

After catching, trapping, and handling many of these leviathans, I have come to see what beautiful creatures they are. The only danger that remains to threaten me lies in my own impulsiveness. I have great admiration for these animals, but I have to keep in mind that I could make another silly mistake as I did years ago while checking a trotline that I could not see. Recently, for example, while examining one particularly large and handsome male alligator snapper that I had just trapped, I started to reach over and pick off some leeches that were attached to the soft tissues around its eyes, forgetting for a moment that the turtle probably would lunge at me and give my hand a terrible crunch. It wouldn't understand that I was trying to help it. Luckily, I caught myself in time. I must force myself to remember that some things in nature are meant to be appreciated at a respectable distance.

11
OUACHITA EARTHWORMS
A Glowing Story

I AM DRIVING A 15-PASSENGER VAN WEST ON APALACHICOLA
National Forest Road FH-13 when I spot a recently prescribe-burned
flatwoods and stomp on the brakes. With a grin, I turn to the students
on my field trip and ask, "Anybody want to grunt?" I get the usual
frowns and gasps. Then I say, "Hop out and we'll all grunt together."
With funny looks on their faces, the students follow me into the
longleaf pine forest.

After a prescribed burn, longleaf pine forests are clean of the
stems of grasses, forbs, and even of most woody plants—except the
pines themselves. The ground, although black with ash, is clean
and easy to see. I pick a spot free of tree trunks and then direct the
students to make a big circle with their arms on the shoulders of those
next to them. When the giggling and laughter have quieted down, I
ask loudly, "Is everybody ready to grunt?"

Again they snigger but I get serious and tell them to follow my
directions exactly: "When I give the command, I want you all to
begin stomping in unison—and watch the ground in front of you."
Following my example, they all begin stomping together and soon are

totally cracking up with laughter. A pickup truck drives slowly by and we all laugh harder imagining what the passersby must be thinking of our crazy behavior.

Then someone shouts, "Look, there's an earthworm crawling up out of the ground!" Then someone else exclaims, "There's another!" And soon everybody is clamoring, "There's an earthworm! There's one!" As we quit stomping and gather up the foot-long, pink worms, I grin widely and tell them that we all just finished grunting together.

"Grunting," "fiddling," and "noodling" are all terms used by earthworm hunters. Usually they do it by pounding a stake into the ground and rubbing it with another stick or with a piece of metal. The stake vibrates, making a *rrrrrrrrrup, rrrrrrrrrup* sound, and up come the worms. The Apalachicola National Forest is famous for its earthworm grunting industry. It sells more than 250 permits a year to locals who make their living by marketing the worms to fishermen. The earthworm they seek is famous as a bait worm for freshwater fishing. It has a mouthful of a scientific name, *Diplocardia mississippiensis*, and is often sold as the "Louisiana Pink." This is not the night crawler or wiggler that is sold as fish bait; both of these are exotics and the latter is raised in worm farms. *Diplocardia mississippiensis* is a native species found only in the Southern states from Mississippi to Georgia. It has not been domesticated and so can't be farmed; it must be grunted. Farm-raised worms are cheaper, so worm grunting wouldn't be economical—except that the Louisiana Pink makes a superior bait. Southern fisherfolk believe it to be the earthworm most likely to bring a fish to the hook.

Some years ago it occurred to me that simply vibrating the ground by almost any means should bring up earthworms. I tried stomping and it worked, but humans are not the first animals to invent worm stomping. While radio-tracking the wood turtle, *Clemmys insculpta*, in Pennsylvania, a researcher observed four adult females and eight males stomping for earthworms on 63 occasions for a total of 32 hours. After taking several slow steps forward, wood turtles stop and then, with one front foot, stamp rhythmically on the ground at a rate of about one stomp per second. They alternate with the other front foot, each bout beginning with a light treading, the force of which increases to a true stomp by about the sixth or eighth step. The force of some stomps is so great they can be heard several yards away. The observer clearly saw worms emerging from the bare mud within one to five inches of the turtle's snout, the turtles quickly snapping them up. One turtle he watched captured fifteen worms in one hour this way.

No less a personage than Charles Darwin conducted the definitive research on earthworm biology. Observing and experimenting on English earthworms on the grounds of his property and elsewhere in Britain, and 22 years after publishing *The Origin of Species* in 1859, Darwin published *The Formation of Vegetable Mould through the Action of Worms, with Observations on Their Habits.* His investigations involved *Lumbricus terrestris,* a member of an earthworm family not native to North America, but now common here following its introduction in the 1600s. That's one of the major stories about earthworms. Many species the world over are alien in many places where they are now found. They have hitch-hiked across the oceans of the world in potted plants, on sailing ships of the fifteenth through the nineteenth centuries. Many of the earthworm species present today in North America, including especially the commonest types we encounter in our lawns and gardens, are exotics.

Because earthworms burrow in and ingest soil, they perform important ecological functions in it. They facilitate aeration and percolation by burrowing, nutrient cycling by the ingestion and excretion of organic matter, and fertilization by the movement of nutrients throughout the soil. Earthworm biomass is significant in vertebrate food webs, providing food for salamanders, frogs, turtles, snakes, lizards, and birds. Mammals, too, such as echidnas, shrews, moles, and other burrowing insectivores, are specialized for burrowing and feeding on earthworms.

During his productive career, taxonomist Gordon Gates, professor at the University of Maine at Orono, was the leading earthworm expert. When he retired in 1961, he effectively withdrew from earthworm research because he had no laboratory or funding for it. Then, by a curious stroke of fate, Gates' research was rejuvenated when young Eddy Komarek asked his father, Edwin V. Komarek Sr., to identify the earthworm he had brought in from out-of-doors. The elder Komarek, then the head of Tall Timbers Research Station, a small biological field station in the north Florida woods, inaugurated a search to find a specialist who could identify his son's worms. Himself a keen naturalist, Komarek was also curious about the worms he had seen all his life in the region. The name of Gordon Gates came up, Komarek contacted him, and Eddy Jr. got his earthworm identification.

Komarek thought it incredible that the southeastern United States' earthworm fauna was so poorly known. He empowered Gates financially to reinvigorate his taxonomic studies and Komarek encouraged the Tall Timbers Research Station staff biologists to collect earthworms and send them to Gates. Komarek himself made some special trips around the Southeast to collect earthworms for Gates and discovered an entire earthworm family, new to science, in the North Carolina Piedmont. Gates promptly named it "Komarekionidae." Altogether, earthworm biologists have honored Komarek by naming species in three genera for him.

Komarek allowed Gates' collections to be housed at the Tall Timbers Research Station Museum, and it grew to include quite a collection of important taxonomic types. Tall Timbers became the publisher of *Megadrilogica*, the leading earthworm scientific journal; staff members did the editing of submitted manuscripts; and Komarek provided a fellowship that enabled John Reynolds, a successor to Gates, to complete his Ph.D. in earthworm biology.

One of my own exciting encounters with earthworms occurs when I am hunting for some rare terrestrial salamanders in midwestern Arkansas. I enter a lovely hardwood forest of oaks, dogwood, elm, and pines growing on a boulder talus slope of Rich Mountain—in the Ouachita Mountains—and begin searching under logs. I spend ten minutes of back-breaking work digging a hole two feet wide, four feet long, and two feet deep, leaving it fringed with a pile of the large boulders that I excavate using my hands and steel-tined potato rake. I sit down on a large log, wipe my sweaty brow, take a deep breath, and relax. Then, out of the corner of my eye, I see something pink oozing into the hole from the far side of my excavation.

Most of the sudden, surprising discoveries of new species of animals and plants in the United States and Canada have already been made. All of the obvious birds, mammals, frogs, turtles, butterflies, and most other animals in familiar groups such as the vertebrates have long ago been found and named. About the only way to find a new species in the US nowadays is to study a group of wide-ranging, similar-looking populations to see if they are a complex of closely related species. Using genetic and biochemical techniques or behavioral studies, one may "discover" that the group is composed of several different species. An experienced naturalist doesn't expect to just go out in the field, even in a remote place, and suddenly roll a log and say, "Eureka! There's a new species."

But what am I seeing in this hole? I watch, spellbound, for a few seconds as something quite amazing takes place. Slowly, inch by inch, a huge earthworm spills into the bottom of my hole like a long skein of toothpaste squeezed from a tube.

As one of those Tall Timbers biologists who participates in collecting earthworms for Gates, I am by now, familiar with most of the known earthworms of the southeastern US. In North Carolina I collected samples of *Komarekiona eatoni;* in Mississippi I collected *Diplocardia mississippiensis* at the site where it was first discovered; and I even found a new species of aquatic earthworm, *Sparganophilus means,* down in the swamps of the Coastal Plain. So, on this day, 11 June 1973 to be exact, I know in an instant that I am looking at an earthworm that is totally new to science.

I pick up the moist worm by its front end and it dangles down a full two feet. This is incredible. It is the longest live earthworm I have ever held in my hand. I say live because I have handled pickled monsters from other parts of the world in museum collections, and some exotic giant worms that Gates sent to Tall Timbers to be stored in our museum collection. But I can clearly see that this is a native *Diplocardia* and it is larger, by far, than any I've seen before.

Adrenaline recharges my energy. I grab my potato rake and

feverishly begin digging another hole. It is as tough to dig as the first one because there is only a six-inch veneer of soil on top of huge boulders in this area. The Jackfork Sandstone that makes up the bedrock of Rich Mountain breaks up into huge blocky boulders that lie all ajumble in big boulder fields that creep downslope from the highest elevations. Geologists call such a talus slope a " rock glacier." No luck in the second hole. I exhaust myself digging a couple of other holes with no further results, but just as I am leaving, I spy another large *Diplocardia* emerging into the first hole from the side of the excavation in the same slow and deliberate manner as the first worm. I take my two specimens, preserve them in the correct fashion, send them to Gates, and am thrilled when he names it after me, *Diplocardia meansi.*

Later, I wonder just why these large earthworms crawled out into my holes. Normally, earthworms take refuge from disturbance by crawling further down in their burrows. It occurs to me that I may have "grunted" the worms by making vibrations in the soil when rolling the boulders together or by vibrating the boulders while scratching them with the hard tines of my potato rake during excavation.

Continuing my salamander field work in the Ouachita Mountains, on subsequent visits I search for additional *Diplocardia meansi* while digging salamanders from the soil, but I have a dickens of a time finding any. Gates used the original two specimens in his type description, and that was sufficient for taxonomic purposes, but I worry that there should be more than two specimens in museum collections for other worm researchers to study. Then, in 1981, I have a breakthrough and my two beautiful sons are with me to share the fun. By now, Harley is thirteen and Ryan, nine.

Our purpose is to do some follow-up research on the Ouachita Mountain dusky salamander, *Desmognathus brimleyorum.* We arrive on Rich Mountain in late May, about five weeks earlier than I normally visit my salamander study sites, and at 8 P.M., we begin a drive west from Mena on the Talimena Scenic Drive. It is a long, paved road that snakes along the ridge crest of two mountains, named Rich and Winding Stair, that straddle the Arkansas-Oklahoma border. East to west, the elongate ridge of these two mountains combined extends about 70 miles, but the ridgeline highway runs along only about 40 miles of it.

Our destination is a secret camping site I have been using for several years during my salamander research. Yesterday, Rich Mountain near Mena received several inches of rain, and today a thundershower has been in progress since 6 P.M. and is just now letting up. We drive the dark night in fog and gusting wind along the summit. As always during a windy, rainy night here, the road is littered with pine needles, so I don't pay much attention to what's on the pavement. There is so much trash that my eyes can't easily resolve a small snake or salamander among the litter. I slow down and try to avoid squashing quite a few Woodhouse's toads (*Bufo woodhousei*) that we see hopping around on the road surface; then, suddenly, we spot a toad struggling with something in its mouth that is thin and much longer than the toad. Aha! What if it's a *D. meansi?* We stop the car and jump out in the chilly 65-degree air to find that it is indeed a *Diplocardia meansi* the toad is struggling to eat.

This is a nice surprise. I have seen no *D. meansi* out on this road—ever—during more than ten years and fifteen field trips. This is the first specimen of my namesake earthworm that I have seen since discovering it, and it gives me a chance to tell the boys my story. While I am doing so, Ryan pipes up, "Dad, here's a big worm over here." Then Harley finds one. Then we see that there are lots of *D. meansi* crawling on the road surface. We jump in the car and slowly drive along, picking them up as we go. Two hours later and only five miles down the road, when we reach the valley that forms a deep notch between Rich and Winding Stair Mountains, we have seen more than a hundred adult earthworms and many Woodhouse's toads. An earthworm migration of sorts seems to be under way. I speculate that finding worms on this particular trip must have to do with the earthworm's breeding season. In the past I've always arrived on the Fourth of July weekend, but this trip we've come five weeks earlier.

We see at least three toads with earthworms dangling from their mouths. We pick up an earthworm and notice that it secretes a very disagreeable, pungent, coelomic fluid when agitated. This is typical earthworm behavior: many species squirt bad-tasting coelomic fluids out of their bodies to deter predators, but the fluid from *Diplocardia meansi* has another anti-predator property. It becomes very sticky and glutinous when it touches one's skin. I lick the fluid along a worm's body to find out what it does to a mammalian predator, and my tongue, even though wet, gets coated with a rubbery, nasty-tasting substance. We notice several toads smacking their mouths after biting a worm, but apparently Woodhouse's toad ingests *D. meansi* nevertheless. Moreover, so must other predators because, although we see numerous dead and squashed *D. meansi* on the road during the next several hours of the night, almost none remain at nine the next morning when we decamp and drive to Mena for breakfast. Instead, we find lots of small animal scats all over the road: fox, skunk, armadillo, raccoon, opossum, and toad.

I've become fascinated with this worm. I know it is common all over Rich Mountain; now I'm keen to know if *D. meansi* ranges all the way down Rich Mountain's sister, Winding Stair Mountain, to its western end in the drier climate of eastern Oklahoma. To find out, the next night, the boys and I drive west again along the same ridge crest highway on Winding Stair. It's obvious from water on the road that it has rained recently, so conditions for toads and worms should be similar to those on Rich Mountain. The drive down Talimena Scenic Highway terminates at US Highway 271, and we see absolutely *no* worms. The number of Woodhouse's toads seems much reduced, too, so at 11:45 we resolve to do a little experiment. We drive back east to the notch between Winding Stair and Rich Mountains counting toads and *D. meansi* along the way. Score: 29 toads, *no* worms, in 19.7 miles of searching on Winding Stair. Then, from 12:20 to 1:20 A.M. we drive 13.9 miles further east down Rich Mountain and score 68 toads and 81 *D. meansi*. This is a highly significant difference. It is possible that *D. meansi* is a species that is strictly endemic to Rich Mountain.

This is fascinating biogeography, if it stands the test of time. Rich and Winding Stair Mountains are really one long mountain with a deep notch separating them. I've discovered that salamanders on

Rich Mountain occur on Winding Stair, but in much reduced numbers because of rapidly increasing aridity going west. It may be the case that the reduced rainfall on Winding Stair Mountain makes the soil uninhabitable by *Diplocardia meansi.*

We have more to learn, something truly amazing, in fact, and we discover it the next night. More afternoon thundershowers have wet the road and soil, and earthworms are out in abundance again. While road-cruising the Talimena Scenic Highway, I pull the vehicle over and dispatch the boys to fetch some *D. meansi* in the auto headlights. They pick up a few and then I douse the headlights just for a prank. The joke is on me. The boys' hands are glowing with a lime green light! We promptly discover that the coelomic fluid, which the worms invariably secrete when picked up, is bioluminescent. I jump out of the car, approach an undisturbed worm, gently prick it with the tips of a pine needle, and watch it squirt coelomic fluid onto the road surface. The glow is quite bright in the dark, but too weak to be seen in daylight or even in the light from our flashlights. When the earthworms are continuously stroked and pricked, their entire bodies light up, beautifully silhouetted against the dark, blacktop highway.

Later, when I bed down for the night, my head is spinning. What on earth kind of benefit does bioluminescence provide for an earthworm?! They have no eyes, so they can't see in the dark. Living underground in the dark, they have no need of eyes. You would think that possessing light has to do with some sort of signaling, some sort of communication between the earthworm and something else. Normally, in sighted animals, bright color of feathers or light reflected from a body part such as the throat fan of a lizard is used to communicate between the sexes or to signal others of the same kind about territorial boundaries. I can think of no direct function that glowing might provide for the blind earthworms, themselves—but maybe I'm thinking about the problem from the wrong perspective. Maybe earthworms glow to signal other species for some reason.

An idea begins to dawn on me as I think back on fieldwork I have done with brightly colored frogs in Central and South America. Brightly colored frogs, as well as butterflies and some other insects, signal to warn potential predators that "if you bite me, you will be sorry." The punishment often is a painful sting or a bitter taste. Having suffered it once, the predator remembers, when it sees the bright color again, that a bite is likely to hurt or taste awful, and soon develops an avoidance response when seeing that animal. Such colors are called warning, or aposematic, coloration. Being conspicuous serves to warn. Now *Diplocardia meansi* does have a bitter-tasting coelomic fluid and its coelomic fluid also becomes glutinous on the tongue or skin. The combination of bitter taste, glutinous secretion, and a flash of green light may all serve to reinforce aversive responses in would-be predators.

I'm getting drowsy. I ask myself, "What sorts of predators need to see an earthworm glowing underground?" I have a difficult time trying to imagine what sighted predators might lurk below the ground surface and would attack earthworms there. Moles burrow and eat earthworms, but their eyes are very tiny. Would a mole see the glow of a luminescent earthworm while burrowing underground? I don't know. Most shrews tunnel underground. So do some rodents and some predatory invertebrates. All of these are sighted and good candidates for subterranean predators. "But," I think, "last night I saw a potential predator, Woodhouse's toad, attempting to prey on *D. meansi* crossing the road. Unfortunately, because my vehicle's headlights overpowered any bioluminescence the worms might have been giving off, I was not aware that any glowing was taking place. It may be that *D. meansi* is warning terrestrial, nocturnal predators during its surface wanderings, especially in times like these when earthworms are on ground surface en masse searching for mates. Now I need to check on whether Woodhouse's toad really eats *Diplocardia meansi*. Those few I saw with worms dangling from their mouths might have been naive youngsters who were getting their first nasty taste of the earthworm."

I'm almost asleep. Bioluminescence in *Diplocardia meansi* may really be aposematic. If so, how wonderful—that in order to give off a visual signal in the darkness underground or at night, this species, which itself cannot see, has evolved a means of using light to warn sighted predators. Sighted animals that are aposematic, however, rely on reflected light to display their bright warning coloration. *Diplocardia meansi*, on the other hand, not able to reflect ambient light because it inhabits dark environments, actually creates its own light!

The evolutionary story gets even more wonderfully complicated because most animals do not create their own bioluminescence. They get it from microbes that produce it. If microbes produce the bioluminescence in *Diplocarida meansi*, then how did the earthworm originally acquire these microbes and hos iw it that the bioluminescence is produced when the worm secretes it in coelomic fluid? And what benefit do the microbes get from the association? Who could have guessed at such wonders in an earthworm?

My two sons have been listening to me speaking of all these thoughts as they drift off. Now they are snuggled next to me, fast asleep. Tonight I shared with them a small experience of the magnificence of nature. Each little beast in the field has its own special qualities and its own worth, independently of how humans might regard it. I am reminded of a song, and I drift off into a deep sleep with the lines running through my mind: "Everything is beautiful, in its own way. . . ."

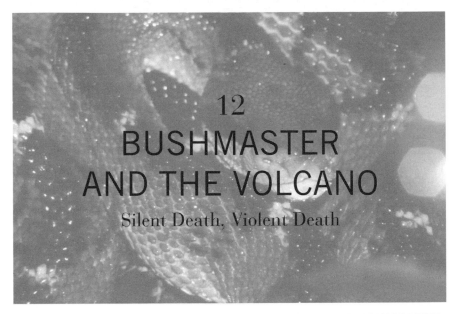

12

BUSHMASTER
AND THE VOLCANO

Silent Death, Violent Death

SINCE IT WAS FIRST DESCRIBED IN 1803, THE BUSHMASTER, *Lachesis muta*, has remained one of the world's most mysterious and fearsome venomous snakes. Even its name evokes dread. *Lachesis* is the Greek Fate responsible for determining the time of death: literally, the whole name means "silent snipper of the thread of life." Possessing beaded scales, a strangely pointed tail, and fangs more than an inch long, this awe-inspiring serpent has stimulated a lust in prominent herpetologists for a chance to see it in the wild. Zoos have vied for the opportunity to display a specimen and expeditions have been mounted—unsuccessfully—to bag one.

The bushmaster is all superlatives. It is the world's largest pitviper, commonly ranging from seven to eight feet and recorded up to 12 feet long. It's venom is among the most toxic of all the vipers, and it is the most dangerous snake in all of Latin America. Even given medical treatment, 80 percent of all people bitten by this snake have died.

Driven to bring back a bushmaster to display in the Bronx Zoo, herpetologist Raymond Ditmars mounted an expedition to Trinidad, the only Caribbean island to support a population. He even published a book about his experience but, alas, he never got to see a single bushmaster in the field.

My own fascination with the bushmaster dates back to the late 1940s when I was a kid. I recall staring at the famous photograph of the preserved head of a bushmaster in Ditmar's classic book, *Snakes of the World*. It is a side view of the snake with its mouth partially open and huge fangs bared. Either the photograph has been touched up to highlight the vertical pupil, or the light reflecting eerily off the iris heightens the impression that this is a sinister and evil reptile. Anyway, this old photograph is downright scary. Coupled with the snake's size and toxicity, the photo has done much to spread the mystique of this magnificent creature.

Comments about the snake's rarity are common in bushmaster literature. Speaking with officials at the Instituto Clodomiro Picado in San Jose, Costa Rica, in 1977, I was told that the bushmaster is, indeed, very difficult to find. In that same week, I visited the field station of the Organization for Tropical Studies (OTS) at La Selva and was told by station workers and biologists alike that bushmasters were rarely seen. In the 24 hours I spent on the trails, day and night, looking for a bushmaster, I never saw one.

Ten years later, in the summer of 1987, I returned to OTS La Selva and looked up Harry Greene of the University of California Berkeley. He was working on the snake fauna there. He told me I was in luck, because for two months he had been studying a five-foot-long male bushmaster that he had equipped with a radiotransmitter. More exciting yet, he invited me along to look for another bushmaster he had heard about that very day. The snake was reported to be just an hour's walk away. I had no idea what I was in for.

It is 8:15 A.M. on July 21, 1987, and the sky is overcast. A small troop of bushmaster enthusiasts—Harry Greene, my sons Harley and Ryan (now 19 and 15 years old, respectively), Dave Hardy, Ian Stone, and I—set out along the central trail into the Atlantic slopes rainforest. We are all toting cameras and backpacks loaded with lenses and film. Before we have walked 15 minutes, a tropical drizzle begins falling. We don ponchos and stow our cameras under them in plastic bags.

Harry has graciously given me his snake hook and allows me the coveted lead position so I can be the first to see and catch anything that we may encounter on the trail. I spearhead the entourage with Ryan and Harley hot on my heels. Our hopes run high for seeing at least the more common fer-de-lance—almost as dangerous as the bushmaster—or some other snake, but most of all we're pumped to see a bushmaster. The forest is gloomy in the drizzle, and I have a hard time seeing the dark forest path at my feet.

Half an hour into our walk Harry cries out from behind me, "Fer-de-lance!" I rush back to see, pinned under Harry's boot, an 18-inch-long, very young male snake with a yellow tail. I must have stepped right on it or just missed it, as did both Harley and Ryan, failing to see it against the dank forest floor in the foggy drizzle. I pin its head and pick it up. We take shots of its open mouth and relatively long fangs, then release it. Its coloration is a study in leaf-litter camouflage. "Well, at least we won't be skunked now," says Harry as we resume our trek. Harry has been apprehensive that the new bushmaster we seek might have moved since it was sighted 48 hours ago.

After about an hour of steady walking, we arrive at a site off the trail where lightning, some time ago, struck a tall tree. The dead tree has lost all its branches and epiphytes. Only the trunk and downfallen limbs and leaves are left beneath a perfect round window of sky in the otherwise dense canopy. The window lets warm sunlight reach the forest floor for short periods, and warmth is very important for deep-forest reptiles. The warmth of direct sunlight helps them digest a big meal, for instance, and during pregnancy it speeds up the physiological processes. A spot like this is an ideal one in which to find a snake.

Two days ago, a botanist was in the area studying seedling colonization and plant succession. As he was struggling over a high horizontal log beyond the edge of this very tree fall, a well-camouflaged bushmaster reared its head back defensively just a few feet away from where the botanist would have stepped. When he had recovered his composure, the startled botanist marked the snake's location.

We head eagerly for the blue flagging in the distance. Approaching stealthily, we whisper in hushed tones. Dave Hardy, in front, peers over a downed log and scans the ground. "I don't think it's here," he says with disappointment. Harry is mumbling words of disgust when Dave shouts, "Wait, there it is!" Jubilant, I move up for a look, but see nothing at the spot some ten feet away where everyone is pointing. Even when I carefully scrutinize every inch of ground, all I see is crinkly leaf litter on the dimly lit forest floor, with a small palm or fallen branch here and there. Suddenly the snake pops into my view—exactly where I am staring. This comes as no surprise to me, recalling how many times an eastern diamondback rattlesnake has suddenly come into my focus in just this way. The diamondback is dark with yellow lines breaking its pattern. The La Selva bushmaster is light tan to light brown with bold black markings. You can spot it by looking for a light patch in the litter.

Its back flush with the top of the leaves, the bushmaster lies coiled with its head on top. I can clearly see its eyes, mouth, and the two heat-sensitive pits that assist it in locating its warm-bodied prey. Harry says this snake looks smaller than the one he has been tracking.

We crowd around to take photographs. I ask Harry if our electronic flashes bother the snake. Bushmasters usually sleep in the daytime, he says, and a flash will rarely cause them to move. Through my camera lens I can admire the snake close up. I thrill to see the beaded scales of its skin. Rather than being flat or smooth like the scales of many snakes, or evenly keeled with a small ridge down each scale, each dorsal scale of the bushmaster is raised to a knobby point, making the skin very bumpy. Such scale morphology might aid this rainforest animal to rid its skin of rainwater by offering a tiny slope to run down, or by increasing the evaporative surface of the scales, or both.

Although we carefully keep our distance, it is clear that we have awakened the magnificent beast. For a long while, I admire this wonderful work of life-art up close through my 200 mm lens. I take about five photographs before Harry begins to worry that we are bothering the snake; then we stop shooting.

Walking back along the boundary trail, we are all elated. Imagine seeing a wild fer-de-lance and a bushmaster within one hour of each other, I chuckle to myself. Little do I know that, before the morning is over, we will have much more to tell of bushmasters.

When we come to the site where the five-foot bushmaster has been sitting with one of Harry's transmitters surgically implanted in it, we make a brief detour to see if it is still there. It isn't! This comes as quite a surprise. A major discovery of Harry's research has been that bushmasters remain coiled in one place for very long periods of time. This particular bushmaster had not moved from this spot for a record 30 days—until this morning.

Harry switches on his radiotelemetry receiver. He seems to be having a little trouble adjusting the 27-megahertz receiver to the frequency of the transmitter in the snake. I am fascinated with his equipment, having done snake radiotelemetry research of my own. We pick up a weak, low frequency signal, about 60 feet away from the spot where he last saw the bushmaster, and take it to mean that the snake is still in range.

We walk around, occasionally picking up a signal, but not the high-pitched tone we want to hear. Harry can't seem to tune in the receiver properly. I follow about ten feet behind him, frustrated that I cannot hear the low-frequency signal. Finally, to hear the signal better, I come up very close behind him.

A discarded plank lies a few inches above the ground on top of some fallen lianas and other debris. We step on it repeatedly as we move back and forth over the terrain searching for a signal, then we move out toward a bare patch on the forest floor. It's not the sort of place you would ever search for a snake because if one were there, it should be obvious to anybody—or so we think. As we move out in lock step across the open spot, I peer over Harry's right shoulder. Suddenly, Harry recoils against me. " Oh, God!" he gasps. As he jerks his right foot back, I see a large, coiled bushmaster immediately in front of him rearing its head to strike. Harry's next step would have been on top of, or next to, this awesome serpent.

We tumble backwards and then gawk in amazement at this huge pile of coiled snake, completely out in the open next to a small philodendron. Had our reptile been so inclined, Harry, at least, would have become a snakebite statistic.

We catch our breath. Dave arrives and the three of us stand a few safe feet away, admiring the large bushmaster as it lies in tight spirals on the bare ground. Whoever would have thought to look for this giant pitviper on a patch of bare ground?

Then Harry says, "That's a new snake." "How do you know?" I ask. "This one is much larger," he says. "It's even bigger than the one we just looked at." Indeed, the sight is impressive – as impressive as I ever imagined the sight of a live bushmaster could be. The bushmaster we've already seen pales in comparison to this huge reptile coiled on bare clay, its head cocked back like the hammer on a pistol. Its heat-sensitive pits tilt towards us at the working end of a long, handsome head. I'm not sure whether I, being so close behind Harry, was in range of those horrible fangs, but I'm perfectly content with the vicarious rush.

Calmed down and having viewed the new snake to our hearts' content, we remember that we have not yet located the telemetered snake and soon find it—under the plank! The plank must have pressed down fairly hard on the snake considering that Harry, Dave, and I have repeatedly walked back and forth across it. The bushmaster never moved.

Considering how difficult it is to find a bushmaster in the field, I ask myself why we found this new monster bushmaster so close to Harry's radiotelemetered snake. I can't help but think that its presence was caused by the other snake, somehow, meaning that trail pheromones left by the first snake might have caught this guy's attention as he passed by. Unfortunately, I have no more time to spend at La Selva and these are Harry's study animals. I can't even disturb one to get an idea about its defensive behavior since I am Harry's guest, and I don't feel comfortable asking Harry if I can try to catch one. I have no reason to complain, however, because on this amazing day I must be one of only a very few people ever to have encountered three wild bushmasters. And we did it all in the space of three hours on one rainy tropical morning!

But that's not the only danger we encountered on this trip. The very next day, my sons and I drive about 50 miles southwest to the foot of the active volcano Arenal where I sit down on a huge lava rock and begin recording the previous morning's events in my daily journal. Before I am halfway through, Harley and Ryan are getting bored, so I agree to meet them at a fumarole (steam vent) that we can see steaming about one-third of the way to the summit. As the day is advancing, I drive to a local village, make arrangements to stay overnight, and then begin driving back to rejoin the boys.

Volcan Arenal erupts with a mighty BOOM. The force of the blast nearly blows me off the road. I look left out my car window and see house-sized chunks of magma catapulting out of the crater and arcing downhill toward the very steam vent where I sent Harley and Ryan only an hour ago to wait for me! I watch, horrified, thinking I have sent my two sons to their death. Instinctively, I grab my camera and take a photograph of the eruption out of the car window.

I gun the car and drive like crazy for the end of the little dirt track where I left them to make their climb. I can see the awful volcanic bombs falling just short of the fumarole, kicking up dust higher beyond the steam vent where my kids may well have climbed. Any of dozens of huge volcanic masses I see raining on the slopes could kill them. "It's just like my kids," I cry internally, "to push the envelope." I worry that they might have climbed beyond the fumarole into the death zone of the molten volcanic bombs. In a panic I nearly spin out of control on the curves of the loose gravel road. I fight back tears and try to suppress my worst fears.

At the end of the track I jam on the brakes, skid to a stop, and fly out of the vehicle while the motor is still coughing to a halt. I grab my backpack and race to the path my boys climbed. When I can still see the flank of the volcano, which is now making ominous rumblings, I glass the slopes trying to spot my beloved sons. They are nowhere in sight. I swallow a large lump in my throat. Then I bolt up the path between two old craggy lava flows, top a rise, and stop and glass the slope above again. No kids. I let out a huge bellow, "HARLEY, RYAN!" I strain my ears for a reply. No answer.

I try to run up the now very steep trail over jagged lava rocks. My breathing comes in huge gasps. My heart pounds. I'm frantic to find my boys. Suddenly I think I hear something. I stop. I listen. Then, miraculously, I hear it, a tiny little sound: "Daaad!" At first I'm not sure of it, but my heart races in eager anticipation. Again, more discernible this time, "Daaad!" Thank God! It's them. We call back and forth. I am reassured that both are alive, but I'm not sure they are OK. Their voices sound as if something is wrong.

Soon I see them scrambling down the side of the rumbling mountain as fast as they dare over the rugged rocks. When they approach I expect to have a grand reunion, hugging and reassuring each other and telling of our mutual panics. I am dumbstruck, however, when they fly by me with hardly as much as eye contact. I can't even get them to slow down. Wide-eyed, they rush by and scream at me to get the heck down off the volcano with them. As they pass, the volcano belches forth again, not so violently this time, but a huge ash cloud billows overhead and I can see it coming toward me. The eruptions have scared the boys badly.

Later, they tell me that as they were nearing the steam vent, the ground started to shake and rumble. Suddenly, overhead, the volcano erupted with a terrible explosion. Looking up, they saw huge masses of red-hot magma hurtling down upon them from a dark ash cloud that seemed to be directly above them. "We're doomed," they both thought. The two of them crouched down and, hugging, said they loved each other. Almost immediately, hot volcanic dust and ash rained down on them, slightly burning their arms. In reality, below the vent where they were huddled, they were in no great danger, but from their perspective on the side of the steep slope looking up, the volcanic bombs appeared to be falling right on top of them. It was obviously a terrifying experience.

From sheer relief, I burst into laughter as they speed by me. They think I am mocking them, but my glee only expresses my joy that my sons are alive. I sit down near where they have passed me about a quarter of the way up the volcano and open my journal to finish recording the events of our encounters with the bushmaster. Grains of hot volcanic ash from the minor eruption rain down on me as I write in my journal. The grains are coarse, about the size of an average sand grain, and hot. I notice that they burn little red spots where they land on my arm. I watch my sons for a while. They don't slow down until they reach the car.

Just now, the summit begins making loud and scary chuff-chuff-chuffing sounds. It must be steam from one of the fumaroles or big bubbles of magma bursting open or something. It sounds like a locomotive, and the interval between sounds grows shorter even as I sit here. I fear another eruption. Harley and Ryan yell up at me to leave. I understand their fear. This massive smoldering mountain "huffing and chuffing" with periodic rumbles and explosions is, indeed, frightening. Thick clouds shroud the peak, parting now and then to reveal an awesome view of the conical summit. In those moments when the volcano is silent, I hear black howler monkeys far off in the distant forest below and to the east.

Still, I think that I probably don't have to fear for my life, and wanting to take in the ambience of an active volcano while it is erupting, I decide to sit tight and use the opportunity to finish recording the bushmaster story.

As I write in my journal, I wonder which would be the worst kind of death, being struck silently by a bushmaster or being bombarded by the hot and violent outpourings of a noisy volcano. One would be slow and painful; the other most likely would be sudden. I'm glad I don't have to choose, and luckily for us, we only flirted with these choices. Somehow, sitting on the side of an erupting volcano and thinking about the beautiful snakes we saw yesterday, I find the flirtations make my life a little sweeter.

13
IS TZABCAN KUKULCAN?
Stalking the Plumed Serpent

WHY DO WE HUMANS LOVE EXPLORING? SOMETIMES THE ONLY
purpose for a hike down an unfamiliar path or a vacation in an exotic
land is the thrill of the new and the unexpected. In 1975 I explored
some ancient Mayan ruins on the Yucatán Peninsula of Mexico and
was fascinated by the "snake art" I saw there. Carvings of a mythical
plumed serpent with rattles on its tail festooned the walls, balustrades,
and columns of the great Mayan city-states of Chichen Itza, Mayapan,
and Uxmal. For years afterward, I lusted to explore more of the Yucatán
Peninsula, find the rattlesnake that the Mayans lived with, and see
some of the Yucatán's relatively unknown herps. I finally did it.

Twenty years before my first trip there, in 1955, Mexican
archaeologist Jose Diaz-Bolio marveled at the beauty of this great
feathered serpent, known as Kukulcan, or Quetzalcoatl, and wondered
why it was so dominant in the art of that ancient Mayan site. He
hypothesized that the model for Kukulcan was a local rattlesnake and
he believed that he saw its diamond pattern in temple architecture,
frieze decorations, and even in Mayan chronology based on the
numbers 13 and 20.

The particular rattlesnake to which Diaz-Bolio ascribed this
tremendous influence was then known as a variety of the species

Crotalus durissus that is found only on the Yucatán Peninsula. Earlier, in 1952, famous rattlesnake biologist Laurence M. Klauber had recognized the uniqueness of this Yucatán variety by giving it a distinct subspecies name, *tzabcan*, which in the Mayan language comes from *tzab*, meaning "rattle," and *can*, meaning "snake". These Yucatán populations appear to be isolated from other Central American populations and are morphologically distinct by certain qualities of the color pattern and differences in the characteristics of the scales. In 2007, DNA studies revealed that the Yucatán populations were, in fact, a full and distinct species, not a race. The correct scientific name is *Crotalus tzabcan*. A common name has not yet been coined, but throughout Latin America, rattlesnakes go by the Spanish word *cascabel*, which means "little bell."

When I visited the Mayan ruins of the Yucatán, I saw that more than 70 percent of the sculptures on the temples represented snakes. An outstanding carving of the plumed serpent, whose tail ends in a distinct rattle, adorns the wall of the Nunnery at Uxmal. It was obvious that the plumed serpent was a rattlesnake, but in all the carvings I saw, its skin was covered with *feathers*, not diamonds. Too, diamonds and squares (diamonds rotated 90 degrees) were prominent on friezes and wall decorations, and I thought these might be based on the diamonds of a rattlesnakes, although I didn't find any rattlesnakes in the surrounding countryside.

How could a rattlesnake be so important in Mayan iconography, and which species inspired the plumed serpent myth? These questions remained in my mind when, in 1976, I undertook a long-term life history and ecology study of the eastern diamondback rattlesnake in the southeastern United States where I lived. I pursued that study for nearly 30 years, and in all that time, in the back of my mind, I yearned to return to the Yucatán to learn more about the roots of Mayan plumed serpent mythology. Especially I wanted to see firsthand, and possibly study, the life history and ecology of *Crotalus tzabcan*, a large rattlesnake for which very little basic life history and ecology knowledge exists.

Fast-forward to October 2004, when I am blessed with an

opportunity to make a 15-day preliminary exploration of Mayan ruins and *C. tzabcan* rattlesnake haunts. According to my correspondence with Julian C. Lee, the author of two books on the amphibians and reptiles of the Yucatán Peninsula, *C. tzabcan* is most likely to be found in the dry thorn forests of the northwestern part of the peninsula. In his publications, Lee goes so far as to hypothesize that *tzabcan* may be more or less confined to the western half of the Yucatán Peninsula and the fer-de-lance to the eastern half, partly because of habitat preferences, but possibly also because of competition between the species.

My wife, Kathy, and I land at the Cancun Airport and rent a tiny Volkswagen Pointer. We immediately drive west down the new Cancun-Mérida toll road to escape the horrendous commercial development and tourism now known as the Mayan Riviera. Our purposes are twofold: to find and photograph *Crotalus tzabcan* and to investigate the relationship of this rattlesnake with the mythical Mayan plumed serpent, Kukulcan.

Right away we get mixed messages and faulty information from the locals. The American proprietor of the hotel we stay in near Chichen Itza on our first night out enthusiastically tells me that he has the skin of a six-foot-long rattlesnake that was killed nearby earlier in the year. I dash upstairs with him to a storage room only to find that it is the skin of a boa constrictor. Next day, I am taken to a Mayan shaman in Piste who is said to have great knowledge about local snakes and who bottles and sells for medicinal cures the snake oil of *tzabcan*. When we find the old gentleman, he is vague about rattlesnakes. He says he hasn't seen one in many months and that the species doesn't occur locally. When I pull out the dead carcass of a small black and white snail sucker (*Sibon fasciatus*) that the gardener of our hotel grounds killed earlier, he nervously tells me that this is a "very dangerous coral snake!" I open its mouth to show him that the harmless snake has no fangs, but he recoils, telling me, "Danger, danger!" I rub my finger across the roof of the snake's mouth with no ill effects, but this does not change his mind; it only heats up his alarm which I sense is becoming mixed with anger. I leave, desiring no more misinformation from this "sham-man."

According to my correspondence with Julian Lee, the best place to look for *C. tzabcan* is in the vicinity of Muna, north of the ruins of Uxmal. Kathy and I drive to Uxmal, take in the ruins, and then ardently cruise the backcountry roads. On our fifth night in the Yucatán, during the magic hour for snake movement, we finally capture our first live snake of the trip. It is the time of crepuscular activity, half an hour before and after sunset, when both diurnal and nocturnal predators have difficulty seeing prey. To my diurnal eyes, it is difficult to see snakes on the road because daylight has dimmed so much and yet the headlights are not effective. But this is the time when nocturnal eyes are somewhat blinded by what, to me, is weak daylight. Everywhere that I have been road-cruising in the world, this is the hour when I usually find some snakes. Note that road-cruise is a specific term used by herpetologists as a method to find herps, which are slow-moving animals, easier to find when they are moving across roads at night.

Roads in the Mexican Yucatán are ideal for road-cruising because uncut vegetation offering protection to small animals grows right up to the edge of the pavement, or to the edge of the tire ruts on dirt roads. Road shoulders do not exist in the Yucatán and motorists are well advised not to let their tires run off the edge of the pavement if they wish not to hit a boulder, to plummet down a hidden precipice, or to flip the car.

We have just passed through the sleepy little village of Abala, when I stomp on the brakes and bolt pell-mell from the driver's seat for a red-, black-, and yellow-banded snake. It could be a giant coral snake or a large and harmless mimic, but I have no time to identify it while it is thrashing wildly to reach the safety of the bushes. Several times I flip it back into the middle of the road with my snake hook; then, as it tires and slows down, I pin its head with the soft rubber handle and grasp the snake by the back of its head. It is difficult to pick up the lovely creature and restrain its muscular head so as not to get bitten, yet not grasp it so tightly as to injure it. It has a coal black nose like an eastern coral snake, but when I open its mouth with the aid of a pencil and see no coral snake fangs, I realize it must be a tropical kingsnake, *Lampropeltis triangulum.* I soon confirm the identification with the field guide I brought with me. It is a big, pretty snake, almost four feet long and many times the bulk of its Florida relative with which I am very familiar. I photograph and release it, and we see no other snakes during the rest of the night.

The next night we forsake a touristic light show at Uxmal for road-cruising. We arrive at the Mayan village of Xcanchakan with the intention of driving the Abala road during the magic hour, but I take the wrong secondary road and we wind up in Mahzucil. The rough, pitted asphalt road passes through some countryside that looks good for *C. tzabcan*, so we turn around and retrace our path. En route, we see an entrepreneur of about 30 years of age selling something to kids out of the back of an old pickup truck. A cooler in the bed of his truck reads "Paleteria," which later we decide means "Popsicle store." I stop and ask him in my pidgin Spanish if he knows of any good roads where we might see the *cascabel* crawling about at night.

I am pleased when he points to two remote roads on our Mexican highways map, one of which is the road we are on. Hoping his information is good, I decide to cruise back and forth on the Xcanchakan-Mahzucil road and not venture any further this night into unfamiliar territory. At 25 mph, a one-way cruise on this stretch of one-lane road takes us 17 minutes. The flat, dried skin and bones of a seven-foot-long boa constrictor lie plastered onto the road at the outskirts of Mahzucil, but we cruise through the magic hour and see no other snake of any kind. We see only two male teacup-sized Mexican red-rumped tarantulas crossing the road, probably out searching for females, and half a dozen caprimulgiform birds (this formal name means goatsucker—which act they do not perform—but I can't bring myself to call them that) flying into the air after insects. After three hours of road-cruising, I am weary of staring at the road with no results. Then it happens.

The waxing three-quarter moon is bright overhead and the air is cooling down. Neither condition favors snake movement. We come over a small rise and suddenly I spot a thick-bodied snake motionless on the road surface with about one-third of its body exposed. I jam on the brakes and begin fumbling for the door and my snake sticks. Kathy shouts, "It's moving!" and when I look I fumble even more and shout, "It's a cantil!" I never thought I would see this snake, but to catch and examine a cantil ranks with *C. tzabcan* as a prize experience for me. The cantil, *Agkistrodon bilineatus*, is one of only three species of the genus in the New World. Its closest relatives are the copperhead, *Agkistrodon contortrix*, and the cottonmouth, *Agkistrodon piscivorus*.

Aware that the cantil is dangerously venomous, I leap from the car with adrenalin pumping furiously through my veins. Then I make a big mistake. The cantil speeds up fast to reach the thick roadside grass, and I make one stab at the cantil with my clampstick and miss the snake. The auto headlights don't penetrate the thick grass and, in the dark of night, the snake quickly disappears. I can't even hear it moving. Only then do I realize that I could have used my snake boots or snake hook to flip the cantil back out into the middle of the road and work with it.

Furious with myself, I get back in the car spitting and fuming. When I calm down, I rationalize that at least I can be proud that I erred on the side of prudence. Kathy is happy that I was overly cautious instead of reckless, but I drive back to our lodgings in a black mood.

Today is the sixth day of our Yucatán snake hunt, and our only catches for the whole six days are one fast-wriggling black snake crossing the toll road that I couldn't stop to identify, one black- and white-banded snail sucker killed by the gardener at the hotel in Piste, one tropical kingsnake caught live, and one missed cantil. These are typical results of snake-hunting efforts in the neotropics of Central and South America, and slim pickings for me. I am growing depressed about the prospects of finding a live *C. tzabcan*. We still have the longer road that the Popsicle man told me about, but after seeing none on the first road he recommended, I doubt that he knew what he was talking about. We decide to scout it out the next morning to see if it looks promising.

The road, an 18-mile stretch of smooth macadam only one and a half lanes wide, looks perfect. Heading north out of a large town called Tikit, it undulates over limestone terrain through alternating patches of corn agriculture, abandoned oldfields, and thorn scrub forest that is reclaiming areas occupied by agriculture in earlier decades. The thorn scrub forest of northwestern Yucatán is not so obviously different from the rainforest of the eastern side of the peninsula. It consists of some trees with spines or thorns on its leafy branches, especially legumes, and when mature it is a closed-canopy forest. We do not drive into thorn forest and say, "Aha, there is thorn scrub." The transition across the Yucatán Peninsula is gradual and I have to get out of the car to examine some of the trees to realize what forest type we are in. This forest is much disturbed by humans, who have cut down trees and pilfered wood from it for centuries.

From the literature, I have the impression that the *Crotalus tzabcan* rattlesnake, like the eastern diamondback, gravitates to a sparsely treed, open-canopied savanna, more a grassland than a forest. For that reason, I am encouraged to see abandoned agricultural fields and active cornfields whose perimeters are dominated more by grasses and forbs than woody shrubs and trees. Halfway down the road, we encounter a brush crew cutting roadside weeds. I stop and ask the straw boss if they encounter many snakes, especially the *cascabel*, on this road. He surprises me by saying, "No, almost no snakes at all, and never the *cascabel*."

This I can hardly believe, but if it is true, our hopes for success later tonight while road-cruising are dashed. For some reason, I feel his answer is untruthful, so when I come upon a man operating a weed-whacker some distance further, I stop and ask him the same question. He answers emphatically, "Yes, we see them all the time and this road is famous for its *cascabeles*." What a puzzle. Two men on the same crew, presumably with the same experience, give me completely contradictory information. Counting the Popsicle man of last night, I think to myself, "Two to one," in favor of my finding a *cascabel* on this road.

After scouting our night's route, we hurry to a roadside restaurant on the new six-laned bypass surrounding Mérida, looking for a light, early supper well off the tourist track. El Tiburon (The Shark) Restaurant thumps loudly to a band playing lively Mexican music and all eyes follow us as we press our way through tables crowded with well-to-do Mayan Indians having their supper. When the band pauses between songs, the lead singer addresses Kathy and me, the only gringos in the place, over the loudspeaker for all to hear. It sounds as though he asks if I speak Spanish, to which I reply that my Spanish is lousy and we are from Florida. Then he asks if I speak Mayan and the place cracks up with laughter. It is a very friendly exchange, and we get smiles from all the patrons. I don't quite understand what the waiter is explaining when I order fried fish for Kathy and shrimp for myself, but as luck would have it, a Mayan man sitting next to us turns and says in perfect English that we are going to be really happy with our order.

Out come four huge plates of ceviches, two plates for each of us in different sauces, and a platter of mixed seafoods in ketchup. Then we are served a plate of empanadas and a saucer of crispy fried tortillas with two kinds of delicious salsa. When I have forced down the last of the ceviche, thinking that supper is over, Kathy is served a huge platter with a large scombrid fish, cross-scored and fried, with french fries and salad, and the waiter places before me a huge plate of fried shrimp with french fried potatoes and a guacamole side salad. Next they serve us a plate of bread and some white, foamy dip that I am loathe to eat, fearing Montezuma's revenge. We wash it all down with Pepsi and stagger out of the place wishing for a stomach pump. We are so overfed that I almost suggest we find a motel and turn in for the night.

We begin our road cruise at 5:56 P.M., about 30 minutes before sundown, just at the onset of the magic hour. I am highly expectant. The road passes through relatively uninhabited terrain broken up by a mosaic of different habitats, most of which would produce rats and mice for rattlesnake food as well as good cover from the sun and predators. Limestone boulders are superabundant, providing rocky hiding places as well. Over the next 45 minutes we drive the 18 miles slowly and with high hopes. I stare hard at the pavement at the far edge of the headlights, trying to force a snake to materialize. Nothing. We turn around at the northern outskirts of Tikit at a place called Finca Kinchahau, a ranch established in 1898, according to a plaque on its over-arching stone gate.

On the return voyage up the road, my hopes are even higher. Full darkness is upon us now, and nocturnal creatures should be moving. From the scant literature on *C. tzabcan*, I get the impression that the rattlesnake is nocturnal at this time of the year and I recall that related rattlesnakes I caught in Costa Rica some years ago moved at night.

The road is a road-cruiser's delight. We see no vehicular traffic and few pedestrians, even near the three little Mayan villages along the way. At 7:42 P.M. we reach the road's northern terminus where it joins Mexico Federal Highway 18. Now I am discouraged. The weather is perfect, the time of day correct, the habitat along the road ideal—but nothing is moving.

We turn around and head south again. We pass all three of the Mayan villages with no luck. At the top of a small hill on the road, we see ahead a single-beam light flashing down the road at us. When we approach, a Mayan man stands on the roadside with a strong light on his head and a rifle over his shoulder, obviously night-lighting for deer and other game. I stop and ask him if this road is good for the *cascabel*, and I am disgusted with his reply. Emphatically, he says that he never sees any *cascabel*s along this road, and only rarely any other kinds of snakes. I am disgusted. If anybody should know whether *C. tzabcan* is common hereabouts, it should be a 60ish Mayan hunter who has lived in the area all his life and knows the fauna well. I drive off in a dark funk. The verbal score for this road is now two to two. I speed back down the road a short distance until we come again to the driveway of Finca Kinchahau where I stop and consult a map, looking for the quickest way to some overnight lodging.

To get to a federal highway, we'll have to pass through some large, unfamiliar towns at night. Kathy remarks that we did not record the names of the three Mayan villages we passed through, which are important locality entries in my field notes, so at her suggestion, I decide to return and get the names. Besides, the quickest way to a bed is back up our road-cruising track. I turn the car around and speed off in disgust, thinking that any more searching of this road is futile.

With disgust on my mind and no expectations for any snakes this night, four minutes later and less than half a mile from where I had spoken with the old hunter, we top a small rise and are greeted with a sight I'll never, *never* forget. I spot a very large snake casually gliding across the lane-and-a-half wide paved road from left to right. Its diamond pattern, rattles held upright, and massive body tell me immediately that it is a rattlesnake. I am so dumbstruck by the totally unexpected sight I can't speak. *Crotalus tzabcan* at last! I stop the car in the middle of the road to block any traffic that might come along, turn on the flasher, and dash out into the night with my snake hook in hand.

I have no idea what behavior to expect from this snake. The books all say that members of the *C. durissus* complex are very aggressive, rising off the ground in an upright defensive posture, but this snake turns out to be as placid as they come. At first, I gently hook the snake back into the middle of the road, expecting it to rattle and coil up. It is unaffected by my touch and continues its leisurely crawl across the road. After several such hookings, I gently clamp the snake about one-third of the way back from its head, and pick up the tail with my free hand. The snake seems completely relaxed and unafraid. I can easily point its head into a pillowcase on the ground and I get the snake bagged with no difficulty at all. So that we will be safe while transporting it inside our rental car, Kathy helps me double-bag it. When this is accomplished, I realize that the snake has not rattled once throughout the capture. "What a sweetheart this snake is," I think. On the drive to overnight lodging in Mérida, I sing and hoot loudly until I get on Kathy's nerves and have to shut up. I am on a really big high.

The next day I take the snake to a secluded place to photograph it. When it crawls onto the dark maroon lateritic soil so typical of many tropical rainforests, my jaw drops. Its color pattern is as beautiful as any I have ever seen on a snake. Its background color is light gray and down the midline of its back is a string of about 20 diamonds outlined boldly in the same maroon color as the soil and set off by a thin fringe of single, cream-colored scales. The middle of each diamond is tan and the diamonds fade toward the tail, which becomes uniformly dark gray. The diamonds are spectacular, but the appearance of the snake is all the more dramatic because, beginning behind each eye, bold, maroon, longitudinal stripes run parallel down the neck and abruptly give way to the first diamond.

Besides the color pattern, there are even more distinctive external differences between *C. tzabcan* and the eastern diamondback rattlesnake that I am so familiar with. The head of *C. tzabcan* is narrower, not set off from the neck as widely as in the eastern diamondback and most other rattlesnakes. And unlike other rattlesnakes, it has two features that remind me of the bushmaster, *Lachesis muta.* For one, its dorsal scales are beaded, that is, a ridge down the middle of each scale is knobby and rises quite high above the scale. For another, and this is what best sets *C. tzabcan* and the races of *Crotalus durissus* apart from other rattlesnakes, its cross-sectional profile is not round, but almost triangular. The back is ridged, like the pitched roof of a house. The beaded scales and ridged back in both *C. tzabcan* and the bushmaster may serve as adaptations for shedding rainwater and allowing the skin to dry quickly in the tropical regions in which they both live.

The scales under the tail of *C. tzabcan* also differ from the eastern diamondback. In *C. tzabcan* they are single, like the belly scales of most snakes, but in the eastern diamondback, the subcaudals are divided. Holding up just the tail with the front of its body restrained by my clampstick, I count 29 subcaudal scales in my specimen of *C. tzabcan.* I am able to palp out a hemipenis and determine that the snake is a male, so the number of subcaudal scales in both *C. tzabcan* and *C. adamanteus* may be similar in differentiating the sexes. In *C. adamanteus*, males always have more than 26 subcaudals and females fewer. I resisted the urge to pin the head and manipulate my live *C. tzabcan* in my hands, in deference to Kathy, who does not like the idea of having to save a dying husband in the boondocks of a foreign country in which she does not speak the language.

Under Kathy's watchful eye, I carefully estimate my *C. tzabcan* to be about 50 inches in total length. This is a respectable size for any rattlesnake and I notice that its string of seven free rattles does not taper by even a millimeter. The rattles can tell you a lot about a rattlesnake. The lack of a taper indicates that this is a mature snake that has reached its ultimate body size. I also see that it has lost its natal button, a distinctive rattle that is easily identified. Had the juvenile button been present, the entire shedding history would have been preserved in the rattle string. Rattlesnakes add one rattle per shedding, so that if the rate of shedding is known for an individual, or generally for a species—and if the season when the species gives birth is known—one can deduce the age of a rattlesnake.

Individual rattles in young eastern diamondbacks can tell a lot about juvenile growth, too, and this may be true in *C. tzabcan* as well. Rattles produced during winter when *C. adamanteus* is dormant and not feeding, are not nearly as wide as in spring and summer when the food supply is good and the little snakes have been feeding well. In *C. tzabcan*, availability of food or weather conducive to hunting may also be governed by climate, in this case, wet versus dry season. Of course, as little rattlesnakes grow, their rattles will be proportionately wider because of growth, but even so, relative differences in growth rate due to nourishment are detectable. In older snakes that have virtually stopped growing in length, differences in the width of rattles are slighter, but are sometimes recognizable and, I presume, are also caused by seasonal availability of food.

When I get all the photographs I want, we release our prize where we caught him. He glides out of the pillowcase container and heads for the roadside vegetation. I watch him go with mixed emotions. I have a powerful desire to possess this beautiful creature. I'd love to take him home with me and install him in a large aquarium where I could enjoy his beauty at my leisure for years to come. On the other hand I realize that, from his point of view, his life will be much better if he ranges free in nature. If he had a conscious choice, I'm sure he would choose living free and wild over being maintained in a cramped aquarium, no matter how abundantly he might be fed and how safeguarded he might be from predators and disease. Still, I struggle to suppress a powerful urge to grab him again as I watch him glide into the grass and disappear noiselessly.

I'm torn, too, watching him go because so little is known about the biology of this species of rattlesnake and I can't help but feel that his return to the wild is a lost opportunity. I'd love to put a radiotransmitter in him and follow him around to learn the secrets of his life history and ecology. I already know that *C. tzabcan* differs substantially from what I discovered about the eastern diamondback. The latter is strictly a diurnal snake but the *C. tzabcan* seems to be somewhat nocturnal. The eastern diamondback is inactive for two or three months while overwintering through cold winters whereas the *tzabcan* lives in a tropical climate. Beyond that, we know very little about its growth, reproductive biology, behavior, physiology, or daily and seasonal habits. I want to learn as much as I can about *tzabcan* while I'm in the Yucatán, so I decide to explore the northern peninsula in the time we have left.

From Mérida, we drive to Puerto Morelos, then east over a long, narrow barrier island protecting a salty bay with stunted mangroves. Much of the woody vegetation is dead, a result of saltwater intrusion from deadly Hurricane Isidore in 2002. We stop at the village of Chicxulub and get out of the car to stand in silence, contemplating the meteorite impact crater that made much of life and all the dinosaurs extinct 65 million years ago. I am impressed by the fact that the monster crater, about 175 miles in diameter, is nowhere visible where we stand. It was buried by about 3,000 feet of limestone that accumulated on top of it during the eons in which we mammals came to dominance. That an asteroid or comet of about six miles in diameter made a monster pucker in the earth's surface, created unimaginable tidal waves, and blotted out the sunlight for weeks or months, wiping out 70 percent of all life on earth is eclipsed in my mind by the fact that Mother Earth has buried all the evidence under 3,000 feet of the shells of trillions of small marine creatures—and she has witnessed the evolutionary replacement of all the lost biodiversity.

We road-cruise day and night for more than 360 miles through some of the most snakey-looking habitat I have seen anywhere. We find dozens of large spiny tailed iguanas, *Ctenosaura similis*, especially in sand dunes. Several hundred pink flamingoes stand on one leg, each with its head buried under a wing, at midday in the lagoon east of Rio Lagartos. A coatimundi crosses the road in our headlights. I see one large, flattened marine toad, *Bufo marinus*, near Chabihau, and reflect with surprise that I have not seen a single live specimen of this ubiquitous species anywhere else on the entire peninsula. This is the cane toad, naturally common from Bolivia to northern Mexico and wreaking havoc on the native biota where it has been introduced into the Antilles and Australia. A large treefrog, *Phrynohyas venulosa*, hops across the road in front of us as we enter the village of Yalsihon. When we arrive in Tulum back on the Mayan Riviera, four days after catching our *C. tzabcan*, we have seen only two live snakes along the way: one beautiful, light gray baby boa constrictor, *Boa constrictor*, crossing a lonely stretch of road through dense, salt-spray-pruned, coastal strand vegetation, and one scorpion-eating snake, *Stenorrhina freminvillei*, hurrying in daylight across a paved road near Piste.

Now we turn toward the Mayan Riviera, which ten days ago we avoided like the plague—and suddenly information about *C. tzabcan* is everywhere. We find people with skins, captive specimens, and road-kills, which convince us that the species is common all up and down the east coast of the Yucatán Peninsula. Then we come upon a real prize. I pull off Mexico Highway 307 onto the small paved road to Chumpon, stop the car, and am studying the road map to get my bearings, when something catches my attention out of the corner of my eye. About 50 feet down the Chumpon Road I see what looks like a large, gray stick lying on the road. Instantly, my brain processes the image and says, "Snake!"

I charge out of the car with my snake stick and run up to a five-foot-long, gorgeous *C. tzabcan*. But alas, it has just been run over and is freshly dead. Blood still oozes from its neck and the carcass is limp with no signs of rigor mortis. A small, .22-caliber bullet hole dimples the back of its head. I take this snake back to the hotel and study it. It measures exactly 60 inches in total length, surprisingly large. When I dissect it, I find that it is a male with the expected 29 subcaudal scales. Most interestingly of all, the juvenile button is still on the rattle string and I am able to count that the snake has shed his skin only ten times in his life. Judging from the expanding widths of the basal rattles, this snake is still growing and, I am amazed to realize that he has probably just become sexually mature. The largest *C. tzabcan* mentioned in the research literature I have read was only 69 inches in total length. This, the second *tzabcan* that we find, is almost as long as the record but is relatively young and has the potential to grow quite a bit larger. The age and growth of this snake contrasts strongly with the rattler I caught six nights ago, which was near its maximum size at 50 inches and was probably several years older.

Soon, I have inspected five *C. tzabcan* specimens all on the east side of the Yucatán Peninsula and believe I have learned something new about *tzabcan*. Every one was killed or collected from rainforest habitat. The habitat in the land surrounding the five-foot road-killed specimen I salvaged was rainforest with no evidence of any open, grassy land nearby, or of any subsistence farms. Apparently, on the east side of the Yucatán Peninsula at least, some *C. tzabcan* populations do inhabit rainforest. This is a new and interesting fact of its biology.

Everything we have learned about snakes during our visit, and especially about *C. tzabcan*, reinforces several conclusions that I have repeatedly drawn about snakes during my 40 years of chasing them. First, local knowledge is often highly unreliable. Second, finding snakes in the neotropics is usually difficult. And third, even published scientific literature is often short on facts. I am content with my small findings for the moment, but I am left wondering about the relationship between *C. tzabcan* and the mythical plumed serpent.

Over the next few days, I read everything I can find about ancient Mayan culture and the plumed serpent. Apparently, Kukulcan is the Mayan name of the plumed serpent and Quetzalcoatl is the Toltec name for it. Archaeologists have determined that Quetzalcoatl was introduced into Mayan mythology by the Toltecs, a tribe of people originally living in the Central Valley of Mexico at Tula and other places after the original Mayan civilization had collapsed. The earliest ruins at Chichen Itza belong to the classic Maya Period and were built between the seventh and tenth centuries A.D. These buildings show no evidence of any plumed serpent, nor of snakes of any kind. Later buildings correspond to the Maya-Toltec Period, from the later part of the tenth century to the beginning of the thirteenth century A.D., and the iconography of these buildings is dominated by Quetzalcoatl, or Kukulcan, the plumed serpent.

The Toltecs imposed their religion on the Itza and expanded their dominions in northern Yucatán by making an alliance with Mayapan and Uxmal. In 1194 A.D., Mayapan broke the alliance and subdued Chichen Itza and Uxmal. Thereafter, Chichen Itza was gradually abandoned.

Rattlesnakes that might have served as a model for Quetzalcoatl, therefore, are likely to have been species of the central valley of the original Toltecs, or the Amerindians who preceded them. I concede, though, that temple design and Kukulcan iconography at Chichen Itza, Uxmal, and Mayapan might have been additively influenced by the blood-red diamond pattern of *C. tzabcan* on the Yucatán Peninsula following Toltec domination.

As so often happens in science, one quest for knowledge branches like a tree into new quests along previously unimagined limbs. To determine which rattlesnake was the inspiration for the snake half of the Quetzalcoatl myth, I should next travel to Tula and the central valley of Mexico. I should learn about the Toltec civilization and its antecedents. I should find out which species of rattlesnake occurred in the region of Toltec influence. Who knows where this quest might lead? The desire for a follow-up trip is firmly planted in my head and heart. Will I ever do it? You bet!

14
ISLAND TREASURES
Nosy Mangabe

MADAGASCAR BROKE AWAY FROM THE ANCIENT SUPER-
continent of Gondwana and has been adrift alone in the Indian Ocean
for 120 million years. Before man arrived only a few thousand years
ago, almost all of Madagascar's plants and animals were endemic
species. There, evolution has fashioned a unique flora and fauna,
which every naturalist dreams of seeing at least once in his or her
life. So in early November, 1999, Kathy and I make a pilgrimage to
marvel at lemurs and chameleons, tomato frogs and baobab trees,
and as many other unique animals and plants as we can stuff into
eleven short days. My first view out the 727 window is about what I
expected: rivers running red with iron-stained silt off barren land long
abused by intense agriculture and pasturage.

The squalid capital city, Antananarivo (Tana for short), teems
with 2.8 million poor people, small frenzied automobiles of European
makes, and garbage left on the street. Traffic chokes the two-laned,
potholed city streets. Dilapidated old buses, trucks, and cars belch
unfiltered exhaust fumes into the air which is so acrid that both of us
quickly develop respiratory problems and burning eyes. The wretched
sights, sounds, and smells of developing-world poverty along the ride
to our hotel are so alien that we are thankful to be back in the air

again soon, flying north to one of the few places in Madagascar where native habitats are somewhat intact.

As soon as we touch down on the Maroantsetra airstrip I like the looks of the place. Lush, tropical verdure colors my vision from all directions, including exotic plants such as mango, papaya, banana, breadfruit, bamboo, and many native plants that I cannot identify. We book a room overnight at the Relais du Masoala and make arrangements for a boat and guide in the morning to escort us to the small island "special reserve" called Nosy Mangabe. It juts up out of the Bay of Antongil, a stranded mountaintop now only about two square miles in area. When sea levels were lower more than 6,000 years ago, Nosy Mangabe was connected by land to the adjacent highlands. Now, because of its rugged relief, which makes agriculture impossible, it has been turned into a small preserve, primarily for the purpose of protecting one of the world's most interesting mammals, the aye-aye, *Daubentonia madagascariensis*, a highly specialized relative of lemurs. This little park also has a great diversity of snakes, lizards, frogs, and other interesting small animals that I'm eager to see.

At 6 P.M. Kathy and I walk out into the darkening evening to look for Madagascan wildlife. We are not disappointed. Within 50 yards of our bungalow, in a ten-foot diameter depression in sandy ground covered with dense grass, we find four bright red, rotund tomato frogs, *Discophus antongili*, belonging to the family Microhylide. Microhylids in North America are narrow-headed burrowers that eat termites and ants, and are rarely seen except when migrating to and from breeding sites. These slow-hopping, beautifully colored tomato frogs are like smooth-bodied toads with wet instead of dry skin, but they have a very different evolutionary history from that of toads. There are no toads in Madagascar, so microhylids have evolved to fill toad niches here.

In a *Eucalyptus* forest near the hotel, in quick succession we spot what we think is a fat-tailed dwarf lemur (*Cheirogaleus medius*), a weasel sportive lemur (*Lepilemur mustelinus*), a brown mouse lemur (*Microcebus rufus*), two female panther chameleons (*Furcifer pardalis)*, and several giant katydids. Such diversity seems ironic to me because species of *Eucalyptus* are alien trees in Madagascar and I wouldn't expect indigenous animals to be very abundant in non-native vegetation. We then walk into an abandoned agricultural field grown up with brush and, while I am slowly walking behind our local guide, I look down at my feet and get a surprise that trumps the tomato frogs. Lying across the path is a three-foot-long Madagascan tree boa (*Sanzinia madagascariensis*), the snake I most wanted to see in this country. It is greenish in color with a pair of white spots on both sides of numerous black saddles down the back. While standing in the dark examining the snake with my flashlight, I can't help thinking about how long this snake and the two other boas of Madagascar have been isolated from their closest relatives in the New World. When Madagascar and Africa broke away from South America, boas survived in Madagascar and South and Central America, but not in Africa.

Cool morning breezes. Soft, low-angle sun. Low tide, rock-strewn beach. Nubile human bodies reflecting a black sheen in the sun, backbones straight as an arrow under various items balanced on their heads. Pirogues passing along the shore—dugouts with two men each—now one turns into the mouth of the freshwater creek and the men get out to wash their nets and fishing gear. Girls in colorful traditional dresses called lamba hoany run to the boat to inspect the catch, which includes two large blue lobsters. I purchase them to be served later today on our lunch table.

We set out for the island at 8:45 A.M. and make a two-hour boat ride to Nosy Mangabe over calm and placid water. We sit comfortably on the bow and get a little too exposed to the sun. Our two guides, Felix and Paul, serve us shrimp in tomato/onion sauce for lunch in spite of our having specially asked for our lobsters. The tent camp at Nosy Mangabe is on the southwest side of the island in a lovely half-moon bay circumscribed by an even lovelier arcing beach of tan-colored sand. A clear, cold stream splashes down from the high peak on the north side of camp. As soon as we arrive, the wildlife begins to pop out at us. Incredibly, I see and hear about a dozen or so large plated lizards (*Zonosaurus madagascariensis*) with two green dorsolateral stripes halfway down their bodies; they scurry about the grounds of camp, rustling the leaves, and are relatively unafraid of our presence. Felix immediately finds a leaf-tailed gecko (*Uroplatus fimbriatus*) hanging vertically on a support of the thatched roof over our tenting location. Shortly afterward, he calls our attention to a large panther chameleon, *Furcifer pardalis.* We pull it gently down from the vines it is ascending and photograph it. While we are milling about, I look toward the cook shack and see a troop of white-fronted brown lemurs (*Eulemur fulvius albifrons*) on the ground in low vegetation begging for easy food. Of course, we spend some time taking close-up photos of them.

About 2 P.M., Felix and I go for a long walk south of camp along a trail following the coast a few hundred feet from the beach. Immediately we begin finding more leaf-tailed geckos. All lie flat, heads facing down, against the trunks of unusually small diameter (three- to five-inch) trees. They are almost perfectly camouflaged against the chiaroscuro patterns of lichens on bark. Nocturnal animals, they spend the day pressed tightly against the bark and are active only at night when they are less vulnerable to predation. There are at least half a dozen species of this genus of geckos, all endemic to Madagascar.

The leaf-tailed gecko is the largest of the group, with large individuals reaching eleven inches in total length. Those I see have some amazing adaptations for camouflage. Not only does their dorsal coloration match the color and blotching of tree bark, but they can change color in a matter of seconds when they move to differently colored bark. The sides of their large chin and edges of their arms and body have flaps of skin that individuals press down on the bark to eliminate their shadow and break up their outline. Moreover, their large, unlidded eyes lack a visible sclera (white of the eye), their irises look like bark, too, and their vertical pupils have four tiny openings that enable them to see in daylight without having an obvious, black, round pupil that diurnal predators could key on.

I catch a couple of the geckos and observe their fascinating defensive behavior. They gape open their mouths and display a white lining and a red tongue to frighten off predators, but their bite is innocuous. A little flap of skin over their eyes, not a true eyelid, rolls up to display a bright white sclera that makes their eyes suddenly bug out and appear frightening to a small predator. Their skinny arms and legs terminate in huge hands and feet with large toepads. The toepads cling tightly to almost any surface, including the skin of my hands and arms. At first, these large lizards are bizarre to look at, but after I inspect them closely and recognize their clever anti-predator adaptations, they suddenly become beautiful. I soon find myself searching the boles of trees and small saplings for more.

We see and hear many plated lizards, *Zonosaurus laticuadatus*, running off the path into adjacent leaf litter. These are large, terrestrial lizards that are said to establish a favored site on a hollow log and wait all day for a meal to come along. When they run, however, they are anything but sedentary. Then we find a patch of bamboo growing along a stream. In the hollow centers of stems that have died and broken off, we find two species of frogs. In one section of the bamboo there are four green-backed mantellas, *Mantella laevigata*. Another frog is light-colored, having a cream back with black vermiculations, but it jumps away and I do not have a chance to identify it. Then we examine a large treefrog that disappears into wet leaf litter that has accumulated in the hollow of a tree. We fish it out and wash it off. It has large, expanded toepads but relatively small eyes for its head. It is a *Boophis*, the first ranid-derived treefrog I have caught with my own hands.

This *Boophis* is another wonderful example of convergent evolution. Treefrogs with expanded toepads of the family Hylidae are thought to have evolved from toads of the family Bufonidae, or at least, both families shared a common ancestor. Here in my hand I have a treefrog with expanded toepads that, if I didn't know I was in Madagascar—and if other herpetologists before me hadn't examined internal anatomy and done DNA studies—I'd never know belongs to its own family, the Rhacophoridae. This group of treefrogs evolved from the ancient frog group that we call the Ranidae. In Africa and

Asia the Rhacophoridae boasts hundreds of species, but they are not related to our hylid treefrogs at all, having evolved their arboreal characteristics entirely independently.

Shortly, a frog well camouflaged against the leaf litter jumps a few times with me hot on its heels. When I catch it, I find it to be a true ranid frog, *Mantidactylus luteus*, perfectly camouflaged against the dead leaves of the forest floor. A pronounced ridge runs down its back from each eye.

Just at the moment when I am changing lenses on my camera to take a panorama of a lovely rainforest scene, Felix calls out that he has a real prize, a species of dwarf chameleon, *Brookesia peyrierasi*. I scramble to change lenses back again but discover that the batteries of my electronic flash are sapped. So I put the lovely creature in an empty plastic film canister and it hardly spans the bottom; it is only about an inch long. How lizards so bizarre and complex as chameleons could have evolved to be so miniaturized is a wonder to contemplate. Back in camp, I photograph the tiny marvel and wonder if I could raise a small colony of these delightful creatures. If they would eat fruit flies and tolerate moderate changes in heat and humidity, it could be a delightful enterprise in miniature.

The sun sets at about 5:30 and it is dark at about 6. At 6:15, when we are finally eating our lobsters for supper, Paul shouts, "Bruce, snake!" I race over to discover a freshly shed Madagascan tree boa crawling slowly along the ground through leaf litter. Its skin has an iridescence in the light of my flashlight. I gently pick it up and we all have a good look. It is a beautiful creature. I am particularly impressed with the looks of its head, which has raised, beaded scales on top and lip pits for infra-red heat detection.

After supper, at 7 P.M., we begin a long night walk down the path I had taken with Felix earlier. Right away we find another species of snake, *Liopholidophis lateralis*, which resembles a garter snake in color pattern. It lies on the boardwalk over a small creek and bulges with a freshly ingested food item that I suspect is the fat plated lizard that I saw earlier right on that same spot. I have no difficulty picking up any snake I see, even if I don't know what species it is, because no venomous snakes are found in Madagascar. Next we find a pair of leaf-tailed geckos mating on a two-inch sapling about twelve inches off the ground.

Felix spots a tiny, white, furry face peeping out from under leaf litter on the ground. When I get there, the leaf litter is moving, so I press my hand down on top of the movement to try to hold it still and find out what it is. We worry that it might be a small spiny tenrec and I might get quills in my hand, but I feel the muscles and warm fur of some small mammal and no pricking quills. I feel it moving down a hole and escaping, so I scoop it up in my other hand and promptly get a sharp bite. In my hand I have a white, mole-like animal with a long shrew- or mole-like snout and white fur. It is as big as a North American mole or bigger, but its hands are not as adapted for burrowing nor as powerful as the mole's. It has no or very tiny pinnae (external ears), and an almost hairless, short tail, about half as long as its body. I believe it is a rice tenrec, *Oryzorictus*, in a subfamily of mammals (Oryzorictinae) endemic to Madagascar. One species has four fingers but this one has five. It is a very interesting insectivore, indeed, because it has converged, morphologically and ecologically, on true moles in a completely different insectivore family. Once again, I am seeing convergent evolution in organisms that have been evolving on the isolated island of Madagascar for millions of years.

The lowland spiny tenrec (*Hemicentetes semispinosus*) that I expected to find here belongs to another subfamily of mammals endemic to Madagascar, and represents an even more spectacular example of convergent evolution. Hedgehogs, porcupines, and echidnas all have modified hairs that serve as protective spines. Amazingly, the five species of spiny tenrecs also have spines that are modified hairs. Tenrecs are among the most primitive of placental mammals, having several primitive characteristics such as largely nocturnal activity, body temperature varying according to ambient temperature like an amphibian or reptile, an opening called a cloaca that is common to both the anus and urogenital tracts, and undescended testes. Tenrecs were probably among the earliest mammals to arrive on Madagascar and are, therefore, the oldest surviving lineage of mammals on the island.

When I release the rice tenrec, Felix tells me that the climax of the night will be finding an aye-aye. We walk to a hardwood tree that Felix showed me earlier in the day in which dozens of small, shallow holes had been bitten into the bark. When we arrive, I am thrilled when we find an aye-aye on the trunk only ten feet off the ground, looking down at us. Related to lemurs, it is the only living member of its own family—and, of course, it's endemic to Madagascar. We creep up and I begin photographing it. The animal soon begins feeding, and seems totally undisturbed by our presence in spite of our three flashlights on it as well as my camera's flash going off repeatedly. We keep at it for about half an hour until I run out of film.

We discover two more snakes on the way back to camp. One is a juvenile of the garter snake look-alike; the other is a long, slender snake with a blunt head and vertical pupils, a species of the genus *Stenophis*. These snakes are taxonomically not yet well known in Madagascar, so the field guides aren't clear about which species this is. Its bulbous head, vertical pupils, large mouth, and arboreal habit make it obviously a member of the Boiginae, or rear-fanged snakes, whose best-known member is the black and yellow mangrove snake, *Boiga dendrophila*, found in southeast Asia. The brown tree snake, *Boiga irregularis*, that has plagued the island of Guam, is probably better known.

We wake to the sounds of Malagasy people giggling and laughing as they sit around in the cooking area. Affectionate coos emanate between a mother and a two-year-old toddler, a very cute little boy named Ibalido. Low-angle sunlight filters through the overarching rainforest. Waves lap gently onto the nearby shore, and we feel on our faces a cool sea breeze waxing and waning. Light brown sands, dark green leaves, thick air, high-pitched bird sounds—these are some of the sensory inputs of a slice of Nosy Mangabe morning.

After breakfast we go out on a five-mile round-trip walk to a beach northwest of the main camp. Only 100 yards from camp, we run into another *Sanzinia* coiled asleep at the base of a log, a greenish male with big spurs. About halfway down the trail, Paul and Felix escort me into the rainforest off the trail to locate a pair of black and white ruffed lemurs (*Varecia variegata*), at which I get a good look.

About three-fourths of the way down the trail we find still another *Sanzinia* coiled on the ground among some sticks next to the trail. It is a male, also, and looks a bit underfed. I am impressed with how many snakes, lizards, and mammals we have been seeing.

Before lunch I walk behind a small building with wooden siding and startle a medium-sized gecko, which begins to run up the wall. I grab it only to have the shock of the day when I open my hand and find that a number of its really large scales have rubbed off, leaving its pink flesh exposed. At first I can't believe I am holding it tightly enough to cause it injury, then I realize that I have an example of one of the fish-scale geckos, *Geckolepis maculata,* in my hand. They readily lose scales in order to escape the clutches of native predators. This is quite a natural history bonus for me. I did not expect to see one of these amazing geckos here. I feel sorry for it, though, because the skin under the scales looks scalped. It will probably regrow the scales sooner than I think. I notice that it is regenerating its tail. That makes two adaptations in a single species involving the easy loss of body parts for use in escaping predators.

We nap for 40 minutes after lunch and then I take off on a solo snorkeling foray in the waters just off camp. I work my way northwest among rocks along the shoreline. Right away, I find a lovely, purple, checkered moray eel, lots of sergeant majors, wrasses, parrotfish, a lionfish or two, a couple of jack crevalle, and many small butterfly fishes. The most impressive sights are some large round and shelf-like corals, about 20 feet in diameter. Other corals are spread out on the seafloor, but branching corals are few. The water is not crystal clear, however; there is only about 50 feet of visibility. No doubt the turbidity is due to agricultural runoff from the mainland across the bay. Sadly, as unnaturally high sediment loads continue to run off into the bay, the coral reef ecosystem here will collapse.

Food in this part of Madagascar is prepared over small charcoal cookers. The cook squats to prepare our food. Out of the corner of my eye, I see him wiping our fresh tuna steaks clean after they have fallen into the dirt, so I am not surprised when I find grit in my meat at supper. I just hope all the smaller stuff that I can't taste—the microorganisms—have been heated sufficiently to keep my stomach from going berserk. We are served boiled carrots and potatoes, and a rubbery quiche on the side. We drink eau vive, which is what the locals call bottled water, accompanied by cut-up hot dog buns for our bread.

After supper, I go out again for a night walk with the guides. We walk up a trail to a place called The Tombs, where the bones of dead people are stored, some in concrete and some in wooden boxes on the ground under a large, overhanging rock. On the trail I find three black snakes with a yellow upper lip stripe and shiny smooth scales that are quite iridescent. My field guides lead me to believe they are *Pseudoxyropus heterurus*, a species with no common name. We also see two new kinds of geckos, a rather large one on a tree with the general looks of a Mediterranean gecko that I never catch and can't identify, and the other on the ground, a slender gecko with a black tail and a yellow tail tip, which is probably *Paroedura homalorhinus*.

We then re-walk last night's trail to the aye-aye tree and see another black snake and a four-foot-long example of the *Liopholidophis lateralis* we caught last night with a food item in its gut—but no aye-aye. The guides say it is too late for it to be active. I arrive back at the tent exhausted and fall into a deep snoring sleep almost as soon as I hit the deck. When I get up to pee in the still darkness of 3:30 A.M., tiny fireflies light the ground and leaves. I stand in the sweet night air of the western Indian Ocean and think how crazy it is that a few aye-ayes had to be transplanted onto this tiny, two-square-mile island because the species is nearly extinct elsewhere in Madagascar, the world's fourth largest island of 226,658 square miles.

We say our goodbyes to the magical little island of Nosy Mangabe and then are ferried by boat across the bay to camp for two nights near the remote village of Ambanizana, home to 800 people who live in ten-foot-square stick huts on pilings with palm thatch roofs. I walk through extensive rice plantations that have usurped all the bottomland soils of the local river valley and learn that the village population has already outgrown its rice supply. Nobody in Ambanizana is fat. In order to generate income to purchase sufficient food, villagers have cleared the steep mountain slopes right into the Masoala National Park where they grow cloves as a trade item. And I see rainforest trees hacked down for use as cooking fuel the first several hundred yards inside the park.

In order to see the endangered ringtail lemur, *Lemur catta*, we fly to the south end of this thousand-mile-long despoiled Eden—three times as large as Florida—just to spend three hours on a puny habitat island of only 660 acres surrounded by 200,000 acres of planted sisal (Mexican agave). We are delighted to see dozens of these beautiful and graceful lemurs, which have been habituated to humans and are all over the place. Inbreeding depression will probably decimate these animals if a single cyclone doesn't get them first.

We then fly back to Tana and use up two days getting through the crush of humanity to reach Perinet, a preserve all of 2,025 acres in size, where we come to see the nearly extinct Indri, largest of lemurs. Flying over Madagascar we often can't see the ground for the dense smoke of fires set to keep the native vegetation suppressed. In the mountains east of Tana I discover that a lot of the few patches of forest we can see from the air are in fact not remnants of the once-extensive rainforests, but alien eucalypts introduced from Australia. Neither fire nor the axe kills these eucalypts, which sprout vigorously from cut stumps or charred stems alike. The pungent litter is highly flammable and when burning, assists in killing native plants, most of which are fire tender.

Alien plants, barren landscapes, rivers of mud, lost native ecosystems, unique but endangered flora and fauna, more than 14 million people and growing with no end in sight—we are only too glad to be leaving Madagascar and flying home to Florida.

Our first view of Florida is the abrupt boundary of developed landscape impinging on the Everglades as we fly into the Miami Airport from the south. Looking down at the sea of roads, houses, parking lots, and other trappings of development, I am struck by how similar the landscape appears with that over Tana. Flying home to Tallahassee at the north end of the peninsula, we see the concrete and asphalt of Greater Miami changing to vast sugar cane plantations.

Soon we see the ugly scars of phosphate mines over hundreds of square miles, and beyond I strain my eyes but can't find any remnant of the longleaf pine forest, once the state's most extensive upland ecosystem, now reduced in Florida to less than ten percent of its original extent.

As we approach Tallahassee over endless rows of planted slash and sand pines, it occurs to me that these pines are, themselves, alien species to the upland sites on which they have been planted. Although they are Florida pines, they are just as alien as *Eucalyptus* would be in replacing longleaf pine that was the native tree there. They form densely stocked forests that do not allow sunlight to reach the forest floor like longleaf pine does. This drastically changes the rich longleaf pine savanna groundcover to a barren land with little else save pine needles. That is part of the reason why the red-cockaded woodpecker, ivory-billed woodpecker, indigo snake, southern hognose snake, gopher tortoise, Florida pine snake, flatwoods salamander, and Florida panther no longer walk or fly in these woods.

Alien plants, barren landscapes, lost native ecosystems, unique but endangered flora and fauna . . . it all seems the same as in Madagascar. Florida, too, has more than 14 million people. We, too, are polluting the atmosphere, soil, and water. Looking down at a new mega-development in southeast Tallahassee, I wonder if there are any fundamental differences between us at all. At least Madagascar reached its condition through natural processes of population growth, of which the people were largely ignorant. Americans are much better educated, however, and should realize that there are ultimate limits to growth.

In Florida, though, we cling to the notion that growth is good. Politicians promote it, developers love it, business supports it, and the working man and woman have clearly benefited from it—so far. This philosophy of growth-based economy is really economy that is based ultimately on human population growth, and it pervades the entire country, not just Florida. Surely people can see that there are limits to population growth that any given area can support.

Will we sit by and allow our numbers to crowd out all the other creatures? Will we wait until our numbers, alone, compel us to react to what surely will be difficult times ahead? Or are we intelligent enough to foresee the future and begin acting now to find an economic philosophy that puts quality of life ahead of unbridled growth? It should be clear to any thinking person that at some point in our future, Americans will be confronted with severe shortages of living space, drinking water, and the good life. At what human population level will that be? 400 million? 500 million? 1 billion? 5 billion? More?

15
TREEFROG DINES ON BATS
Prey Turns Predator

THE STENCH OF AMMONIA RISING OFF WET BAT GUANO BURNS
my nose and the acrid vapors nearly choke me as I try to inhale. I hear
a muffled roar deep in the abyss below me. Listening carefully, I can
distinguish myriad clicks and squeaks amidst the rush of beating wings.
I peer down the beam of my headlight into the 70-foot shaft and see
blurred movement, but the light is nearly absorbed in the blackness.
My excitement is at a high pitch. I have been here before and know
well what will happen in the next few minutes. Crouching down in a
tiny alcove just below and back a few inches from the mouth of this
Crack of Doom, I am poised to photograph some spectacular predation
events as 110,000 little bent-wing bats (*Miniopterus australis*) begin
an evening's emergence from Bat Cleft, a small 8-by-30-foot fissure
in the limestone sidewall of Mt. Etna near Rockhampton, Queensland.
It's late in the bat's maternity season when the young of the year are
first learning to fly.

At 7 P.M. sharp, the first bats spiral upward, furtively shoot
out of the maw of the cleft, and disappear into the waning twilight.
Immediately the furor begins. Now ten bats, then 20, 50, and soon
hundreds are fluttering around me, their wingtips brushing my face
and arms. Bat Cleft is so narrow that the bats have to fly zig zag

paths from one end of the cleft to the other in order to gain sufficient altitude to reach the open sky. So many bats are exiting the maternity chambers 70 feet below that they interfere with each other's flight. I hear the tiny flicking of hundreds of wings hitting wings and brushing against the rough limestone sidewalls as they fly around me. To my amazement, my breathing is soon easier because so many beating wings are mixing the thick ammonia-laden cavern air with outside fresh air. Myriad bats spiraling upwards create a continuous wind in my face and a low-pitched roar like the sound inside a conch shell.

Now come the predators. Noel Sands, my Queensland Parks and Wildlife Service designated guide, shouts down, "Bruce, here comes a spotted python behind you." I slowly turn my head and see a small dark snake (*Liasis maculosus*), about 30 inches long, moving over the limestone boulders of the cramped side-chamber I am squatting in. On one of the boulders that the snake passes sits a big green treefrog, *Litoria cerulea*. The snake crawls in a straight line, reaches my boot, crawls over it without hesitating, and finally comes to a stop on a jagged piece of limestone that juts out into the cleft. It anchors its body on the rough rock, then stretches its head and the front half of its body out over the abyss. The flying bats are making a turn at this point and some of them bump into the limestone, and the snake. Soon the little python nabs one in the air by biting sideways when it feels touched. It begins constricting the bat.

I am lucky to observe this drama. The numbers of spotted pythons and other snakes that feed annually on these bats have declined drastically. The Queensland Parks and Wildlife Service suspects that reptile poachers have been at work. They have a plan to insert little pit tags under the skin of the snakes so that the unwitting poachers, not knowing they possess marked snakes, can be caught and prosecuted. Another benefit of the pit tags will be to learn if the same snakes return each year.

I feel a thud on my boot. The treefrog is moving forward, too. I look back and see another treefrog coming into my small alcove from a crack in the limestone behind me that leads to the outside world. Eventually, both frogs make their way around me and take up positions at the edge of the abyss. One of them sits on a flat part of the spotted python's rock, just inches from the snake. Now here comes another spotted python. It moves along the side of my cramped space at the level of my head, then reaches the sidewall of the abyss and anchors itself about fifteen feet away from me. The limestone is rough and provides a pitted and bumpy surface that the snakes can cling to. This snake holds onto a nearly vertical sidewall and dangles in the air among the bats. I watch it snap at bats that brush against it. Soon, it, too, hangs down with a bat coiled in strangling loops.

In the frenzy of the main exodus, many bats alight on the limestone sidewalls for a few seconds before renewing their upward progress. Some land on me, crawl around briefly on my chest, arms, and face, and get in my hair. I remain frozen, trying to observe and not interfere with their activities. There are so many bats that they knock each other out of the air. A few land on the flat rock near the treefrog. It stares glumly at them. Each bat flies off. And now I see a new kind of snake on the left sidewall of the abyss, orange-brown, skinnier and longer than the spotted python. It is the brown tree snake, *Boiga irregularis*, a species that has wrought great havoc on the native fauna of the mid-Pacific island of Guam, but here in Australia it is in its native home. It has a bulbous head and red-reflective eyes, and like the second python, it takes a position hanging from the sloping sidewall and dangling out into the air to intercept bats. Soon it has one. It seems not so efficient as the little python in killing and ingesting its prey because it tries to swallow the bat alive without constricting it. The struggling bat manages to inflict some good bites on its assailant, but loses the ultimate battle.

While transfixed watching the bat/tree-snake drama, I forget to check the treefrogs. I look down and am aghast! The posterior of a little bent-wing bat hangs limply out of the mouth of the frog on the flat rock! "Eureka!" I want to shout. Instantly I realize that this is a momentous observation. Years ago the discovery of some Central American bats that eat treefrogs set herpetology abuzz with excitement. This scene, of frogs eating bats, however, is something altogether different, and to my knowledge, the only known example. I can't believe my good luck at being present at such a unique predation event.

I struggle to bend down in the cramped space to get photographs of the event on a level with the frog. The frog sits facing me with the bat sticking out of its big mouth. The frog is not much larger than the bat, which is no bigger than a large house mouse. While I watch the frog, the first python works at finding the head of the second bat it has caught and constricted. Frog and python are inches apart eating bats simultaneously. In the next two minutes, the frog makes three gulping movements and the bat disappears. Altogether on three different nights, I see frogs eating bats four times, and snakes at least thirty times. A frog simply snaps up the front part of a bat when one crawls up to it. The bat struggles for ten or fifteen seconds, then goes limp, probably from suffocation. A few gulps by the treefrog and the event is over.

A snake predation event involves much more action. The snake holds itself out in the air and waits until it is touched, at which time it snaps right or left to catch the unsuspecting bat. A python constricts the bat, killing it by suffocation, and then holds the dead and immobile bat with its coils while searching for the bat's head with its snout. The brown tree snake simply holds the bat in its mouth and tries to swallow it by whatever part it has grasped. Both snakes eventually have to swallow a bat head first. This becomes tricky when the snake's mouth reaches the wings, which must be forced backward as the advancing jaws press them to the rear. Altogether the time required for a spotted python or a brown tree snake to eat a little bent-wing bat is on the order of ten to twenty minutes. The green treefrog does it in less than five.

Bat Cleft is the centerpiece of Mt. Etna Caves National Park, created out of a great political conflict between champions of bat conservation and limestone-mining interests. Bat Cleft was discovered in 1965, and almost immediately thereafter was threatened by the quarrying of limestone from Mt. Etna's eastern face. Symmetrical Mt. Etna, 923 feet in elevation, reminded early settlers of the silhouette of its namesake in Sicily. For more than twenty years, heated battles flared and there was even a blockade of mining trucks by human bodies. Thanks to the resulting international attention, the National Park was created.

Bat Cleft supports the largest known maternity colony of the little bent-wing bat, whose naked young require warm air when their mothers are out foraging at night. The required warmth is trapped in domes or closed vertical shafts in the ceiling of the large cave. Bat Cleft is unusual, also, in having a large pool of rainwater in the floor of the main cave. This prevents closure of the cave by the build-up of bat guano, because fresh guano decomposes and dissolves in the rainwater and is carried away in solution when the water seeps into the ground.

Australian scientists have documented that the 110,000 female little bent-wings at Bat Cleft produce about 82,000 young each year. In late January, newly volant young bats, first trying out their wings, make easy pickings for predators. Snakes and treefrogs have only to sit and wait until the clumsy young bats land near them or brush against them. Ten years ago, the carpet python (*Morelia spilota*) was a common snake predator seen feeding on the bats here, but the cane toad (*Bufo marinus*) arrived and this seems to have led to the disappearance of the carpet python. Cane toads have anti-predator toxins in their skin. It is thought that the carpet python dies by poisoning when it eats a toad. Fortunately, I have not seen any cane toads near the mouth of Bat Cleft, but days earlier, while being escorted underground in adjacent caves, I saw many big ones.

Noel Sands and his Central Queensland Speleological Society colleagues, Peter Berrill and Clive Kavanagh, led the struggle to save Bat Cleft and create Mt. Etna National Park. Sitting around the mouth of the cave one night, they tell me that only a few years ago they witnessed as many as 30 or 40 snakes of all three species feeding on emerging bats. Records of frogs eating bats have been only occasional, however. After getting special permits to film here and with the eyes of three National Park representatives helping, we see no more than five or six snakes attempting to feed during any one of six nights in a two-week period. Apparently the snake poachers have made an impact.

Crudely calculating, 30 snakes times three feeds per night times sixty nights equals about 5,400 bats, or about 3 percent (5,400/190,000) of the bats in those years when snake predation was at its zenith. This year the predation from snakes may have declined to about 900 bats or roughly one half of one percent of the bat population. If these figures are anywhere close to correct, predation by snakes on the little bent-wing bat at Bat Cleft is insignificant. Predation by the green treefrog, in contrast, is an order of magnitude smaller.

The green treefrog is Australia's most famous frog. It is the most common Australian frog sold in the pet trade around the world. Bright green in color with large toepads and a thick, glandular ridge over the eye and ear, older well-fed ones look like stuffed bell peppers. This is the frog most likely to stimulate a scream from restrooms in Australian caravan parks when a startled user spots two bulging eyes peering out of the loo. It ranges widely from the Kimberley in extreme northwestern Australia to most of the populated east coast. The green treefrog is a ubiquitous animal whose own plight might be threatened by the highly competitive and cannibalistic cane toad were it not for the fact that the green treefrog can climb and the cane toad cannot.

Two nights later, I get another chance to witness the spectacle of treefrogs eating bats. Hunkering down in my cramped rockhole, I see another green treefrog waiting on the flat ledge at the edge of the abyss. Spotted pythons and brown tree snakes come and go. Then, during the heaviest outpouring of bats, a number of young drop onto the rock where the treefrog sits. As one of the bats nervously struggles forward directly toward the frog, I see the frog's large mouth quickly open and, in a blur, snap shut leaving the posterior half of the bat protruding. The frog sits there making no movement. The little bat's legs struggle and kick a while, then go limp. The frog seems unperturbed at my camera's flashes. Soon the frog makes a swallowing movement and some of the bat moves beyond its lips. Then, before I am ready to fire the camera, the frog uses one hand to push the bat's wing forward so the wing will lie parallel with the body. Two more gulps and the bat disappears down its throat.

I sit in the dark, turning on my headlight only periodically so as not to disturb the bats too much. The frog sits there for two hours and eats no more. Its belly appears quite full. Other green treefrogs appear. One night I see five, but do not witness any feeding events. In the dark I can concentrate on my thoughts. I'm amazed that I got to see an amphibian swallowing a mammal, and now my attention is riveted on the bats. The rush of air, the muffled roar of wingbeats, the soft caress of batwings, and the smell of guano all combine to make me feel insignificant in the immensity of this great outpouring of life from the mountain. When I look up, I see dozens of W-shapes streaming skyward through the beam of my headlight.

Grateful to have had such close contact with these beautiful animals, I feel humbled in their presence. I think of all the tribulations the bats must endure to survive: snakes, frogs, long flights to find food, cold winter hibernation, and bulldozers that would destroy their ancient breeding enclaves. Then I remember that the other creatures that operated those bulldozers have recognized the importance of Bat Cleft to the little bent-wing bat by establishing a national park. That's the major difference between us and the bats and the frogs and the snakes. We can contemplate the beauty of other creatures. We can be emotionally uplifted by them. And we can take actions, sometimes, to diminish our own impacts on them, such as making a national park out of a small mountain that is vital to the survival of a species of bat. This is a good thing.

I can't help but wonder, though: in the long run, will it be enough?

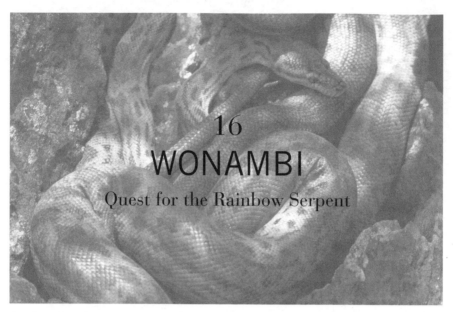

16
WONAMBI
Quest for the Rainbow Serpent

DURING DREAMTIME, IN THE BEGINNING OF ALL THINGS, A giant serpent is said to have emerged from the ocean. Wherever it crawled about on land, it gouged out the canyons and riverbeds of the world. When it rose into the sky, it brought down the life-giving rains. Where it came to rest, its body made up the mountains. Today Aboriginal people of Australia call that mythological snake " rainbow serpent." It is the guardian of all fresh water. You can see it in the skies when it rains, in the mists of waterfalls, in billabongs, and even in shallow wells that you dig in the sand.

Among the nearly 500 tribes of Aboriginal peoples, the rainbow serpent story is the most widespread creation myth. I came to Australia in 2000 to learn about the rainbow serpent, and to discover the origin of the myth. Which snake was the model for the rainbow serpent? Was it one of the splendidly iridescent pythons, of which Australia has 17 of the world's 30 species? Was it a giant extinct snake that died out following the arrival of man? Did the story come to Australia following the migrations of ancient man out of Africa? Or is there another explanation that is not readily apparent?

These questions are foremost in my mind when David Wright and Mimi Magee accompany me to seek answers. We have a splendid time, over a period of several months, meeting interesting people and chasing down leads—and what we discover about which snake might have been the origin of the rainbow serpent myth is wholly unexpected.

Our first stop is Naracoorte Caves National Park, a World Heritage fossil site at the southeastern corner of the continent.

Naracoorte and Wonambi. The weather this May morning is drizzly, alternating with clearing skies, off and on all day. We get on the road to Naracoorte about 11:30 A.M., taking the Glenelg Highway from Ballarat to Casterton, then north through Penola to Naracoorte. The scenery is rural farms for most of the way, lots of sheep and cattle, some pine plantations, and agriculture.

We pass at least five flocks of more than a hundred white cockatoos milling about in pastures. Along the roadside many magpies and galah parrots sit on fence wires and forage in the bush. Lunch is fish and chips at a small takeout cafe in Lake Bolac. We cross into South Australia about 4 P.M. and, from horizon to horizon, little else is visible but grape arbors with grape leaves turning yellow, brown, and red. At this latitude (38° S), May is the equivalent of November in the northern hemisphere.

Next morning, Cecelia Carter and Andrew Bourne meet us at Naracoorte Caves National Park. We are first shown Victoria Cave, where a huge cone of mixed sediment and animal bones has accumulated over the millennia, the animals having fallen through a hole in the ceiling of a large room in the cave. Cecelia tells us that of the estimated 5,000 tons of such sediments, less than about 5% of them have been scientifically excavated. Bones of extinct animals are found in the floor sediments all over this and other local caves, in addition to the talus cones. The carcasses of animals that died following a fall of about 30 feet onto the talus cone became disarticulated, for the most part, because they slowly were washed down the slope by rains, but animals that survived the fall wandered off into the recesses of the cave, died, and later were covered with clay and silt. In the far back of one cave we find a mummified opossum that fell in a few months ago and is in the process of being added to the fossil fauna of the cave. Many caves have beautiful speleothems of all kinds, including soda straws, stalactites, stalagmites, curtains, and rimstone pools.

Inside Victoria Cave paleontologists have erected the complete skeleton of an extinct marsupial "lion," *Thylacoleo carnifex*. It stands next to the skeleton of *Macropus rufogriseus*, a present-day kangaroo. The marsupial lion is about the size of a leopard with large incisors that project forward and served to stab its prey, while a single, large premolar has a long, shearing surface for slicing flesh, skin, and maybe even bones. Its strong, opposable thumbs have very long, curved nails that probably sliced through prey like scimitar blades. It is thought that the lion actually filled the leopard niche by dragging its prey up into low trees to escape marauding competitors such as tazzie devils and the thylacine.

In addition to the present-day living Tasmanian devil, there was a larger, extinct devil in the fossil fauna. Also, bones of the modern koala are present with those of a giant koala that was about 25 percent larger than the modern species. My favorite extinct giant marsupial, the size of a small black bear, was *Palorchestes azeal*, a large herbivore with a long snout, somewhat like that of a tapir. The similarity ends there, however, because its powerful forelimbs and koala-like claws indicate that it may have occupied the same ecological niche as the extinct American ground sloths.

Then there was *Zygomaturus trilobus*, a giant marsupial cow that was about the size of a small hippopotamus. It may have had similar habits, living in small herds in swamps and around water. It possessed strong tusks in its lower jaw that may have been used in scooping up aquatic plants to eat. Its nostrils were raised up on the skull, which would have assisted it while submerged or feeding in water. Another extinct marsupial monster was *Diprotodon australis*, the largest marsupial ever known to have lived anywhere in the world. It was a huge herbivore weighing at least 4,000 pounds and it stood as tall as a man at its shoulders. The mocked-up individual on display in the Naracoorte Center is impressive, indeed, dwarfing me with its bulk of a small elephant.

The fossil deposits of the Naracoorte Caves contain an amazing number of kangaroos. In addition to the bones of living species, there are remains of no less than nine species of extinct, leaf-eating kangaroos, including *Procoptodon goliah* that stood nine feet tall in order to reach up for leaves, and may have weighed around 600 pounds. Others were in the genus *Sthenurus*, meaning "strong-tailed," with a single-toed foot and large, hard nails. The top of one deposit under study has been dated at about 70,000 years ago and the bottom at about 205,000 years, giving these deposits extra value because they aren't a small slice of time, but offer continuous information over a long period of time.

In a gridded-off area, graduate student Rebecca Gresham shows us what we have come here to see: two vertebrae of *Wonambi naracoortensis*, the huge fossil snake for which this site is famous. Wonambi is the last species of an ancient snake family, the Madtsoiidae, a group of snakes known only from the southern continents that once formed the ancient mega-continent of Gondwana. Fossils of the Madtsoiidae are known as early as 90 million years ago in the late Cretaceous of South America, Africa, Madagascar, and Australia—25 million years before the dinosaurs went extinct. No Madtsoiid snakes survive anywhere today, but fossils of *Wonambi naracoortensis* indicate that this species was present in Australia until the late Pleistocene, only about 40,000 years ago, and maybe even more recently. Aboriginal man is known to have arrived in Australia at least 60,000 years ago, so it's highly probable that man was in Australia at the same time as the giant *Wonambi naracoortensis*. Was *Wonambi* the source of the rainbow serpent myth?

Wonambi is a local Aboriginal word meaning giant snake or rainbow serpent, which is why paleontologist Meredith Smith used that name when she described the snake in 1976. A chill goes up my spine as I stare down in my hand at a vertebra of *Wonambi*. This giant snake, estimated to be about 18 feet long and thick as a telegraph pole, was the last of a long line of snakes in a primitive snake family whose evolutionary history was longer than the rise and domination of Earth by modern mammals and flowering plants. Dozen of thoughts flash through my mind. Was *Wonambi* an aquatic snake? Did it have rainbowlike iridescence like so many modern snakes, and especially the Australian pythons? Was it an easy prey for hunter-gather humans? And isn't it ironic that Australia lost its megafaunal marsupials—as well as this giant snake—*after* the arrival of man?

I probably won't learn much more about the origin of the rainbow serpent myth in southeastern Australia. We learn that fossils of *Wonambi* are also known from northern Queensland and that rainbow serpent rock paintings are common on the Cape York Peninsula in Queensland where Aboriginal people still have knowledge of their traditional culture. Years ago I had a too-short visit to the 750-mile Cape York Peninsula, so I'm keen to return. We pack up the Land Cruiser and head north.

17 years earlier. Roaring into Laura, northern Queensland, in a cloud of bulldust, I lean the Kawasaki motorcycle over on its kickstand, walk into the old Laura Pub, sit down at the bar, and order a cold beer. My left knee burns from the scrape it got earlier when the small termite mound I kicked had unceremoniously dismounted me from the cycle. It was thus that I rudely discovered that the damned things are as hard as concrete. And my right middle finger is throbbing.

"Hey, mate, looks like you could use a doctor for that finger," blurts a nice old Aboriginal man sitting next to me.

"Yeah, I cut the tip of the fleshy part off on a sharp piece of metal on my cycle a little while ago" I volunteer. The finger is wrapped tightly in a handkerchief, red with my blood and full of dirty bulldust. "Today has not been one of my better days. Look at what I did to my knee," I say.

We strike up a conversation and I tell him that I am a biologist on a mission to see the Cape York Peninsula from its base to the tip and that I am especially interested in amphibians and reptiles. I inquire about where I might go to see these animals. He tells me I should be able to see snakes and lizards most anywhere, but wouldn't I like to see some Aboriginal rock art? He'll be glad to escort me to some places off the beaten track.

A walkabout with this nice old man is very tempting. He promises a treasure-trove of beautiful rock art with pictures of plenty of reptiles. I think it over during a second can of beer, and then tell him I am quite interested in his proposition, but I have to try to get to the tip of the peninsula first. If I make it to the "Top," as the Aussies call it, and have the time when I return, I will take him up on his offer. I shake his weather-beaten hand and roar off into the dreaded bulldust, deep accumulations of very fine, silty Cape York Peninsula dust that can surprise the unwary driver. I don't have time to get back and figure it's another of life's missed opportunities. Little do I know that our life paths are destined to cross again.

Laura and George Musgrave. Now it's 17 years later and I'm back on the Cape York Peninsula with David and Mimi trying to learn about the origin of the rainbow serpent myth. We're following a man named Victor and another man I am told is his grandfather, George Musgrave. We follow Victor's vehicle to the end of the bitumen (Aussie word for asphalt) south of Laura and then onto a one-lane track into the eucalypt woodlands on the east side of the main road. Immediately, we need four-wheel drive because of the deep sand and very rough, rutted, rocky stretches up steep slopes. We pass through an extensive stand of grass trees rising three to five feet tall on naked stems—they are like palms except that the filamentous leaves bursting out of the top of the small trunks look like clumps of long grass. The flowering structure, a woody stalk, rises vertically five to six feet above the grassy tuft at the top of some of the plants.

When we reach the end of the track at the Aboriginal rock art site known as "Mushroom," I squeeze myself out of the Land Cruiser, walk up to George, and hold out my hand in introduction. "Hi, George, I'm Bruce. It's a real pleasure to meet you," I say. Before I can continue, George startles me by calmly replying, "I'm glad to see you, but I've met you before."

I hesitate a little, not knowing how to take this, and then I say, "I'm not sure what you mean. You've met me before?"

"Yes," he says, "when you were here before."

I puzzle over this a minute, then a dawning begins rising in my brain. "George," I say, "I was here seventeen years ago in nineteen-eighty-three. I drove through Laura on a motorcycle. You remember that!?"

"Yes," he says, "but you were a lot younger-looking then!" Everybody has a good laugh on me. Then Victor chimes in and says, "Yes, Poppy told us in the car after he spotted you when we picked him up that he remembered you from years ago."

I am dumbstruck. It seems incredible that this man, who is now 80 years of age, could remember me from that long ago. Then George says, "Yes, you came in town on a motorcycle and talked to me about taking you to see some Aboriginal rock art. I told you I would take you, but you said you were in a hurry to get up to Bamaga, and would look me up on your way back. You never did!"

You could bowl me over with a cough. How incredible that this wonderful old, white-haired man with the twinkling black eyes and wizened body remembers me after all these years. All the rest of our day together I can't help musing about the irony of his recollection of me. We couldn't have spoken together for more than 30 minutes, if that, such a long time ago. I certainly don't remember his face, and I had to consult my journal of 17 years ago to discover that I had written about the meeting. The difference in our memories may have to do with our cultural backgrounds.

You'd never know that George is 80. He moves around on gnarled, bare feet nimble as a cat. He was born in Musgrave, about 135 km north of Laura where he now lives. When a boy, he had a young dingo for a pet. Every day—morning, midday, and afternoon—he says, his father taught him the ways of the bush, and he learned tracking by watching the dingo. When he was a young man, he drove cattle by horse from Musgrave to Mareeba. At one time he was a crocodile shooter. Eventually, thanks to his tracking skills, he was hired as a police tracker. He tells me of many occasions when he successfully tracked people lost in the bush. With such mental and visual acuity, it's no wonder his memory of faces is more vivid than mine. At least that's what I tell myself.

A little later, while I am still shaking my head over my surprise at this second meeting, he repeats that when I had hurried off, he'd been expecting me to come back. I blurt out, "George, yes, I did say I'd come back, but I didn't say when. Here I am!" We all have a hearty laugh on George.

Then we get to the business of what we came here for. George leads us to a huge rock about 30 yards in diameter that is undercut all the way around and provides an overhang up to 20 feet wide —a veritable mushroom, as its name implies. On the short walk there George shows me at least four different plants that have medicinal or other utilitarian value. He is a walking encyclopedia of herbal information and among the last remaining elderly custodians of the secrets of Australian nature in the Laura area.

Before we enter the sacred zone under the overhang, George stops us and sings out a few incantations, apparently hailing the spirit guardians. I get the impression that he is asking permission for us to come forward.

Under "Mushroom Rock" we examine many different Aboriginal art figures, including yams, crocodile, kangaroo, fishes, echidna, people, eel, and a snake. It is the snake that I want to focus on, mostly, and when I ask about the snake, I learn that George's people belong to the Taipan Tribe. He is evasive, though, in talking about the rainbow serpent.

I am delighted to learn firsthand from this elder the local significance of Aboriginal rock paintings. For one thing, George tells me that the animals figured are pictures of what was eaten here. It was common practice to paint a picture of a kangaroo, for instance, after one had been killed and eaten at the rock shelter.

Then George shows us something very touching—little handprints on the wall, the size of a baby's. These, George says, are the prints of a newborn child. Mothers would birth their babies under the rock and mark the birthplace with the prints of the child's hands. The hands were held against the rock, and ochre in water was blown or sprinkled against the hand so that the hand was stenciled on the rock. Ochre is a fine red powder obtained locally by grinding limonite, a form of reddish iron ore found in clay soils. People living in traditional times in Australia always had a real "birthplace" with which they could identify because their birth was commemorated this way by leaving their handprints on the walls of the rock shelter at which they entered

the world. What a lovely practice. I never had the yen to return the
Queen of Angels Hospital in downtown Los Angeles where I was born
to reflect on the mysteries of life, but I envy people who can return to
the "Mushroom" or any of the hundreds of other such sites all around
Laura to commune spiritually with their origins in idyllic natural
surroundings.

Next we drive to an even more hauntingly beautiful place called
"Giant Horse." This is an overhanging rock shelter along the top of
an escarpment overlooking the east side of the Laura River. We climb
down the cliff through huge broken blocks of sandstone and come to
a ledge with a high overhang. There George shows me a 20-foot-long
snake in red ochre. This, he acknowledges, is a rainbow snake, but I
can't get more information out of him about its significance to him or
his people.

George ushers us around to another rock face and an even better
gallery of wonderful rock art. A huge overhang shields a 50-foot-long
vertical wall that is about 15 feet high. On it we see dozens of creatures,
yams, other bushtucker (which means food items), people, and at one
end, a huge horse. The horse motif must have been painted in the past
150 years or so after European contact. A man is represented upside
down, which is an indication that he is dead. This wall is so busy with
paintings and paintings on top of paintings that I go crazy trying to
decipher all the individual animals and plant foods.

George says that all these beautiful pictographs can be interpreted
as a kind of writing. Consider a family group occupying the shelter.
The young children, too small to go out into the bush to forage, could
learn about the local food items by looking at the walls of their house.
What they learn from looking at rock art and some of the elements
of survival are reinforced by stories and legends told around the
campfire.

When we finish at Giant Horse, George breaks off a wattle branch
and sweeps all our footsteps clean. The last man out, he turns to the
site and chants to the spirits again, thanking them for allowing our
trespass.

On the track out, two emus run in front of the vehicle in plain view for at least two minutes. I have had the privilege of seeing ostriches in the wild in southern Africa, but somehow flushing the two emus from the eucalypt bush and watching them run along with their thick hairlike feathers flapping in time with their gait is a more thrilling experience for me. Emus are more primitive-looking anyway, like medium-sized dinosaurs—which they actually are! I am particularly aware of their large, clubby legs, which are stockier than those of ostriches.

We stop at the old Laura Pub, still there, and settle up with Victor and what we owe the Aboriginal community for permission to film at the rock art sites. I sit down with George and ask him again about the rainbow serpent. He pauses for a few moments, realizing that I am not going to give this topic a rest. Then he perks up and says that yesterday, two little ones came out of the tap when he was drawing water in a bucket. He carried them down to the river and poured them into the bigger water. "Rainbow snake is main story," he says, "Everybody knows *that* story. Keeps water, brings rain, makes rainbows, comes out spigots . . . keeps water." After a brief pause, he says, "Every place you go in sand, dig water and see rainbow . . . must pick it up and throw in main water."

After nearly an hour of trying to learn about the rainbow serpent, I have extracted no more out of George. I have the impression that there is something taboo about my inquiry. In fact, I am fast learning that elders and the few Aboriginal people that have knowledge of ancient customs are loath to speak directly about them. I let it slide, but this only piques my curiosity to learn more. I feel like the kid from whom the other kids are openly keeping a secret. On reflection, however, I realize that to George, I may be poking my nose into matters of his culture where it doesn't belong.

I'd been hoping to get some insights about the rainbow serpent from George. I'd hoped maybe he'd make some comments to the effect that way back in time there was a giant monster snake that ate people. Or maybe I wanted to hear what George had to say about the amethystine python, Australia's largest, and the world's third longest, snake, which is found on the Cape York Peninsula. But George is too tight-lipped. I suppose it's ignorant of me to think that I might learn the truth about a mythical story that has been passed down by word of mouth for hundreds of generations. Instead of prying into George's religion and spiritual beliefs, I'd really rather spend a month with George on foot out in the bush learning what he knows about the wonderful natural history of his country. Alas, I am here on another mission, again, and must take my leave of this pleasant old gentleman while once again wishing to share more of his company.

All the literature we have consulted points to Arnhem Land as the place we next should visit. A particularly large sample of Rainbow Serpent rock paintings can be found in western Arnhem Land, which is also the place that has been the focus of a good deal of archaeological study.

Mt. Borradaile and Aburga—The drive to Kakadu National Park is long and hot. We spend a couple of days viewing the rock paintings elbow to elbow with hundreds of foreign tourists who are shuttled around the sites in diesel-belching buses. Then our luck changes.

At suppertime in Jabiru, a young Australian named Adrian Parker regales patrons of the hotel restaurant by playing the didgeridoo. After he finishes, I walk up to purchase one of his musical CDs and thank him for the splendid entertainment. When he learns that we are in Kakadu to see rainbow serpent rock art, he shows me a fine photography book he has published on the Aboriginal art and craft of the region. He asks me if I am aware of the rainbow serpent cave painting outside the national park on Aboriginal lands at Mt. Borradaile. It is the largest and possibly most spectacular of all the rainbow serpent Aboriginal rock paintings. Adrian, a young art historian and musician, is fascinated by Arnhem Land culture and art. He soon convinces David, Mimi, and me to let him guide us to Mt. Borradaile Camp, a concession developed and operated by Max Davidson, who has a permit from the Aboriginal Land Council.

We pick up Adrian early the next morning and then make arrangements with the local Aboriginal Land Council to enter Arnhem Land. We cross the border of Kakadu National Park, drive east past the village of Oenpelli, and then turn left onto a very rough one-lane dirt track, over which we grind along in four-wheel drive for an hour

1 The author returning an 85-pound alligator snapping turtle to the Apalachicola River. Photo by Harley Means.

Faces of herptiles. Giant southern toad, black-belly salamander, coastal taipan, pig frog, frilled lizard, shingleback, rain frog, and mole salamander. What's not to love?

10 An eastern diamondback rattlesnake—the largest rattler and most dangerous snake in the US and Canada.

11 Fish-scale gecko having shed some scales during capture, Nosy Mangabe, Madagascar.

12 Timucuan Amerindians smoking miscellaneous animals, including the eastern diamondback rattlesnake, the first illustrated New World snake. Theodore De Bry, 1591.

13 Alabama red hills salamander, *Phaeognathus hubrichti*. This old adult male is 11 inches long.

14 The Apalachicola kingsnake, *Lampropeltis getula meansi*, discovered in 1968, named in 2006.

15 A cottonmouth in typical defensive pose, exposing the white lining of its mouth.

16 Cotton rat,
Sigmodon hispidus.
Important member
of southeastern
U.S. vertebrate food
webs.

17 Leaf-tailed gecko
on Nosy Mangabe,
showing its bizarre looks
and adaptations for
camouflage.

18
Large
bushmaster
found on a
hike in La
Selva, Costa
Rica.

19
Quetzalcoatl or
Kukulcan on
the facade of the
Nunnery, Uxmal,
Yucatán Peninsula,
Mexico with a rattle
on the end of its tail.

20 *Crotalus tzabcan*, an adult male specimen I caught north of Tikit.

21 Eastern indigo snake from Fort Stewart, Georgia.

22 Green treefrog eating a little bent-wing bat. [This is the first photograph taken of this unique phenomenon and it has been published in major nature magazines in the United States and Europe.]

23 World's largest rainbow serpent rock art painting, Mt. Borradaile, Arnhem Land, Australia.

24 Black tiger snake, glutton of Chappell Island.

25 The extremely rare rough-scaled python from the Kimberley region of Australia, displaying its large teeth.

26 The eastern diamondback rattlesnake thrives on US barrier islands.

27 The fierce snake, or inland taipan, the world's most toxic venomous snake, on the Gibber Plains of western Queensland. Photo by David Wright.

28 Rich Mountain giant earthworm, *Diplocardia meansi*, Polk County,
Arkansas.

29 Green tree python, one of the world's most beautiful snakes, Iron Range National Park, Queensland.

30
Giant treefrog, *Litorea infrafrenata*, in Australia's Iron Range National Park

31 Alligator lurking underwater, waiting for prey to swim overhead, Shepherd Spring, Florida.

32
Reddish-colored western cottonmouth retaining juvenile pattern against the light-colored substrate of its home ravine, Tunica Hills, Mississippi.

33 Australia's most dangerous snake, the coastal taipan, threatening me after I turned it loose.

34 Author with a seven-foot olive python that was caught trying to ingest a rough-scaled python. Photo by David Wright.

and a half. We arrive at the outback camp about 10:15 A.M., drink a cup of tea, and then drive to a dry creek bed with occasional billabongs (stagnant waterholes) near some mesalike, sandstone hillocks left over from general widespread erosion of what was once a higher plain.

After a short walk into the hills, Adrian leaves me at a massive wall of sandstone through the middle of which water and wind have eroded a large, irregular cavity, about 50 feet wide and five to ten feet high that is open to the air on two sides. The floor is deep in charcoal. To get from one side of the shelter to the other you have to sit down and slide on your duff over some breakdown ceiling rocks, which have an amazingly high-gloss black shine. While sliding over the slippery sandstone I wonder to myself what in the world caused them to be so highly polished.

On the other side of the shiny rocks I find myself standing on a ledge facing the sun. The ledge is strangely pitted with half-tennis-ball–shaped depressions and I am puzzled at what made them. Then I see, nestled perfectly in one depression, a loose round stone. Suddenly it dawns on me what I am looking at. The pits are depressions rubbed into the hard sandstone over millennia by grindstones, busily grinding away at plant seeds. The loose rock is clearly a grindstone. I sit down, humbled to think about how many years would be required for each depression to be made. Then a light goes off in my head about what the lustrous black polish is all about. For gosh sakes, the polish was created by thousands of human buttocks that slid over the rocks, just as I did without thinking about it, for hundreds of generations and who knows for how many thousands of years.

The day is hot and I'm sweating. Adrian startles me from deep thought with a tossed pebble. I look up and he silently beckons me to follow him. Without having discussed it, we speak in hushed tones. Something about this place is mystical. We both feel it and I think I know why: it's the ghosts. We walk on soil and rocks that were trod by the feet of no telling how many people over the ages, but few people walk here today, and nobody lives here. We both realize that the de-peopling of this and so many other sites in Australia has taken place only in the very recent past, say within about a hundred years or so.

And what Adrian is about to show me will soon reveal some rock art that I will shortly see is evidence that people lived and died here for at least 15,000 years and probably much longer.

We walk on flat ground at the base of a vertical, rocky cliff rising in places to 50 feet in height. The cliff is pocked with horizontal, wind-blown caves and notched by vertical canyons eroded by eons of rainfall. The little canyons and caves often coalesce, leaving a rocky labyrinth of passages and rooms. An occasional round-topped *Eucalyptus* tree grows here or there out of the cracks in bare rock or sandy and gravelly soil. Groundcover plants and grasses are abundant, but the soil is hot, cracked, and dusty now in the dry season.

Adrian leads me into a wide place in a small canyon, turns to me, and stands still. The look on his face is like someone saying, "*Taa daa!*" I guess that he wants me to discover something without being told where to look. I scan the surroundings and see nothing of note. Then I look up. Gasp! What I see takes my breath away, and I can imagine that it did the same for Aboriginal people, too. It is Aburga, the rainbow serpent of the now extinct Malakiri people.

I almost want to shade my face and peep at the scary image through cracks between my fingers. Its fearsome head with gaping, toothed jaws glares out from the ceiling of a cave with a wide rectangular opening, about 20 feet high above the ground we are standing on. A sheer vertical rock wall protects the cave mouth, but we gain access by working our way through tunnels and caves behind the visage. Crouching down, I move under Aburga and sit down with Adrian. This rainbow serpent, painted in white ochre and outlined in red hematite, stretches back into the cave a full 20 feet. It is the largest known rainbow serpent painting in Australia.

This fat, toothy serpent could be patterned after *Wonambi*, I tell Adrian. No doubt the dragonlike head and one flipper are stylized embellishments, but a *Wonambi*-like snake could surely inspire such a painting. Adrian thinks for a moment, then tells me that archaeologist George Chaloupka, one of the principal authorities on Aboriginal cultures of Arnhem Land, believes the painting to be no more than 1500 years old. We sit in silence for a few more minutes, contemplating what ceremonial significance this visual manifestation of the rainbow serpent may have had on its original viewers, then Adrian jumps up and says, "Follow me."

Less than a hundred yards away, on a vertical wall in an adjacent small canyon, Adrian points to a faded painting that looks perfectly like a crocodile. "Bruce," he says, "this is a naturalistic painting that typifies the oldest rock art in Arnhem Land. Naturalistic paintings are thought to represent the first period of rock art and are the oldest images, possibly dating as far back as fifteen thousand or more years. If an extinct mega-snake like *Wonambi* were the inspiration for the rainbow serpent, one would expect some rock art of this period to display such a snake. There are no rainbow serpents in the naturalistic style."

Then Adrian leads me not far away to some sticklike images of humans in red hematite. Although highly stylized, the figures of men hunting with spears and boomerangs are graceful and beautiful because they portray action. Adrian says, "Archaeologists call these Dynamic Figures. They are the second phase of rock art and they have been estimated to be about ten thousand years old. Only one large snake painting has ever been identified in this style, and the archaeologists don't think it is a rainbow serpent." It is a bit disappointing to learn that rainbow serpent images are not found in these two early stages of Aboriginal rock art because the giant snake, *Wonambi*, probably went extinct well before 10,000 years ago. It means, therefore, that the rainbow serpent mythology probably wasn't based on *Wonambi*. I ask Adrian when the rainbow serpent images first show up in rock paintings.

With a spring in his step, he leads me to yet another rock wall, this one no more than 50 yards from Aburga. And there he shows me a strange, thin-line drawing called a Yam Figure, of the third recognizable period of Aboriginal rock art in Arnhem Land. "This," Adrian pronounces, "is one of the first rainbow serpents known in any rock art and it has been estimated at around six thousand years of age." I stare at the image and have a difficult time imagining that I am seeing a snake at all. Certainly, it is not a large, monster of a snake like Aburga.

When I complain that I cannot believe this is a rainbow serpent, Adrian sits me down and gives me a lesson in recent archaeological research. Australian archaeologist Paul Tacon and others analyzed the details of 107 rainbow serpent rock paintings in Arnhem Land. What their analyses revealed, and their hypotheses about which animal might have served as the origin of the rainbow serpent figures, totally blindsides me.

First, rainbow serpent paintings from the next and last period, the Modern Period (4,000 years ago to the present), are highly variable and stylized, and do look more like large snakes than earlier paintings. Second, the first rainbow snake images (of the Yam Period, 6,000–4,000 years ago) are all quite similar and relatively small. Third—and here's the kicker—the animal that most resembles the earliest rainbow serpent paintings is not a snake at all, but a seahorse or its close relative, a pipefish.

A pipefish! Adrian sees the disappointment in my face. He gets up and wanders off to find David and Mimi, leaving me sitting befuddled in the dirt. How, or why, in the world would the ancient people of Arnhem Land have come to deify a pipefish? This is a marine animal, to begin with, and people, in general, are landlubbers.

David wants to record Adrian playing the didgeridoo, so we walk to a rock shelter with obvious signs that people once lived there. The shelter is an undercut cliff somewhat shaped like the inside of a shell, with perfect acoustics for a wind instrument. Before Adrian starts playing, he relates Paul Tacon's hypothesis about why a pipefish might have been the focus of the oldest images of what came later to be the rainbow serpent.

Ten thousand years ago, sea levels were at least 300 feet lower than today and Arnhem Land was broadly connected to New Guinea across the seawater of the shallow Torres Strait that today separates the two landmasses. At that time natural global warming began melting continental ice sheets and slowly raised sea level until it stabilized at today's beach lines between 6,000 and 4,000 years ago. As sea levels rose, 25 to 45 yards of Old Arnhem Land coastline were being drowned per year in some periods, pushing people ever farther inland in their lifetimes. This had profound cultural and physical, if not psychological, impacts on people. They would have experienced serious, life-threatening flooding and would have seen some strange, snakelike, pipefish creatures washed up on the newly formed shores. These experiences and observations came to have supernatural significance, and probably the Yam Period rainbow serpent images were born and first symbolized what was taking place on migrating coastlines. Over time, the pipefish images, already elongated, became more snakelike, and as one might expect, much more variable in shape, size, and embellishments. It's a great hypothesis, but one must always remember that it is just a theory. However, the hard facts that the earliest rainbow serpent images are most like seahorses and pipefishes puts the snake hypothesis to rest, whatever the truth really is.

Some of the naturalistic art in northern Australia may be 30,000 years old, as old as any cave art in Europe. *Homo sapiens* has occupied Europe for only about 40,000 years, but the earliest Australians arrived here about 60,000 years ago. In Europe, cave art vanishes after about 10,000 years and the earliest writing only dates back to about 5,500 years. Arnhem Land may have been more or less continuously occupied throughout the history of man in Australia and so may possess a continuous stream of rock art down to the present day. As George Musgrave once told me, rock art is Aboriginal writing. Don't I wish I could precisely read its every page!

Adrian sits cross-legged and begins playing the didgeridoo in the cave mouth as the setting sun bathes us with an orange-red glow. It's one of those precious moments in my life I'll never forget: the sound of the didgeridoo, the sunset, amazing thoughts flying around in my mind, and my awareness that many generations of people have lived, loved, and died at this shelter. More than anything else, I am overwhelmed by the realization that the entire history of the rainbow serpent mythology may be painted on rock walls and ceilings all around us. Within only a few hundred feet of where I sit, humanity's oldest continuously documented story is recorded in the red iron dust called ochre.

17
BLACK TIGER SNAKE
Glutton of Chappell

SITTING ON A LOW, GRANITE RIDGE LOOKING WEST, I WATCH
the sun set at exactly 8:30 P.M. Twilight dwindles and then at 8:43, as
if by magic, the first short-tailed shearwaters, *Puffinus tenuirostris*,
sail over the promontory and begin their nightly migration to their
burrows. By 8:45, just two minutes later, the sky is filled with the
silhouettes of thousands of these birds. Some 250,000 will probably
land here tonight. I watch spellbound as they wheel in the air overhead
and spiral down toward the ground. They sail in at high speed and
then flop into the low bushes or bounce clumsily onto the ground.
Their small feet and long, narrow wings are not well adapted either
for landing or for taking off from the ground. Once they start digging,
however, they can burrow like moles. It is quite comical to see plumes
of dirt arcing into the air as webbed feet sweep it backward out of
nesting burrows.

Twilight lasts a long time here on a lonely island between Australia
and Tasmania. Faint light still glows on the horizon at 9:45 P.M. when
I leave the promontory. By this time, most of the birds have made it
to the ground and only a few still circle overhead. Once bedded down,
their incessant, wheezy, yapping calls make a deafening cacophony.
Picking my way carefully to the camp to avoid collapsing their

burrows, I notice many birds sitting on the ground or in the bushes not looking for burrows. Maybe these are unmated birds, or birds whose burrows were raided by the long black death that lurks here.

It's not the birds, but the long black death that I have come to see. The short-tailed shearwater is one of several seabirds called "muttonbird" because the oily flesh of their huge, downy chicks reminded early explorers of mutton. The long black death is the Mt. Chappell Island tiger snake, *Notechis ater serventyi*, a giant among Australian tiger snakes, and it is especially adapted for living on this one island. It has to be a giant because, as an adult, its principal food is the large, ungainly chicks of the muttonbird.

Possessing considerable variation in color patterns, two species groups of tiger snakes are recognized and both are confined to the temperate zone of southern Australia and nearby islands. Races of the eastern tiger snake, *N. scutatus*, are found on the southeastern mainland while races of the black tiger snake, *N. ater*, are distributed in western Australia, Tasmania, offshore islands, and an isolated gorge in the Flinders Ranges. All are stout-bodied snakes with highly neurotoxic venom and, until the development of antivenin, they were responsible for many of the snake-bite deaths in Australia. Tiger snakes get their common name from populations of the eastern tiger snake, which usually have crossbands (but sometimes don't) of lighter yellow scales on a darker background color ranging from light gray through olive, brown, or reddish.

Black tiger snakes are usually black, but on Mt. Chappell Island, some individuals range to olive brown. Young snakes are often banded, but lose the bands as they grow. Adults of mainland populations in western Australia may have narrow yellow bands. Mainland populations of both species and populations of the black tiger snake on large islands vary little in adult size, running to a little over three feet in total length. It's on small islands that populations have become really large. The giants of the genus live on Mt. Chappell Island, where they have been measured at more than five and a half feet long. It is these giants that I have come to see.

My camp is located on the south side of the island in the abandoned cabin of a sheep ranch. There are no trees on Chappell, but a plague of woody box-thorn bushes has been taking it over. Box-thorn is the bush that Africans use to make lion-proof fences around their huts. The nuisance part of this plant is its many terminal branchlets that end in stout prickles. This type of plant is well adapted to defend itself against browsing herbivores. Unfortunately, it impales many short-tailed shearwaters that fly into it and it grows so densely and so low to the ground that it takes over the bird's nesting habitat.

Besides places dominated by the impenetrable box-thorn, other sites have a high percentage of a pungent horehound introduced from England. A native bunchgrass still grows in some places but many sites are overgrown with the low, sprawling horehound subshrubs about 12 to 24 inches tall. The dark brown soil is often bare, or vegetated with low-growing herbs. All these different sites have muttonbird burrows in them. I wander away from camp and enter a grassy field riddled with muttonbird burrows.

Suddenly I see my first black tiger snake coiled in the shade of a box-thorn. I move toward it quickly and clamp it gently with my snake tongs before it can make a move. I pull the snake out into the open where I can work with it, then hold its head down in soft soil using the handle of my five-foot-long snake hook.

I grasp the snake's head in my left hand with the rear of its jaws pressed between my forefinger and thumb. I am impressed by its skull and lower jawbones, which feel sturdier than in most snakes. The head is short and broad relative to its body size and bears large, glossy black scales called shields. I deduce that the snake is a male by the shape and length of its tail. The snake deposits some oily fecal matter on my legs as my punishment for disturbing his grace. The diamond-shaped scales are smooth and lustrous but his skin is stretched by a full belly, revealing softer, non-lustrous skin between the scales. I take a few photographs and release him. He crawls into low shrubbery and disappears into a muttonbird burrow.

At one point just before sundown I sit down on a large, flat piece of exposed granite, and am startled to see a 12-inch-long juvenile black tiger snake speeding off from the tuft of grass my feet are in. I quickly clamp him and drag the feisty little snake out into the open where I can get a good look at him. He stands up tall like a cobra and makes numerous strikes towards me, even feinting at me by striking and crawling in my direction a few inches as he parries. This little guy is clearly banded with narrow yellowish lines on his black background color. Young snakes are said not to be very common on Mt. Chappell Island. They subsist on five species of terrestrial lizards until they are large enough to ingest small muttonbird chicks.

I enter a loamy area with lots of bare brown soil and muttonbird holes. Loose bones lie everywhere, mostly of muttonbirds, but also of the Cape Barren goose, *Cereopsis novaehollandiae*, and quite a few sheep. Strangely, I have seen very few snake bones, maybe because snakes usually die underground. I come around the end of a large box-thorn and see the head and neck of another tiger snake. As I watch, he suddenly bolts downhill and I get a full view of him. He is stout and has a snubbed-off tail. One report claims that a snub-tail is an indication that a snake is quite old because it dates back to the days when people were paid bounty for snakes by turning in only the tails. Not more than two minutes later I spot another large snake sitting in the shade of a box-thorn with just a little part of its body in the sun. I leave it alone.

From 9:23 A.M. until 4:30 P.M. I see nine tiger snakes. Apparently they are out all day, although many are resting and thermoregulating in shade from about noon until four in the afternoon. It gets hottest today from two to four P.M.

God, I love exploring—just walking around with no particular motive except to look at scenery, animals, plants, water, and sky and to be at one with the planet. Around the western end of the island, I see how severely wind and salt spray have pruned the box-thorn bushes, making some into huge rounded sculptures, as if someone had deliberately taken a shrub-trimmer to them. As I walk through shady passageways between the box-thorns, suddenly I spot a large black tiger snake lying lazily in the shade as if it has not a care in the world. I creep up and take some photographs while he sleeps, and then I slowly reach for him with my clampstick. He doesn't move until

I touch him at midbody. When he recoils from the touch, he reacts exactly like someone who has been startled from sleep.

Ambling on, I walk around the west end of Chappell Island and begin working my way east along the south shore. Soon I come to a lovely white sandy beach. I stop to take a photograph and spook five Cape Barren geese lounging on the white sand. At 1:39 P.M. I catch a four-and-a-half-foot-long, but very skinny, tiger snake lying in the shade cast by large box-thorn bushes. About 200 ticks are attached to the delicate skin between the scales of his neck. In addition, his eye and the left side of his face are all crusty with dried blood from an injury. The eye is nonfunctional, and the snake may be permanently blind. Thinking about what might have caused his injury, I get the idea that he might have been pecked hard on the face by an adult muttonbird defending its nest. The injury appears to be a week or two old, and this would correspond with the time that the adult birds were sitting on their underground nests. It would seem, if I am correct, that occasionally the muttonbirds win the underground struggle in their dank burrows.

The frontispiece of *Song of the Snake*, the classic book written by Australian herpetologist Eric Worrell, shows Sir Eric standing on a flat rock outcrop facing a nearly six-foot-long black tiger snake that has reared up in front of him. I find the outcrop and feel lucky to stand in Sir Eric's place. I have with me research papers by my friend and colleague, American herpetologist Terry Schwaner. Terry spent a number of years studying island populations of tiger snakes and he marked and released about 1,650 individuals on Chappell Island. It's from Terry's work, and that of others who have preceded me here, that I know something of the biology of these giant snakes.

Seventy percent of Australia's snakes belong to the cobra and coral snake family, the Elapidae. Many elapid snakes in Australia and elsewhere lay eggs, but a large number in several genera, including tiger snakes, give live birth by retaining the eggs in the oviducts until they are ready to hatch. Mating and birth in the black tiger snake takes place in autumn and early winter. Brood size ranges from ten to 31 with a mean of about 19. Chappell Island young snakes feed mainly on lizards and a few rodents, switching to muttonbirds when they are large enough to eat them. Terry Schwaner believes that adult Chappell Island snakes may have a window of only five to six weeks in which they can eat muttonbird chicks before the chicks become too large to be swallowed. The snakes then have to coast all the rest of the year on the fat reserves they store up in those few weeks. Black tiger snakes on another island that has no muttonbirds grow much more slowly over a longer period of time. Sexual maturity there was estimated to be reached at ten to 12 years of age.

At eight the next morning, I spot a six-inch-long White's skink (*Egernia whitii*) sunning in the mouth of a muttonbird burrow. The five species of skinks that occur on Chappell Island are very skittish and quick to dart to cover, so that if you are not watching carefully, you won't realize just how many there are. Their numbers must be abundant because they form the important food base of the young tiger snakes until the snakes are large enough to take muttonbird chicks. I notice lots of grasshoppers, too, which would be one of the important foods of the lizards.

Around noon I find what I believe must be a two-year-old tiger snake (about 24 inches long) crawling in full sunlight on bare ground among tufts of the exotic horehound. This pugnacious little snake is only as big around as my middle finger, but it acts like the mean kid on the block. It rears up and repeatedly strikes to intimidate me. It spreads its little hood and crawls around with its head and neck about an inch off the ground and cocked so I can see the widest part. I shoot off half a roll of film and enjoy the show immensely. This little toughy is tiger snake number four for the day.

A few hours later I find myself walking on a white sandy beach at the head of an azure lagoon. It is hot, the lagoon is beautiful, and I am all alone. I throw off my clothes and walk into the water. Strangely, as hot as the sun is, I am instantly cold standing naked in the wind! And the water is really icy. I sit down on a warm and smooth granite rock and splash myself to get used to the water. Then I submerge fully and take the best bath I can without soap. Lying down on the warm, flat granite to dry, I luxuriate in my nudity, the tranquility and privacy of the lagoon, and the remoteness of Mt. Chappell Island. I think how fortunate I am to be one of only three people on this beautiful island, while more than six billion other people swarm over the habitable parts of the planet.

About 3 P.M. I see another two-foot-long juvenile tiger snake crawling along the edge of a box-thorn bush in full sunlight. It is stump-tailed, too. Now I realize that, since the proportion of stump-tailed juveniles is pretty high (half of the four I saw today), something must be happening in early life to cut off their tails. The obvious predator here that might do such a thing is sea gulls or some other bird that might peck at a snake. Any hawks or owls that are here would swallow a little snake whole. Kelp gulls (*Larus dominicanus*) scavenge the freshly dead muttonbird adults every morning. These are my candidates for the tail-pecking culprits. They also would explain the strange appearance of the carcass of a two-foot juvenile I saw yesterday. The snake was lying dead with all its flesh pecked off in the same manner that the gulls deflesh dead muttonbird adults, leaving bones and flaps of defleshed skin.

By the fourth day, I have tallied sightings of about 55 black tiger snakes. Today, however, I decide not to focus on snake sightings but to tackle Mt. Chappell. I set off at about 11:30 from the saddle in the central spine of the island. The going is not difficult. I see no muttonbird burrows all the way to the summit as I zig-zag through patches of brush alternating with grassy/rocky stretches. I expect the mountainside will be full of muttonbird burrows, but along the route of my ascent and descent I find none. The reason, I believe, is that the soil is too thin over the underlying bedrock. On the very summit, however, I find one small patch of deeper soil with about eight burrows clustered together. And while on the very top, I find a tiger snake! It is a small adult about four feet long with a congenitally deformed right eye. It looks reasonably healthy, but not nearly so fat as many of those at the base of the mountain.

Sitting on a large summit rock, I enjoy a breathtaking panorama of the surrounding ocean. Behind me to the west, sky meets water at the curvature of the earth. Eastward, I see mountains of Cape Barren and Flinders Islands jutting into the sky. From my vantage point, I can easily imagine that Mt. Chapell Island and the high points on the other islands were once part of a larger land mass. When post-Pleistocene sea level rose and invaded the margins of the world's continents, salt water flooded the broad plain connecting Tasmania with southeastern Australia. Most of the populations of animals and plants that lived on the plain 10,000 years ago shifted their distributions north or south to accommodate the encroaching seas. Some populations, however, became stranded on the high places that are the islands of the Bass Strait today.

Life on a sea island is not as easy as on the mainland for most creatures, especially for predators like snakes. As the size of an island shrinks, according to the rules of island biogeography, the number of species that it can support falls off faster than the rate at which island size declines. Many islets in the range of a few acres in size are too small to support minimum viable populations of most large animals, especially predators whose population sizes are necessarily smaller than those of their prey.

Half-moon, starry sky, Orion, and the Southern Cross overhead; a 20-mph steady but chilly sea breeze blowing in my face; a cup of warm tea to sip alone in the dark: not a bad scenario for ending a day. I crawl into my tent and snuggle into my sleeping bag for a deep rest. Lying there in the dark, I picture a black tiger snake coiled next to a fluffy muttonbird chick to get warm, as biologists before me have reported. This diurnal snake won't be surprising me in my sleeping bag tonight, thank goodness. I try to imagine what those cold, smooth black scales would feel like against my bare skin. I get drowsy and wonder if the neurotoxic venom acts this mercilessly on its victims. I shudder and then fall asleep.

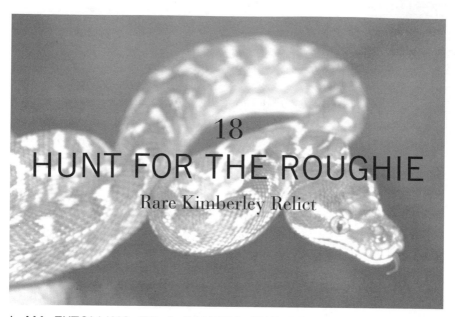

18
HUNT FOR THE ROUGHIE
Rare Kimberley Relict

I AM EXTOLLING TO A CAMERA THE BEAUTY OF A GREEN superb dragon, *Diporiphora superba*, when suddenly my partner and cameraman, David Wright, and I hear Al Britton hollering at us from down-canyon. "John is snake-bit! I'll rush to camp and begin erecting the emergency radio. You help him back to camp." Across the riverbed David and I see John slowly working his way upstream toward us among huge granite boulders, holding his left forearm in his right hand. I drop the lizard and David and I wade across the river, and work our way downstream among the monster boulders.

When John sees us approaching he says with a little quaver in his voice, "Don't worry, I'm OK. I don't think the bite's serious."

I think to myself: Yeah, right! We're in the remotest part of Australia's Kimberley wilderness, a long helicopter ride from the dirt airstrip, a two-hour small-plane flight back to the nearest hospital in Kununara, and you have just been nailed by an Australian elapid snake! Even if the helicopter was standing by—which it is *not*—and even if a small plane was on the airstrip—which it is *not*—and even if we had radio contact with any sort of help—which we *don't*—there's a good chance we might not be able to get you to a hospital for a day or two.

"My main worry," he says, "is not the envenomation, but my allergic reaction to it." John works with snake venom that he extracts and dries into powder at the Australian Reptile Park, minute quantities of which he inhales. Over a long period of time, he, like many other venom extractors, has become allergic to the venoms he has been exposed to. "I have a tightness in my throat and am experiencing difficulty swallowing," he says.

I think: Oh great! We might be able to delay the effects of the venom for a couple of days with appropriate first aid, but you could die from an acute allergic response in the next few minutes if we haven't brought an allergy kit to administer to you!

John has not pushed his panic-button and is calmly calculating his moves, but the rest of us are stifling screams. His life may be in our hands and we are trying to hide from John that we are frantic about what we should do in case he passes out.

Struggling along the steep bank fifty feet above the murky estuarine water where saltwater crocodiles lurk, we help John walk to camp. The camp is located in the floodplain where the clear, fresh waters of Hunter River meet the silty tidal waters of the deep canyon it has eroded. We work our way upstream above the high tide line beyond the croc danger zone of the silty waters, then cross the clear waters of the river bed among huge, round, slippery rocks. We then pick our way back downstream on the other side of the river to our base camp through a couple of acres of smashed mangroves lying like matchsticks in the sand, the result of floods caused by a monster cyclone (Australian hurricane) that hit earlier in the year. John sits down on a log in the shade. He has wrapped his left arm with a compression bandage from the bitten hand to the armpit, which is the proper first aid for elapid snakebites.

Forty-something, John Weigel is quite a character. A long and lanky expatriate American with a full head of red hair, he emigrated to Australia in the 1960s to chase his passion—snakes. He wound up working for famous Australian herpetologist Eric Worrell and fell in love with Australia and the abundant opportunities to make contributions to herpetology on a continent where lots of new species were still to be found.

John tells me I can find some antihistamines and other medicines left over from the flood near his tent several hundred yards up the gorge from our base camp, so I hot-foot it up there to retrieve what I can find. When I get back he seems stable and is talkative, and we go over the details of the snakebite. He starts out by describing his mission for the day: he is hunting for what he thinks may be an undescribed whipsnake, a glossy black species of *Demansia*, he thinks.

By our base camp, sandstone makes up the vertical walls of the gorge, but across the river are masses of igneous rocks that welled up under the sandstone eons ago. The vegetation on the igneous rock is starkly different from that on the sandstone. It is nearly treeless and grassy—good habitat for such an elapid whipsnake that John is searching for. So he set out about 8 A.M.

At about 8:40 he spied one in a pile of dead-stick flotsam along a small, dry creek bed. He pressed down what he could see of it with his "girlie stick" as he calls it, a piece of leather stretched across the end of a Y that allows a snake to be gently pinned. The girlie stick did not hold and the snake was about to get away into deep grass, so John grabbed what was still in view with his left hand, not seeing that the snake's head was in position in the grass to defend itself. It struck him with both fangs on top of the joint above the base of his little finger. He jumped back, startled, and the snake made its getaway. Even though snakebit, John was more peeved at losing the snake than at having suffered envenomation.

Right away he felt a sharp pain at the site of the bite, and when he squeezed the suspect area, he saw tiny little droplets of blood oozing. He quickly wrapped his hand and arm to the elbow with two Ace-type compression bandages. Elapid venom travels through the lymphatic system, whose vessels are under the skin, and muscular movement is what pumps lymph to the heart. If one ceases to move and keeps the affected limb still and below the level of the heart, the compression bandages usually retain the venom at the site of the bite. At this juncture his symptoms were the pain in his hand and a strong ache that went up his arm to about the elbow. *Demansia* bites are usually not fatal in adults, so John did the unthinkable—he continued his snake hunt.

About 30 minutes later he noticed two other symptoms that made him change his mind about the gravity of the situation. His throat became dry and tight and he began having difficulty swallowing. These are symptoms of allergic reactions, and he knew that if these symptoms continued to develop, he could be in real trouble. That's when he began walking back to camp.

We monitor his symptoms throughout the morning, starting at about 9:40 A.M. when we arrive at base camp. Fortunately, once he sits down in camp in the shade, he seems to get better, and all morning he improves. We get a dose of epinephrine ready in case he lapses into anaphylactic shock, and we wait. At 10:37 A.M. he tries a quick experiment to assess whether the envenomation will require medical treatment. He unwraps the outer compression bandage to see what will happen. Nothing does. Then at 10:55 A.M. he unwraps the lower compression bandage, completely freeing the lymphatic system to circulate, but he quickly re-wraps it after 30 seconds. The top of his hand swells a little while we watch it, probably because he has re-wrapped the compression bandage too tightly. Otherwise, nothing.

At 11:05 A.M. John unwraps the compression bandage for two minutes, then re-wraps it. No response. Finally, at 11:12 A.M. he removes the compression bandage and leaves it off for good. Shortly, the swelling begins to decline, his overall symptoms improve, and for all the rest of the day he continues to improve. When I last speak with him at about 9:30 P.M. he is totally recovered save for a little swelling and soreness in the lymph nodes under his left arm. As he walks off in the night following the beam of his headlight, I hear him swearing that he is "Gonna get out in the morning and catch that bastard!"

Meanwhile, David and I continue our hunt for the rare rough-scaled python, *Morelia carinata*. David and I have been here two days already with only John's snake bite to show for all the efforts of six herpers intent on catching a "roughie," as the python's name has been Aussy-fied. John, Al, Craig Adams, and John's son, Arnie, have been here for two weeks. The morning before we arrived, Al found a roughie entwined in the coils of a seven-foot-long olive python intent on eating the roughie. That was only the sixth specimen of a roughie known to have been captured by humans in modern times.

David and I are here to help John find a breeding pair of roughies and to film the interesting biology of this mysterious rare creature to be included in a National Geographic Explorer documentary that we are making about the snakes of Australia. The breeding pair will enable John to study the breeding biology of the species and contribute to the knowledge needed for its conservation. All of our activities are being conducted under permits John labored long to acquire from the Western Australia Parks and Wildlife Department.

Pythons are highly esteemed among snake aficionados and nothing is more valued than something that is rare. The rough-scaled python not only is rare but also unique among pythons for having keeled scales: each dorsal scale has a little raised ridge running down its center. The snake's common name, therefore, is rough-scaled python, and its scientific name, *carinata*, also means "ridged." All other pythons in the world have smooth scales. Only discovered in 1976 and named in 1981, the roughie is presently known only from two localities in remote canyons of that part of the northwestern coast of Australia called the Kimberley. It is one of Australia's rarest vertebrate species.

In the afternoon I go exploring up the gorge. Shortly upstream beyond the tidal area where we have located our base camp, the canyon gets really difficult to walk in. All the soil and sand have been scoured off the river valley bottom and washed out to sea in two recent floods, leaving the floodplain ajumble with large boulders. And judging from the size of the trees that were uprooted and tossed about like so many straws, such severe flooding must happen only once in a century. No doubt high waters rage through this canyon every wet season, but the two recent floods were highly unusual considering the ecological changes that they wrought.

Walking upstream is a rock-hopping feat. I am barely able to hop and jump across the top of large boulders most of the way, but worse obstacles are deep-water pools and mammoth rocks the size of houses. At many places in the canyon I come to rocks so big that neither can I ascend them nor let myself down on the other side, so I have to backtrack and find another passage. Furthermore, in one hand I am carrying my fully extended tripod and my camera dangles from my neck. This makes the going even more tricky.

The canyon is truly spectacular. Huge vertical cliffs overhang both valley sides, coming right down to the water in places, or with scree slopes comprised of rectangular erosional blocks off the cliff. Bedding planes and vertical cracks in the sediments forming the canyon sidewalls are deeply etched into the cliff face, forming great microhabitats for lizards, frogs, invertebrates and—snakes. Vegetation grows on the ledges and out of the cracks. Large, V-shaped nicks in the cliff faces reveal where small freshets have cut their own little valleys in the sidewalls of the bigger canyon. In these alcoves nestle broadleaf forests—remnants of ancient rainforests—in which John believes the rough-scaled python lives.

The gorge curves first one way and then the other, so I can't see the end of the box canyon until I get past the last turn, but oh my, what a lovely sight my eyes feast upon when I get there. A large plume of white water cascades down the nearly sheer cliff face into a lake-sized plunge pool. The solitude and magnificence of the location is spiritual. Looking at the waterfall in the late afternoon sun, I get a visual bonus. A bright rainbow arcs across the scene from the spray created by the cascading waters.

When I get back to camp, David is cooking some nan bread he has whipped up. It goes down deliciously with his deep skillet of garlic, onions, Greek olives, and tomato sauce that all six of us devour with gusto. After a short rest until twilight, four of us go out for a snake hunt. David and Craig cross the river and work their way up the scree along a cliff together. John leads me to the promising small rainforest enclave where Al earlier found the olive python about to swallow a roughie. I search alone while he goes off to hunt another location by himself.

My rainforest patch is a scrubby little forest with all the tops blown out of the trees from cyclonic winds that accompanied the awful floods. There are lots of leafy limbs, however, and vines growing in large tangles rising from thickets they make on the ground. It's surprisingly lush inside my little alcove and soon I learn why. As I ascend the middle of the steep little side canyon and rise above river-bottom talus, I soon come into a magical place of wet vertical rockfaces, tumbling water, small crystal pools, and froggy/lizardy/snakey/insecty-looking habitat, all canopied over with dense verdure. Big and little roots of *Ficus* trees snake up and down the small watercourse. I ascend a series of such magical places, which stair-step uphill for several hundred feet. In each one I can stand or sit in the open and beam my light up into the limbs of the overarching trees or scrutinize the ground and wet cliff faces for critters. It's so beautiful in these pretty places that I get carried away admiring them, not really caring if I see a snake—and I don't.

David and Craig find a nine-foot-long olive python, but neither John nor I encounter any snake. The moon tonight is nearly full, casting its light brightly down. Moonlight is bad for small animals because nocturnal predators can see them. When I reach the river bottom I find Al and Arnie dipnetting some atyid shrimps, called "yabbies," from the stream. The guys intend to use them tomorrow to fish for barramundi to feed the camp. They have a small bucketful when I reach them. Al helps me replace my battery pack. I take a long drink of water back in camp, sit around for 30 minutes, then crawl gratefully into my tent and go to sleep right away.

Just before dawn a pesky little quoll, a marsupial "cat," comes sniffing and scratching around my tent and wakes me. I scare it off so I can get a few more minutes of groggy sleep. It visits base camp every night and often gets into foodstuffs and gear.

David and I film in the morning and early afternoon, then I put my camera and lenses in my daypack and head off up the gorge telling the others that I won't be back until they see me, and not to wait on me for supper. The sun is quite low when I arrive at the northern side of the canyon where the largest rainforest patch exists. This north side receives little sunlight at this time of the year, mid-June, so John calls it a cool rainforest. Since I believe there won't be as much of a chance finding the rough-scaled python there at night when it is even cooler, I hope maybe the warm late afternoon will be a good time. Besides, I have another motivation: I want to see the rainforest.

I work my way across the river again and reach the cliff, then start navigating the contact line between the cliff and the talus slopes. The going is full of obstacles, large rocks and vines, but quite snakey-looking. I expect to see one at every glance. The air is warm, but not hot. At first, as I work upslope, there are enough small broadleaf trees to shade out most undergrowth, so the walking is quite pleasant for a while. Then I get to a huge cliff with large boulder breakdown lying along its base, so I begin walking upriver following the base of the cliff where possible. I go up and up, around a shoulder of rock, then find a narrow defile that seems to lead to the top. Up I climb, searching every one of the many nooks and crannies in the cliff and looking on the ground, on top of rocks, and in vines and branches.

Eventually the defile in the boulder scree I am ascending pinches out under a huge rock making a little cave. I climb in to look for snakes and find nothing, and when I look up, the huge rock overhead gives me the willies. It looks like it will come down on my head with the slightest disturbance. I can't see how it is perched there without falling. I make a quick but soft exit. I next work along the vertical face of the cliff, hanging on to cracks and crevices and with the toes of my feet on a narrow ledge. Soon I am on top of a huge outlier of the cliff with a spectacular view of the upper gorge and waterfall. It is so glorious a sight that I take off my daypack and just sit in awe of the vision. The sun has already set, so the red canyon has a soft grayness settling over it. Above me is a clear blue sky and beyond me, the gorge cradles the almost full moon shining brightly down over the waterfall. The scene is so lovely that I linger for a few minutes and enjoy it.

I descend the cliff and work upcanyon, staying along the base of the cliff in the rainforest growing on the talus slope below it. I am hoping the cliff will act like a huge drift fence and form a causeway for animals going upslope who will turn left or right and move along the cliff when they reach it. Soon I find the way strewn with monstrous squarish and rectangular boulders that are part of the cliff breakdown. They are so large that I can squeeze through the cracks between some of them or go under others that are tilted. Mostly, however, I climb up and over them, down and across gaps between them, then up and over again. Often I come to sheer rock faces I can't scale, requiring that I backtrack and try another path. On this longest part of the night's sojourn, I am constantly entangled in vines and threading my body with difficulty among the branches of wild fig trees, a sure sign of rainforest.

I search the vines, limbs of trees, rocks, and every nook that might hold a snake to no avail. After about two hours of bending my body like a pretzel, I am exhausted, and I still have to make the difficult journey back to camp in moonlight. Then the night suddenly goes pitch black when a cloud—the only one I have seen in three days—forms and slides across the face of the moon. I struggle along carefully, keeping in mind that now that I am tired is when an accident such as slipping and breaking a leg is most likely. I arrive in camp at about 8 P.M. and discover that John has bagged a roughie, the seventh known specimen.

We sit around the campfire and John pulls out the roughie for our inspection. What a fantastic snake. It is quite skinny with a pronounced arrow-shaped head strongly set off from a pencil-thin neck. The color pattern is beige with bold, wormlike, brick-red marks. In our lights, its eyes are vertical slits. I gently pick it up and am handling it when suddenly it lunges and clamps down on the soft flesh of my right arm in the crook of the elbow. Instead of biting and releasing as most snakes do, it chomps hard, holds on, and pulls up a whole mouthful of my skin and underlying adipose tissue. It looks really weird, this triangular snakehead with a mouthful of my flesh. Its body, wrapped around my left hand, squeezes ever more tightly as if constricting prey. The whole thing is pretty amusing, this little snake thinking it is overcoming my huge self. The bite is surprisingly painless and the only thing to do is sit and wait until it decides to release me. Eventually, the snake releases me, and then the bite bleeds copiously from the little pinpricks of a couple of dozen teeth. The bleeding stops quickly, though, as such pinpricks do.

Then a most amazing thing happens. The snake, still in my left hand, opens its mouth about as wide as it is able and displays its mouth toward any moving target such as a hand or someone wielding a camera. Many snakes use their open mouths to threaten, but this one keeps its mouth open for five, ten, or twenty seconds at a time, brandishing its extremely long, very visible teeth. Like most snakes, it strikes at any movement, but it is unique in holding its mouth open so long, presumably so that its enemy will see the long, needlelike teeth and the white buccal lining. Most snake teeth are enveloped in a white sheath of the buccal tissues, but these teeth are fully exposed like little needles.

We sit around camp and talk about the strange biology of the rough-scaled python. John thinks, and I agree, that the roughie is a relict of wetter times when rainforests were more widespread in northern Australia. There are several reasons for this. First, the roughie is morphologically a tree snake or, one could argue, a vine snake, considering its long, skinny body and prehensile tail. Next, its teeth are exceedingly long, just like those of the tree boas and green tree python, teeth that are thought necessary to grasp prey that might leap or fly off of branches. Third, the two presumably disjunct localities from which the rough-scaled python is presently known are deep canyons with scraggly rainforest relict plant communities. And it is from these isolated patches of rainforests in the canyons that all seven of the world's known specimens of this snake come from.

Plant and animal fossils from wonderful sites such as Riversleigh or Narracoorte Caves in Australia tell us that, millions of years ago, the entire continent of Australia was clothed in rainforest. Then, the climate began to dry out as the glacial events of the Pleistocene approached and rainforest became increasingly restricted to protected places, or to where tropical rains still fall, such as in northeastern Queensland. Looking into the eyes of John's most recent roughie is like looking back into the past. The roughie's ancestors probably were more widespread several million years ago, but as the climate dried out and its rainforest habitat shrank into protected enclaves, populations of the rough-scaled python shrank, as well. It's pretty amazing that this spectacular snake still survives, but simple population biology tells us that any animal found in only two small places in the world and that are probably not in touch with each other faces a very uncertain future. It's a wonder that monster cyclones, a once-in-a-millennium deep-freeze, or a ten-year severe drought hasn't already wiped out the roughie purely by natural happenstance.

Enter modern man. We already know that canyon-filling hydroelectric projects, pollution-filled stormwater runoff from mining or agriculture, and a dozen other actions of mankind could wipe out these two remaining enclaves and all the roughies in them. In fact, the python lovers of the world would pay big bucks to own a roughie. A few snake hunters working the two known enclaves of this rare species could probably wipe out the naturally occurring populations. That is why the Western Australia Parks and Wildlife Department considers the rough-scaled python a threatened species, and why the WAPWD has issued John permits to collect a breeding pair of this rare species. And that is why John, himself, wants to try to breed the species in captivity and learn as much as possible about its breeding biology and other behavior as he can. The more knowledge we have about the biology of the rough-scaled python, the better are our chances of helping it to survive into the future. A future without unspoiled canyons, remote rainforest patches, and rare rough-scaled pythons, is one I do not care to be part of.

19
THE FIERCEY
World's Deadliest

WE MOTOR WEST FROM WYNDORAH ON AUSTRALIA'S WARREGO
Highway, a narrow strip of bitumen with wide dirt shoulders. It's a two-
way road, but only one lane wide, so when you meet an approaching
vehicle, both cars have to move left and put their passenger-side tires
in the dirt, keeping only the driver's side wheels on the bitumen.
Problem is, the monstrous trucks called road trains rarely move over,
so you are forced to drive entirely off the bitumen and give them
a wide berth. I am traveling with my colleagues, David Wright and
his wife, Mimi, and we are here to film the world's most venomous
terrestrial snake, *Oxyuranus microlepidotus.*

Oxyuranus microlepidotus has at least four common names:
fierce snake, inland taipan, small-scaled snake, and western taipan.
Inland taipan seems to be emerging as the most accepted common
name, but the Aussies sometimes call it simply the fiercey.

The fiercey was an enigma for many years. The first one was
discovered and given its scientific name in 1879, but no other
specimens came to light until 1974. The principal reason is that the
fiercey lives in the remote interior of Australia in forbidding habitats in
which one would never expect to find an endemic snake. The habitats
are vast waterless plains called ashy downs, or gibber plains—flat to

gently undulating lands with shallow to deep, brown, cracking clays and stony surfaces. The plains are generally treeless with fluctuating climaxes of saltbush, Mitchell grass, annual grasses, and cockleburs. Occasionally, when it rains, the cracks fill up with water; then the terrain is called the Channel Country after the braided channels of streams made during rare floods across the flat terrain.

Temperatures run well above 100 degrees Fahrenheit in summer, and below freezing in winter. Mid-September is one of the best times of the year to find the fiercey because it emerges from winter hibernation at about this time of year and moves around for a few weeks. Then the really oppressive heat of summer arrives and the snake no longer can be found.

Rainfall is highly unreliable, averaging less than about five inches a year, but every seven to ten years severe floods occur. The floods bring about a population explosion of a rat whose geographic distribution largely coincides with that of the inland taipan, and the rat serves as the principal food of the snake. The large population outbreaks of the rat are the reason for one of its common names, plague rat. It is also called the long-haired rat because its hair is somewhat soft and fluffy, rather unusual for an Old World rat, an endemic Australian species whose scientific name, *Rattus villosissimus*, refers to its long hair.

The rat, a large, strong, nocturnal rodent, follows the deep cracks down into the soil when excavating its burrows. The fiercey hunts by day, searching out the rats for a meal while they sleep. It is thought that the snake's extremely potent venom assists it in killing its prey quickly before the rat can inflict retaliatory bites with its sharp teeth in the narrow and confining spaces of the rat burrows.

The fiercey is a relatively large snake (up to six feet long) and its venom, as measured by the number of mice it kills in comparison with other snakes, is twice as toxic as that of its closest relative, the eastern taipan (*Oxyuranus scutellatus*), about 20 times as toxic as that of the king cobra, and about 90 times more toxic than the venom of North America's most dangerous snake, the eastern diamondback rattlesnake! Following the two eastern diamondback snake bites that I barely survived with the aid of antivenin, I can verify that the eastern diamondback is deadly, so how deadly is 90 times more toxic? Or put another way, how dead is dead?

We have learned that one of the best places to find the fiercey is along a stretch of the Diamantina Development Road near the Birdsville cutoff. At our destination, a flat plain spreads monotonously as far as we can see. Two-inch-wide cracks fracture the brown clays like a checkerboard. I poke my snake hook into several cracks and discover that they are up to 30 inches deep, and probably deeper. It is obvious that there is a thriving colony of rodents here because the ground is criss-crossed with their runs. Abundant food and cover: what more could a population of predatory snakes want?

We establish camp on a muddy billabong—a segment of a river that maintains water during seasonal drought when the rest of the river is bone dry. Then we go out on our first fiercey hunt at 5 P.M. We road-cruise by driving parallel with the highway on a dirt track across the cracking clay soils. I stand on the passenger-side running board and see nothing of note by good dark at 7 P.M.

Next morning we road-cruise again with our headlights on, just after first light at 6 A.M. Holding on to the running board and cartop rack is tiring because I can fit only the balls of my feet on the metal strip of the running board and I have to lean back from the vertical and grip the rack tightly. We drive and strain our eyes all morning and late afternoon, but again see nothing.

We are exhausted from the heat when we get back to camp, but David made supper before we left, so all we have to do is warm it up and eat it. It is a delicious stew of chicken, dried tomatoes, cut up sweet potatoes, regular potatoes, carrots, parsnips, and vegetable stock. No sooner do I begin greedily supping my stew when David, standing by the camp stove and butane light, turns his head to the dark shadows behind him and mutters, "Snake." He is so quiet about it that what he says doesn't register in my brain. When he is more emphatic, I jump out of my camp chair and race to the car for my snake hook and clamp stick. David keeps his headlight on the snake and I finally get the snake in sight. I am thrilled. It is a splendid king brown snake, *Pseudechis australis*.

This is my first snake of this kind, one of Australia's most impressive venomous snakes, and a herpetologist's dream. I work with the snake and make mental notes of all its behaviors. Most noticeable is its docility. It seems not at all troubled by my efforts to clamp it gently. I make a very determined effort not to scare it, but then I notice something quite remarkable. I am not able to hold it with my clamp stick. It glides easily out of the grip of the scissor-like metal rods. This is a bit disconcerting because I usually can gently pick up any snake using the clamp stick and lift it into a holding bag. Not this king brownie. No matter how hard I clamp it, it slides right out! As I manipulate the snake, it becomes more active trying to escape, but is still determined to go in the direction it chooses rather than stop and fight. Many snakes will coil up and act defensively aggressive, pulling themselves into an S-loop so they can strike out at their assailant. This guy is having none of that.

After several unsuccessful attempts to clamp it, I realize I must capture the snake by hand in order to examine it more closely. I place the soft handle of the hook on its head and pin it against soft earth, then grasp the snake firmly by the neck. It is a male and immediately I realize why he has been difficult to hold with the clampstick. He is a powerful constrictor. Nothing I have read forewarned me of this. The muscles of his body are hard, not flabby like those of some snakes. He wraps his body around my arm and I realize I must be careful to keep him from using the leverage to twist his head in my grip and drive a fang into one of my fingers. Ounce for ounce, I think this king brown snake has about the most powerful neck muscles I have encountered in a snake. Holding him is difficult, too, because his head is not wide like a viper's head and there is not much to hold onto. After examining him in the light of the campfire, I carry him away from camp and release him into the warm Australian evening. I hear him sliding away from me on dry leaves for a little while, then all is silent.

The next day we drive around slowly in prime fiercey habitat. I stand on the rear bumper eyeballing the flat, cracked clay terrain—and see absolutely nothing! By 10 A.M. the temperature is in the upper 80s and the ground is beginning to get too hot for a snake's belly, so we pack up and make our way back to camp. We repeat the search, adding a couple of hours on foot, in the late afternoon, When the last light of day is gone from the western horizon, we spot a small snake in the road. It's a twelve-inch-long elapid called the curl snake, *Suta suta*, a reddish-brown snake with a flat head and tan cheeks. It gets its common name from the fact that it often curls up into a ball when frightened. Within three minutes we encounter another curl snake, and that is all the snakes we see for this day. Before we retire we place six live-animal traps in prime plague rat habitat. I bait the traps with peanut butter and we put orange surveyor's flagging on them so we can find them tomorrow. I'm curious to examine one of these rats, whose populations are supposed to be the main fare of the fiercey.

About 7:30 the next morning, we check our rat traps. I know from all the rodent trails and other signs I have seen that there is a dense population here, but I am not prepared for four out of six traps, spaced only 50 feet apart, each to contain a rat. Each rat is a grizzled olive brown and tan, and has the classic naked rat tail with a few short, stiff black hairs on it. In my gloved hand, the rats demonstrate their very sharp teeth and feisty demeanor. All four squeal loudly, lay back their ears, and chew my gloved hand with great passion. We film them and then are glad to give them their freedom. I don't yet know how fierce the fierce snake is, but this rat easily qualifies to be called the "fierce rat."

Next morning, clad in snake boots and snake chaps, I place one foot in front of the other, plodding across the brown, cracked, clayey soils of the gibber plain, peering a foot or more down into each of dozens of two-inch-wide cracks. My footfalls are soft, but often I break through many cracks that are roofed over with dirt. Apparently the ground can crack open at depth, forming a long mini-tunnel. I use my snake hook as a ski-pole in my left hand and my clamp stick similarly in the other. If I grasp a snake with this clamp stick, it rarely gets away. It also saves me the split seconds lost trying to correctly identify a venomous snake before diving headfirst to grab it by hand, a move that often results in an escaped snake and a frustrated snake hunter. Furthermore, most Australian snakes are fast and very dangerous. I especially like the safety aspect of using the clamp stick on snakes new to my experience. Besides, the stick is more gentle on the snake than grabbing by hand if one operates the clamping device carefully.

At 8:15 A.M. the air is already hot and I am sweaty. I have been trudging incessantly through prime fierce snake habitat since 6:45. I turn right and begin walking into the sun. Suddenly, I get a thrilling rush when my eyes fall on a long, robust snake whose scales are glowing with reflected sunlight. The sight is beautiful, but the glare of his scales is too bright to discern color or any pattern that would enable me to make an identification. The snake is relatively straight except for two slight kinks. I shout in my mind to myself, with expletives, "Holy #@+!!#! Is *that* a fierce snake?"

The snake isn't moving; it lies still, as snakes commonly do to avoid being seen. I have no idea how fast it will move, but I am prepared to pounce. It is at least 20 feet away, and it may make a dash for a hole. Pumped full of adrenalin, I am eager to close the gap before it gets entirely underground. Unfortunately for the snake, there are no holes nearby, so it remains frozen. I casually saunter obliquely toward it, not directly at it, but to a position about five feet to its side; and I keep my head facing away from the snake. I also squint my eyes so it can't see if I am looking at it. This usually keeps a snake from freaking out and abandoning its freeze posture. Snakes, like most animals, are keen observers of eyes and body language. If I tense up and begin stalking movements, or stare at it directly, it will most certainly dash off, but I amble like a dumb cow, getting very close to it without giving any clues that I am aware of it. Then I place the clamp stick on the upper one-third of its body and gently grasp it.

The snake looks puzzled. It is only gently touched by this silly, inanimate stick and not very alarmingly at that. It turns and investigates the clamp stick. Then I orient toward the snake and all hell breaks loose. The snake tries to dash away, but my clamp stick holds it fast. Tremendous thrashing. Biting the stick. Striking at me. More wild thrashing. I am quickly learning that this is a very flexible and fast-moving snake. But I am puzzled. It has neither the black head nor the pepper spots on its back that are typical of the inland taipan. The sides of its head are almost vertical, which is reminiscent of taipans, but something tells me this is not the special prize we have been so assiduously hunting.

Realizing I cannot control this snake at the end of the clamp stick with it thrashing about wildly and maybe biting me, I decide to grab it by hand. This will be the most dangerous of operations. Any slipups here and I could be doomed. I take my time, trying to place the soft rubber handle of my snake hook on the back of its head or neck, but it is thrashing and biting so wildly that this seems impossible. Then, realizing I have snake boots and chaps on, it occurs to me that I can use my feet to advantage. I gently step down on its head and neck, pressing the dangerous head firmly into soft soil, then I move my clamp stick to the back of the neck and release the pressure of my foot. Simultaneously, I place the fingers of my left hand on the back of its head, pinning the head with my fingers. Then I work the fingers around the back of the head so that I have the rear of the jaws pinched between my left index finger and thumb. This is the way I taught myself to grip the head of a venomous snake. I do not use the three-finger method of holding a snake's head, with the index finger on top of the head and the snake's head between middle finger and thumb.

Finally I get the lovely creature's head restrained and discover that it has backed its entire body up into my shirt through one of the spaces between buttons. After pulling it out and examining the snake closely, I am pretty certain that I do not have the inland taipan. Darn! Although it looks similar to the king brown snake I caught a couple of nights ago, it is quite different in temperament. The king brown almost totally ignored my attempts to catch it, except that it made rapid movements to run away. This snake is very aggressive, rearing up in an S-curve and displaying a small hood, then striking, biting, and thrashing furiously when clamped in midbody. Moreover, while my clamp stick could not restrain the king brownie, the device grips this snake easily. In fact, I learn that I have caught what many herpetologists believe is the second most venomous snake in the world, the eastern brown snake, *Pseudonaja textilis*. We prepare to film its release.

I've got to say that this is one of the most dangerous snakes I have ever handled. I let it begin to crawl out of the snake bag with the intention of pinning the head, but it takes three tries because he yanks his head back into the bag so quickly each time. When I finally do get the head restrained in my fingers, the snake writhes and thrashes so violently I think he is going to wrench himself out of my grip. To release him safely, I gently toss his body away from me, releasing his body first and then his head. While he is airborne he makes a lunge back at me. Had I not first given his body momentum, he would have nailed me in mid-air. When he hits the ground, he takes off as fast as a coachwhip. I trot along about 20 feet behind him and watch as he frantically investigates several shallow cracks. Then he finds a deep one and I am mesmerized by the liquid beauty of his long, straw-colored body disappearing underground.

Two more long and uneventful days pass without spotting so much as a lizard. I'd give nearly anything to find and catch a fierce snake, especially now after seven days of effort. Then, on the last morning, I tell David, "It's prime time for snake movement. Let's get in one more round of road-cruising before we declare this trip a complete failure." David agrees, so we pack up the camera equipment and I jump onto the back bumper. About three minutes down the road, my eye catches something really large lying perpendicular to the road and about 75 feet from it. It seems too large to be a snake. I look away, then it dawns on me that I have not seen this object while road-cruising earlier. I look back, and the next couple of seconds tick by like five minutes.

At first I have the fleeting notion that this thing does not look like any snake. Then a tiny thrill flashes by, "What if this *is* a snake? The *fiercey?*" Then my mind says, "Naw, you only want it to be a snake so bad that your mind's playing a trick on you, but #@%#!, if this thing is a snake, *it's huge!*" Under normal circumstances I would bang on the car for David to stop, but I am so doubtful that it might actually be a fierce snake that I let the vehicle go past the thing while I am making double sure. Finally, *bang, bang, bang,* I pound the side of the Land Cruiser as loud as I can whack it! My god, there is no doubt about it. *It is a snake—a fierce snake—and a monster of a fierce snake at that!*

I bang on the side of the truck so hard that I startle David. He stomps on the brakes and I almost lose my front teeth on the cartop rack as I lurch forward. I bolt off the bumper with clamp stick in one hand and snake hook in the other and run as fast as I can toward where I last saw the amazing creature. Racing pell-mell for the spot, I see nothing at first and almost run past it. Stretched out going away from me is the largest snake I have seen in weeks. Bigger than the noble king brown, bigger than the large and dangerous eastern brownie, this snake is a veritable hoss!

Amidst shouts of glee and amazement, I wonder how in the devil I am going to capture this snake gently and without getting bitten. It is so large. If I grasp it below midbody with my clamp stick, I fear it may be able to reach my hand. Yelling my glee at the top of my lungs, I work with the snake, which by now is bolting for cover. It moves fairly fast, not nearly so fast as the eastern brown, but speedily for a big snake, and it makes occasional dangerous swipes back at me with the forward one-third of its body.

I soon discover that I can hook it and lift it half off the ground without scaring it terribly. Eventually the snake calms down and moves in deliberate fashion without the frantic dashing and thrashing movements it made at first. This response is typical of many snakes. At first touch they are frightened and try to dash away or defend themselves by biting and feinting. When they learn that the only thing that is happening to them is the annoying touching by the innocuous hook, or even gentle pressure of the clampstick, they calm down and you can work with them. Soon I learn that I can walk along and herd the snake in the direction I want it to go. David runs the camera and gets lots of good footage of my encounter with my very first fiercey.

A large snake like this tires easily, and I am soon able to lift it off the ground in the crook of my snake hook. It is heavy, however, and my arm tires quickly: I can't hold it high for very long. Eventually I decide to "tail" the snake, which is the Aussie preferred method of snake handling. You grab the snake by the tail and lift it off the ground, holding it as far away from you as possible. The only trouble is that the snake tries to climb up its own body, lunge at you, and bite your hand. The tactic to prevent this snake maneuver is to give the snake a quick twirl or two, which makes it fall into a straight down position. Many handlers have been snake-bitten, however, using this dangerous tactic. Using the snake hook or clamp stick is safer because, with the front of the snake on a hook or restrained by the clamp, you can keep the biting end at bay while lifting the whole snake by the tail. I do this for the camera and we are able to estimate that this fiercey is about five-and-one-half feet long. Shortly after releasing the fiercy, we find and film a second one about three-fourths the size of the first fiercey. Finding snakes is like catching fish. Some days you don't get a bite. Other days you fill the boat.

We drive back to camp in high spirits. After a long week of day-and-night herping, we finally caught a very impressive adult inland taipan or fierce snake. That, along with the king brown and eastern brown, makes this week a superlative one in my life. In one week I have experienced finding and capturing in the wild, three of Australia's—and the world's—most famous and most venomous elapid snakes. What most appeals to me is that the harsh environment in which these snakes live is likely to remain unspoiled. The bizarre but amazingly diverse flora and fauna of the gibber plains will likely survive the human onslaught of the future because of the hot and dry desert conditions, interrupted by episodic floods. I hope it remains true that herp aficionados of the future can come to Australia's Channel Country and find the fierce snake and fierce rat still thriving.

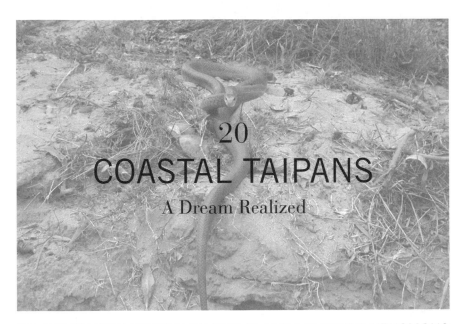

20
COASTAL TAIPANS
A Dream Realized

NO DOUBT FEW PEOPLE ON THE PLANET CHERISH VENOMOUS snakes, but for those of us who do, the chance to get field experience with Australia's venomous elapids is a lifetime dream. After spending a week searching for and capturing the inland taipan—the world's most venomous terrestrial snake—I lusted for equal time with the coastal taipan (*Oxyuranus scutellatus*), the most famous of Australia's snakes. It is a fast-moving, mean-tempered, coachwhiplike snake that reaches a maximum of 11 feet in length and has very toxic venom. By all evaluations of its more aggressive behavior, larger size, and highly toxic venom, the coastal taipan is considered Australia's most dangerous snake. And having caught and handled a couple of inland taipans, I didn't think they were especially dangerous, even in comparison with the more irascible eastern brown snakes that I caught.

After three trips to Australia and several months in the range of the coastal taipan, including two weeks actively searching for this species from Rockhampton to Cooktown, Queensland, however, it seems that such an experience is not to come my way. The coastal taipan has declined in the sugar-growing areas along Australia's northeast coast. The reasons may be habitat loss to sugar cane plantations and development, habitat fragmentation by roads, agricultural fields, and homesites, and no doubt just plain old herpetophobia. Australians are as willing to kill a dangerous snake when they see it as Americans are. Then, improbably, I get another chance because I organize and lead natural history tours to exotic places. In August 2001, I escort eight Americans to Australia on a three-week natural history tour that includes geology, ecology, plant communities, birds, mammals, and at the very bottom of the totem pole, reptiles. We spend a wonderful three weeks together touring Queensland and the Northern Territory and then I say goodbye to my friends in Alice Springs. Before returning home, I decide to make a solo exploration of the Down-Under continent. That is where this story begins.

I drive north to Darwin, trade my rental van for a Toyota Land Cruiser, and then head east. The Land Cruiser has a pop-up top that makes into a spacious queen-sized bed. It is outfitted for a long stay in the boondocks with stove, refrigerator, breakfast nook (good for writing), 50 gallons of petrol, and 50 gallons of water storage capacity.

When I reach the Cape York Peninsula, I drive north out of Coen through some impressive hills—in fact, "mountains" by Australian standards. Smoke from annual bushfires fills the air, hanging low in the valleys. Soon I approach about 15 very dirty motorcycles parked off to the side under some shade trees. Next to them is a van with "Bike Ride Australia" lettered on the side. I hail the first biker and talk a while, learning that the group has just come down from "The Top," which is what the extreme northern tip of the peninsula is called. I inquire about the road. He says the old telegraph track still exists, but has two dangerous river passages. He thinks, though, that I should be able to navigate them in the Land Cruiser. The problem is not with fording the waters, but with driving up and down the steep and dangerously rutted valley sidewalls.

Three and a half hours later, I turn east off the main road onto a dirt track leading to Iron Range National Park, about 85 miles away. Immediately I fall in love with this narrow, one-lane track, winding through a fantastically beautiful sclerophyll (leathery-leaved) forest, also called open eucalypt woodland. The road moves up and down hills, navigates through deep gullies, crosses creek and river beds with no culverts or bridges, and runs diagonally along slopes and down the middle of ridges. Where the tall spear grass has been burned off permitting close visibility of the ground, I see that the landscape is littered with boulders. Then, while driving along slowly, not worrying about making any time, just enjoying the scenery and thinking about things ecological, I see my first snake in days.

It's 2:45 P.M. and my Land Cruiser crawls obliquely down a slope trending left to right. The snake is half out in the dirt track and lies very still; it appears to be nothing but a thin, dead twig—but I know better. I get the vehicle stopped about ten feet from the snake and my blood pressure shoots way up. In a frenzy to get the engine turned off and the car secured from rolling downhill, I hastily grope for my snake clamp stick and throw open the door. Knowing how fast these Aussie snakes can bolt when they decide to, I dash out of the door and lurch toward the snake. It turns back on itself and attempts a quick escape upwards into dense roadside foliage. I lunge at it with the clamp stick, but the snake escapes the grip easily because leaves and twigs of an overhanging eucalypt become entangled with the stick. As the snake runs up into the branches, it flashes in my consciousness that it might be a nonvenomous tree snake. In my fever to catch it, I make another lunge with the clamp stick.

Just as the clampstick closes on the rear end of the snake, a terrible thing happens. My right foot gives way through a wall of green leaves and I find myself plunging, feet first, down a nearly vertical slope. The roadside verdure was so thick that I had no idea there was a cliff just under it. No soft soil here. My left leg, hip, rib cage, and arm get banged up and abraded by the unforgiving roughness of rock. I end up fifteen feet below the car where, fortunately, some vines and roots sticking out of the side of the cliff break my fall. Otherwise I would have dropped another ten feet and hit rugged rocks pointing up from the gully bed below me.

Of course, the snake gets completely away. I never see where it goes, but there are so many vines and branches intermingled overhead that it could easily have kept going for dozens of yards.

My scrapes and bruises hurt and little balls of blood are growing where my skin has broken. I have a difficult time extricating myself from the gully up the steep slope. Then, when I reach the top, I discover that some important items in my shirt pocket—notebook and address book—fell out and are lying at the bottom of the gully. Painfully, hand over hand, I carefully climb all the way down and up again. Back on the road I search in vain for the snake, which I believe was a green tree snake, although it was more golden than I recall other greens being and, for that reason, it might have been a northern tree snake. Back in the car, I try not to be discouraged. "At least," I chuckle to myself, "I finally saw a snake and my streak of bad luck has broken." I scrawl in my pocket notebook, "Damn! First snake in sev. days. Gets away!"

Then, just a few minutes later at 3 P.M., Lady Luck shines on me as I approach a fairly wide, shallow pool of water that marks the bottom of a creek bed that the road crosses. In the sandy road bed on the far side of the pool I spy a dark snake lying crosswise in the road. It is facing the right valley sidewall that the road parallels after it crosses the pool. The snake will have to climb a six-feet high, nearly vertical bank to get away, unless it turns and heads in the opposite direction and into the tangle of deadwood and vegetation in the valley bottom. This time I am better prepared. I jerk the Land Cruiser to a dusty stop, grab my clamp stick, and bolt out of the door. At the same moment, the snake shoots up the bank and crawls under some dry leaves and exposed roots of a *Pandanus* palm. The small palm has fallen from the top of the bank and dangles, top down, just under the overhanging turf on top of the bank. Drat! I worry that in all the excitement the snake will get away.

I stop and listen for rustling. Yes! It is moving under the *Pandanus* and apparently hasn't found a hole to disappear into yet. I take a chance and thrust the clamp stick into the leaves, then see a part of the snake's body moving to my right. I move right to block its exit from the *Pandanus*, then see a little section of the snake and thrust again. After a couple of these back-and-forth maneuvers on both our parts, I finally have the snake grasped in midbody and begin gently pulling it out of the *Pandanus* litter.

At first I see a relatively large, reddish or purplish brown, uniformly colored snake body. Then the head comes out and lunges at me repeatedly and with great speed. I'm glad I have it by midbody, but to really control it and not hurt it with undue pressure, I need the snake hook, which is still in the cab of the Land Cruiser. I am loathe to release the snake for fear that it will get away, even from the middle of the wide, sandy track in the bottom of the creek bed.

The snake is quite heavy and I estimate it to be almost six feet long. I wrestle it to the passenger door so I can reach in the car and get my snake hook, but the door is locked so I have to go around the car to get the keys from the ignition, go back and open the door, and finally seize the hook—all the while carrying the thrashing snake at the end of my clampstick. I gently release the snake in the middle of the largest patch of bare ground and it dashes off, but I hook it. It instantly lunges at me, but I hold it far enough away from my body so as not to get nailed. Then I realize that I am in sandals and shorts with bare legs. (Kathy would not be happy with this. I promised her I would keep myself safe.)

While working with the snake I begin trying to identify it. In the far recesses of my mind I have a hunch that I keep suppressing so I won't be disappointed if it's not what I really want it to be, but the head is definitely "coffinlike" with a strong ridge over the eyes and a groove in which they are set. And those eyes: they are beautiful orange-red in color, very striking to look at. The lips are cream-colored. I just begin hoping I might have caught the coastal taipan that I have lusted to see in the field for so many months—and then I get a look at its venter. The posterior three-fourths is uniformly light yellow or cream, but the anterior one-fourth has some faint little rusty smudges, reminiscent of the brown snakes of the genus *Pseudonaja*. Its upper lip scales are not at all arranged as in *Pseudonaja*, however, but as in *Pseudechis*, the genus of the king brown snake. I know this latter genus very well by now, and this is *not* a *Pseudechis*. So it comes down to the necessity: I'll have to hold the snake in hand and examine it close up. Besides,

I want to photograph it closely, anyway. I work with it awhile by repeatedly letting it run and then pulling it back to the middle of the sandy bare spot until it begins tiring. This helps me to get hold of its head, which I pin in the soft sand—and now I have the beauty's head in my left hand. I pick it up and admire it. It sure looks like a taipan and my hopes are rising. Holding the snake in my left hand, I reach for my camera with my right.

Now I discover that my camera is out of film! Somehow I manage to change the film with only my right hand and begin taking photos of its head, face, neck, body, tail. Oh yes, then it dawns on me. If this is a taipan, it is supposed to have an undivided anal scale. It is one of the few elapids with this condition. I am scared to look for fear of finding a split anal. Now I really want this to be a taipan. And then I see that the anal scale *is* whole! "Wow!" I shout in my mind. "A real taipan, and in its natural habitat and not in some old canefield!" Man, oh man, am I happy. I finish photographing the snake, then replace it under the *Pandanus* litter and walk back to the truck on an emotional high.

Back at the truck, however, I begin worrying about the rusty *Pseudonaja*-like smudges on its fore-belly. I scrutinize the only book I have with me on snakes of Australia, Peter Mirtschin's guide, and then dash back, recatch the poor snake, pin its head, and pick it up again. I have just *got* to make sure. I sit down and count 235 ventrals, which agrees with Mirtschin's data. I count 65 divided subcaudals with a couple missing because of a missing tail-tip, which is commonplace in wild snakes. That agrees. I count 21 midbody dorsal scale rows. That agrees. It has small neck scales and very weakly keeled mid-dorsal scales, which agrees. Finally, I look at Mirtschin's photo of a coastal taipan to see the disposition of the lip scales. His photo is not revealing. Then I remember that Peter kindly let me take some digital photographs of a couple of his captive coastal taipans when I was at his venom production laboratory in February, and they are in my laptop. On examining my photos, I clinch the ID without any shadow of a doubt. The taipan has a temporal scale that comes down nearly to the lip between the last and the penultimate posterior lip scale, just as in snakes of the genus *Pseudechis*. It *is* a coastal taipan. I have finally struck paydirt. I release the fantastic creature a second time and watch it quickly disappear into the ground vegetation. If, as books claim, this species grows to eight or ten feet long, and considering how animated this individual was today, I have no doubt that the coastal taipan, especially a large one, is Australia's most dangerous snake.

Twelve days later, after making a supply run to Cairns, I am en route back to the Iron Range National Park. I'm not thinking about the coastal taipan at all. I get up at sunrise and work on my journal. I am running late for my meeting with Steve Trezise, who has agreed to take me to see some Aboriginal rock art on his property, so I pack everything away, pull down the pop-up roof, turn off the gas to the cookstove, latch the hinges to the roof, stow my one big bag of clothing and tripod on the floor of the campervan, and leave camp on the Kennedy River at a quarter to 8. I am supposed to meet with Steve at his homestead at 10 A.M. and I know from past experience that it takes about one and a half hours to get there from Laura. I am making good time and not thinking about snakes.

I round a bend in the dirt road, not a quarter-mile past the Laura Pub, pulling a trail of dust behind me, when what to my wondering eyes should appear smack in the road in front of me? A great big snake that looks silvery in the morning light. Its shape and general appearance tell me it is a large elapid. Instantly I decide to capture this snake and not let it run away into the bushes. I jam on the breaks, switch off the motor, let the dead engine chug the vehicle to a stop, pull up the emergency brake, grab both snake sticks, throw open the door, pile out, and run around behind the campervan to see if the large snake is still there. My Toyota Land Cruiser is parked squarely in the middle of the road, right in the bend—a very dangerous place. And there lies the snake, a little confused in the dust, but still on the road. "Jesus!" I shout. "Are you a taipan?!" I can't believe it, but I am facing what looks just like a large, six-foot-long coastal taipan. It begins to run off the road, but I clamp it gently about midbody. Damn! That leaves too much snake available to reach toward my hand. It speedily makes a turn for me and would easily have bitten the fool out of me if I hadn't had it clamped. This snake is *fast*! It rears up and charges me again. It has a coffin-shaped head with red eyes and looks every bit as much a taipan as the taipan I caught ten days ago, the live ones I have seen in captivity, and the photos I have looked at in books. And it is very quick.

I ease the snake out into the middle of the road away from the campervan to gain some space in which to work with it and observe its behavior. Twice I am not fast enough on foot to avoid its lunges at me, but I am saved by my clamp stick and the snake hook that I use to fend the thing off. Then I realize I am again standing bare-legged and in sandals with my bare feet exposed. Unfortunately, I can't take time out to go remedy the situation.

Then I hear the drone of a big motor fast approaching. "Oh God, not now. I want to photograph this dangerous beauty, but I don't want an audience of motorists, and I don't want my vehicle involved in a mid-road collision, especially with one of the road-trains that are active in the early morning." I panic. What to do? I must move my vehicle—soon—but I will lose my prize if I have to release it. There seems nothing else to do but bite the bullet and capture the snake. I attempt to place the soft handle of my snake hook gently down on the nape of its neck, but the snake is so fast that it is able to snatch its head back, biting the snake hook at each attempt, and giving it a good dose of venom.

Venom trickles down the handle. A huge squirt of it runs across the snake's right eye and over the top of its head and promptly gets red road dust in it. It dries quickly, and makes the snake look bloody. Not only is it difficult to place the handle on the back of the snake's neck, but the road is awfully hard. I don't want to injure the snake by trying to pin it on the hard substrate, so I use both the clamp stick and snake hook to move the beautiful, writhing animal over to softer dirt on a bank at the side of the road. Finally, I get the head pinned and grab it just behind the jaws, picking up some dirt and grass with the snake. I stand back and lift the exquisite creature by the neck in my left hand, holding the bulk of its body in my right hand.

Motor sound coming nearer. Big, angry, venomous taipan head in my left hand. I wrap the snake's long body around my left arm, grab the snake sticks, and then—for a moment I do not know what to do. I have the snake, but the campervan is in a dangerous place in the road. I can't hide myself behind the vehicle as I sometimes do to avoid attention because the vehicle might get crunched and me with it. Or, if someone comes up and stops and asks me to move the car, how is it going to look if I sheepishly walk out into view with what is Australia's most dangerous snake coiled around my left arm?

Now the oncoming vehicle is getting very close, approaching rapidly from behind around the bend where it can't see my campervan parked in the middle of the gravel road. I make my choice: I dash for the driver's door, open it, jump in, and spend one helluva time pulling off to safety with a six-foot taipan dominating my left hand and arm, trying to go through all the necessary motions quickly so as not to get rear-ended or fanged. I can start the engine easily with my right hand, but I must release the emergency brake, which is on my left side. I reach across my body with my right hand and release the emergency brake, holding the snake's head up out of reach of my right arm that has to cross under my left. To shift the gear, I must also use my right hand to reach under my left and under the deadly serpent's body (the gearshift is on left hand side in Aussie cars).

In my side mirror, I now see the other car, a four-wheel-drive vehicle, coming up fast behind me as I accelerate down the road. Less than a tenth of a mile from the spot where I just caught the taipan, I gun the vehicle to the right off the road and into the gravel bed of the Laura River as the driver of the passing vehicle lays on his horn. Then I realize that, in my urgent and potentially deadly situation, I was driving down the right side of the road, which is the wrong side in Australia! "Damned idiot," he must have been thinking. I chuckle, imagining what he would have said had he known what I am clutching in my left hand. I fantasize about what it would be like if he had pulled over to knock my block off and I had stepped out of the campervan with an angry taipan in my hand.

I drive down the riverbed about a hundred yards away from the road. Now I am far enough away from passing motorists so as not to attract attention. As I roll to a stop, I look at the snake and realize how bizarre the snake and I must look. I take a couple of digital photos of the snake and myself as we sit in the front seat just to document the crazy episode.

I examine its body and determine that the snake is a male. Next, I take him to water and wash off the red mud and venom that has dried on his head. He doesn't like this one bit. When I closely examine his noble head and face, there is no doubt about it: I have my second wild coastal taipan in hand. This one is quite a bit lighter colored than the female I caught and examined outside Iron Range National Park ten days earlier. His light reddish-brown dorsal color is beautiful. His belly, however, is yellow-orange and has lots of rusty round blotches on it from head to tail. Of course, he has the single anal scale and facial scales arranged exactly like many captive taipans I have photographed. And the habitat on both sides of the road where I caught the snake was rocky, grassy, open eucalypt woodlands along the Laura River. This is an excellent transition zone between aquatic and upland habitats, with rocks ensuring good cover for rodents. It is very similar to the kind of habitat in which I caught coastal taipan number one.

Gently, but cautiously, I turn loose the taipan on a bare flat in the floodplain where I can keep an eye (and a snake hook) on him so he won't get away. I shoot off two rolls of slide film and about 50 digital exposures of the lovely creature. He is quite quick and I have to be really careful not to get into biting range. Several times he makes aggressive feints at me, to back me up. As he tires out, I get braver standing my ground. His forward "aggressive advances" are just that, feints that have the purpose of backing up the animal that threatens him. When he does these parries, he rears up, spreads his cheeks and neck, and comes forward a foot or two before stopping. Finally, the snake is calmed down and tired enough so that he poses nicely for me and I get all the photographs I want.

Using my snake hook and clamp stick to guide him, I walk him through the woods very close to the spot where I first caught him. Then I stop and watch him slowly crawl away from the road and disappear into the spear grass among the tree boles of an open eucalupt woodland.

I arrive at Steve Trezise's homestead an hour and a quarter late. When I walk in I blurt out, "I'm sorry I'm late, but I have a good excuse." When Steve asks what it is, I say, "I had an unexpected meeting with the Grim Reaper this morning for an hour, and I took some photographs of the encounter." I then show Steve some of my digital photographs and he accepts my excuse without any argument.

21
GREENIES AND THE
CAPE YORK PYTHON TROVE

I ARRIVE AT THE PRETTY PASCOE RIVER ABOUT 4:30 P.M. I guide the campervan slowly down the narrow dirt track that runs obliquely down the western valley sidewall into a large pool of water, about three feet deep. At the other end of the pool, tire tracks make a sharp right turn perpendicular to the river and cross a long, shallow stretch that is about two feet deep. I shift the Land Cruiser into four-wheel drive and crawl slowly through the current, riding on top of shifting, fist-sized cobbles, gravel, and sand. The passage is scary, but this is how one crosses rivers on Australia's Cape York Peninsula. Vehicular travel to Iron Range National Park is possible only in the dry season. During the wet, the Pascoe is an impassable, raging torrent.

The warm weather was perfect for reptiles earlier, but the temperature is now falling and I have ceased looking for snakes this afternoon. Beyond the Pascoe, the vegetation changes from open eucalypt woodland with lots of spear grass to a low scrubby vegetation, very heathlike. I'm not sure how many of these woody plants are true heaths of the family Ericaceae, but the vegetation has leathery leaves and consists of low shrubs. When I come to some filamentous-leaved grevillias, I stop and suck nectar from some flowers that are dripping with it. At one place I cross a broad, sandy area with massive termite mounds. I have been told that this stretch of road is *the* place to see the black-headed python, but I pass over it and see none.

Hanging from the eucalypt trees are huge wads of green leaves balled up by green weaver ants. They make these nests by cementing live leaves together with a whitish silk. Green weaver ants are one of the most successful social insects of the Old World tropics, sometimes living in huge colonies that consist of hundreds of nests in several trees. The informed traveler knows to avoid brushing against one of their nests because the ants will burst out of it, swarming down your neck and all through your hair and clothes, biting furiously.

A few miles further I drive through a small creek and see my first rainforest hardwoods. As I approach Iron Range National Park and the eastern Queensland coast, I'm definitely traversing different ecological zones. I next pass through a paperbark swamp and see my first Queensland tropical pitcher plant, *Nepenthes mirabilis.*

By about sundown, 6:25 P.M., the air has become cold on my arm outside the window. I think to myself that this inhibits snake activity. The road becomes windy and twisty, descending through a beautiful rainforest of hardwood trees. Darkness falls and it becomes difficult to see what is rainforest and what is open eucalypt woodland, but I can sense an elevation change and warmer evening temperatures as I drive downhill.

Somewhere in the dark I pass into Iron Range National Park, and eventually take a left fork that leads 14 miles to a small village called Portland Roads on the Pacific shore. I pass over several bridges, run through stretches of rainforest, and at one point pass a low fire burning through an open eucalypt woodland along a grassy ridge top. Ahead of me on the road, at about 7 P.M., I am surprised but pleased to find a small slatey gray snake (*Stegonotis cucullatus*), a member of the harmless snake family, Colubridae. I am getting pretty good at identifying Australian snakes because when this snake comes into view, I know right away what it is. The slatey-gray snake has relatively small eyes and smooth, glossy, dark gray scales. It is a long, slender, semiaquatic snake, occurring mostly around water, where it eats a broad range of prey, including insects, fish, frogs, lizards, small mammals, and snake and lizard eggs.

I drive slowly along the dirt road searching for nocturnal animals. At 7:32 P.M., I spot a dull, pink reflection from eyes about three feet off the ground on a three-inch-diameter rainforest tree. It turns out to be a giant green rainforest treefrog with white lips, *Litoria infrafrenta*. It is perched head down, probably watching the ground for litter insects to eat.

Close to Portland Roads, I'm getting drowsy, so I pull off the road for the night, parking about 300 yards from the main track. While I'm preparing my supper, three canines begin howling nearby. It is a wonderful sound, like coyotes, and I like listening to it while I attend to my evening tasks. At one point I walk barefoot up the road about 50 yards and spot their eyeshines in a bright dive light I have brought with me. They appear to be dingos, but I am puzzled by their cries. It was my impression that pure-blooded dingos don't bark. Maybe these are interbred with dogs and have a voice. Then I settle in for a peaceful night's sleep with a feeling of deep satisfaction about the coastal Taipan I encountered earlier today.

The main reason I have come to Iron Range National Park is to see the green tree python, *Chondropython viridis.* This little arboreal python is one of the world's most beautiful snakes. It occurs primarily on New Guinea, the world's second-largest island, but it is also found on a few small islands between Australia and New Guinea and in pockets of rainforest in the northeastern part of the Cape York Peninsula. Its range does not extend south into the more extensive rainforests of the Atherton Tablelands or the Daintree area north of Cairns, where most natural habitats are now obliterated by European settlement. The green tree python is a prime example of a whole suite of New Guinea animals and plants that are relicts in northern Queensland. Only a few thousand years ago, New Guinea was connected to Australia across the shallow Torres Strait. Despite its popularity as an expensive captive pet, few people ever see a green tree python in the wild.

In the morning, I drive about twenty miles back up the dirt road from Portland Roads and check in at Iron Range National Park headquarters for a permit to camp in the park and for information about the laws governing wildlife viewing. As luck would have it, I meet Karl Goetze and Andrea Cook, both of whom work for the Park Service and have been doing a radiotelemetry study of the green tree python for about eight months. When Karl offers to take me on a road cruise tonight and talk of his work with the green tree python, I am thrilled. Rainforest traversed by the 20-mile-long road between park headquarters and Portland Roads—the very dirt road I just drove twice—is good habitat for the species.

I drive back down the main dirt road towards Portland Roads, and then take a right fork to Chili Beach, a long stretch of sandy coastline with coconut palms and a morning view of the rising sun. I spend midday washing out my clothes, walking the beach, and catching up on my journal. I long to swim in the clear blue-green ocean but heed the warning signs that crocodiles lurk along the shore.

I leave Chili Beach en route to join Karl at the park ranger headquarters, a full hour's drive away. I have high expectations of seeing a green tree python this evening, and shortly, at 5:18 P.M. in early twilight, I screech to a halt in front of a small snake lying in the road. I have been so preoccupied with seeing a green tree python in rainforest patches that occur along this road, that I haven't considered that I might encounter other kinds of pythons. This one is a spotted python, *Liasis maculosus*. The habitat on both sides of the road here is grassy, open eucalypt woodland, not rainforest.

The spotted python is the python most commonly seen in Australia because it is distributed up and down the east coast where the human population is also dense. It lives in all available habitats from dry savanna to rainforest, and thrives near towns. Mostly nocturnal, it feeds upon a wide variety of small lizards, birds, and mammals. This little python is one of the most common Australian snakes available in the commercial pet trade around the world. It is closely related to three other small pythons that are also common in Australia, the children's python (*L. childreni*), Stimson's python (*L. stimsoni*), and anthill python (*L. perthensis*). I watch the little python cross the dirt road and I notice a purplish iridescence in its scales.

Shortly afterward, out of the same kind of habitat, a very long, thin northern tree snake (*Dendrelaphis calligastra*) crawls fast across the road ahead of me and tries to climb the banked roadside. I stop quickly and fly out of the car to try to get photographs of it. Like many snakes, it expands its jaws to make its mouth appear bigger. A white streak around its lips accentuates the mouth. The snake also expands its neck and opens up a small "hood," somewhat as a cobra does.

I stop on the road for a quick peanut butter and strawberry jam sandwich and then arrive at Karl's a little after 7 P.M. He rigs up a hand-held, seal beam light for each of us, one operating off the car battery directly and the other out of the cigarette lighter. Thus outfitted, we drive down the road spotting out of the side windows for snakes in the bushes. At night, green tree pythons hang down within striking range of the ground or over a log where small mammals are likely to be passing. Karl says you can often see one dangling from a small-diameter sapling or from slender stems or vines, hanging in one location all night long.

We wonder aloud just how a greenie chooses its spots to lie in ambush for prey. I volunteer that this is an arboreal version of the sit-and-wait ambush behavior that is common in many large pitvipers that I have studied. Surely the snake doesn't pick its ambush sites at random. Its choice must have to do with its chemosensory abilities, but since the snake is arboreal and rarely touches the ground, how does it determine that one site is better than another? Snakes are not thought to have very good olfactory ability, but their tongue tips deliver odor particles to the vomeronasal organs in the roof of their mouths. Possibly the chemosensory ability of vomeronasal organs is more discriminating than we know.

Karl tells me that green tree pythons are common in Iron Range National Park. Only yesterday he and Andrea released six recaptures back into the wild where they found them. One of the park's concerns is that the roadside through the park is a "sink" for the green tree python—that is, a place of death—because the grassy edge between the rainforest and the road, and the road itself, is an unnatural habitat that the arboreal snake may be loathe to cross. The Park Service is concerned, too, that poachers are taking the snakes, so it is desirable to know how abundant or rare the species is.

The telemetry data that Karl and Andrea recently gathered have provided important information bearing on these questions. Rarely did any green tree python they studied along the roadside remain for long near the road. The snakes moved off soon after being released into the forest—one small snake traveling an amazing mile plus! Ironically, they see plenty of green tree pythons along the road, which means that the species may not be that rare and its population seems to be relatively abundant. Karl tells me that occasionally he sees green tree pythons crossing the road. This is an important observation because it demonstrates that the road itself is not a barrier to the movements of this arboreal animal.

While we are talking about snakes, Karl calmly says, "There's one." On Karl's side of the road, wrapped around a downfallen log about four inches in diameter, lies a beautiful, lime-green-colored green tree python, my very first one in the wild. I can't turn the vehicle around on the narrow road, which is cut into a steep slope along the Claudie River, so I back up and park the campervan 50 yards behind the snake in case any traffic comes by. We walk up to it and I am thrilled with a close-up view of one of the world's most beautiful snakes. It faces the ground under the log, clearly in position to strike and grab any unsuspecting rodent or other small mammal that may come along.

I start to take photographs, but the log rests on a steep slope, and I find it a challenge to photograph the snake without disturbing it. I keep slipping downhill and scraping my legs on jagged rocks.

The green tree python I am fondly examining has a lemon-yellow belly and a lime-green back. Its throat and chin are white and a lovely broken series of single, diamond-shaped white scales runs down the midline of its back, standing out starkly against adjacent lime-green scales. Karl tells me that occasional adult specimens of the Iron Range National Park population have some blue color along the midline of the back.

The heat-sensitive pits along the sides of the lower lip and in the forwardmost part of the upper lip are incised very deeply into the scales in which they reside. This is in marked contrast with the shallow pits in the lip scales of the spotted python I photographed earlier today. I suppose this means that they function better in the green tree python, allowing greater sensitivity. The two snakes' snouts are also quite distinct. The spotted python has a rounded snout, tapering both top to bottom and from side to side, whereas the tip of the green tree python's snout appears as though it has been smashed into a brick wall. It is decidedly squared off and the lip scales are expanded to accommodate the large and deep heat-sensing pits.

Karl finishes road-cruising at 9 P.M., but he graciously loans me one of his spotlights so I can continue to indulge in my favorite activity. I drive in first gear and shine into the bushes along the road as I travel back toward Chili Beach, but I see no other snakes. I do, however, find a beautiful treefrog hiding in the leaf litter on the ground. It is so well camouflaged against the litter—repeatedly hopping once, then freezing—that I believe its is adapted for hiding in ground litter. The little flaps of skin at the sides and backs of its heels are reminiscent of those I've seen in some species of New World *Hyla*. This one is *Litoria genimaculata*.

By 11:45 P.M. my eyes are so tired from peering down the beam of the searchlight that I turn into Rainforest Campground and terminate my snake hunt before reaching Chili Beach. I whip up a package of satay rice and call it a night—following another great day in wild Australia.

Overnight I am serenaded by dozens of squeaky calls of a species of frog that hollers its head off in the creek bottom. I trudge into the night, catch one, and discover it to be the wood frog, *Rana daemeli*, most of whose range is in New Guinea. The wood frog is the only frog of the family Ranidae in all of Australia, having migrated onto the Cape York Peninsula before the land bridge between Australia and New Guinea was drowned about 6,000 years ago. It is a New Guinea relict here just as is the green tree python.

I wake up in cool morning air as first light inspires a whole symphony of bird calls from the rainforest, quite different from those

I am used to hearing in the open eucalypt woodlands. A couple of calls are so amazing that I lie listening to them for about 30 minutes, marveling that such loud melodious notes are emanating from small birds. Then I hear the relatively heavy footsteps of some two-footed creatures outside in the leaf litter. I peek out a window and see two brush turkeys moving about. Brush turkeys are megapode birds with very strong feet and legs that they use to scrape up huge mounds of dirt in which to incubate their eggs. The male has a large flap of skin hanging down from his neck, which appears to tighten up and help him make a low-pitched, mooing call. Periodically he runs like blue blazes, chasing another brush turkey. At least a couple of times the pursued bird turns out to be a hen. The two make a great fluttering of wings—I can't tell whether for rapid fornication or for dominance pecking. The hen always stays nearby, even though I think I see her running from the tom at least once.

At 7 p.m., I begin another nighttime road cruise. Ten minutes later I see a four-foot-long snake in the road. I stop and my heart pounds. It is a new snake for me, one I have been waiting eagerly to see in Australia for months, and one I never guessed I'd see here. It is my first carpet python, *Morelia spilota*, lying still in the headlights and looking as pretty as can be with reddish-brown squares linked down its back. What surprises me about finding it here is that wherever the introduced cane toad, *Bufo marinus*, is found—as here in the Iron Range National Park—Australian naturalists have noticed that the carpet python disappears. It is thought that the toxic skin secretions of the toad kill the python, which won't hesitate to eat a toad. I am finding the cane toad abundant here, but this carpet python has survived nonetheless.

I have seen lots of photographs and captive specimens of the carpet python. Many are drab or have unattractive patterns. This one is a real beauty because its blotches are a rich russet color and are arranged in lovely squares down the back. Adults average six feet long or less, but some are known to reach twelve feet long. This individual is crawling out of open eucalypt woodland with lots of brush and stony ground. Longer and stouter than the spotted python, the carpet python was once widespread in eastern and northern Australia, with populations in southern New Guinea, but locally in its Australian range, where once it was common in many areas, it has declined due to the cane toad. The python occupies many different habitat types, from river floodplains and rocky cliffs to rainforest and open eucalypt woodland. Its diet is also broad, including many species of birds and mammals. Young carpet pythons favor lizards.

I turn down the road to Chili Beach and when I get to a culvert that crosses a swampy creek, I stop, put the searchlight out the window, and click it on. The light falls on the full length of a six-foot-long water python, *Liasis fuscus*, looking up at me. This lovely female is so large in diameter that I believe she has the remains of a meal in her gut. I park the car off the road, then wade into the water and follow her.

The water python is the most aquatic of Australia's pythons, found in marshes, swamps, and floodplains. This one is typically dark olive brown with no hint of any pattern, and I can see that she has a plain, yellow belly—but she is not drab. A pretty, iridescent sheen reflects off her body scales in my night light. She blends well with the darkly colored, decomposing leaf litter of the swamp. I have to search hard in deeper pools to see her because, although the water is free of silt and clay that would make it muddy, it is tea-stained with organic acids that have leached out of the decomposing leaf litter of the swamp. I take some photographs of her while she swims, then watch her glide into a hole at the base of a tree. I stand silent in a pool of squishy muck listening to night sounds and observing the beauty of myriad wetland plants all around me, some emerging from the water, some floating, some epiphytic on swamp trees. After a little while, I spot a green treefrog, *Litoria cerulea*, sitting on a branch over water. With some effort, I locate two others within the range of my headlight. This must be a breeding place for the species, and it seems also to be good adult habitat. Here in the northern part of the Cape York Peninsula is one of the few places in the dry continent of Australia where swamps and bogs are common.

Next, I drive down to Chili Beach and back. I see nothing of note for a while, but then I encounter a juvenile brown tree snake, *Boiga irregularis*, crossing the road. This is the snake whose numbers have wreaked so much havoc on the mid-Pacific island of Guam. Here, it is a native species whose natural foods, competitors, and predators hold its population in check. There, it is an alien invader with few natural checks on its population growth.

I continue west to the main road and then one and a half miles to the crossing of Chili Creek. Spotting into the rainforest with the bright searchlight just after I cross the creek, I think I see something shiny about a foot off the ground and 100 feet deep in the forest. I stop the car and stare at it. Suddenly, what I'm looking at becomes a loop of snake belly hanging down from a small, dead tree lying on the ground. I get out my cameras, thinking it might be another green tree python, then see that the belly is cream-colored, not lemon-yellow. As I approach, my heart jumps into my mouth! It is way larger than any green tree python could be. Then I recognize it. Oh my god, it is my first amethystine python, *Liasis amethistinus*, also called the scrub python. I feel like hollering, "FANTASTIC!!" or "EUREKA!" This is a *big* snake and it is lying in a perfect hunting posture. Its body loosely loops up the inclined, dead sapling, while its head and neck hang down looking at the ground as though it is waiting, poised for some unsuspecting little bandicoot to pass within lunging range.

Amethystine pythons have blocky heads with large, well-defined scales on top. Heat-sensitive pits, pinkish in color, lie deep in the lip scales. In light reflected from my flashlight, my eyes catch flashes of purple iridescence, presumably the source of the snake's common name. This is Australia's largest snake, and one of the world's largest as well, reaching to more than 25 feet long. It is distributed mainly in New Guinea and on many nearby islands, with a small part of its range in northeastern Queensland. In Australia, the amethystine python is primarily an inhabitant of rainforest, where it is found in trees as well as on the ground, especially in the vicinity of water. Clutches of about a dozen large eggs are brooded by their mothers, who lie coiled around the clutch and shiver to produce a high enough body temperature for the eggs to develop. When the snake begins to crawl away, I carefully estimate it to be at least nine, maybe ten feet long. Three species of pythons in the short space of about one and a half hours! What next?

I return to road-cruising fully expecting to see more wildlife. The weather has been cloudy all afternoon, but it is muggy and a little breezy tonight. Something about the weather seems to have triggered snake movement, and I now expect to see a bucketful of green tree pythons. I drive for the next three hours, carefully peering down the bright spotlight in anticipation of seeing more snakes, but zilch! Nada! I see no more—that is, until I reach the spot where Karl and I saw the green tree python last night. There lies his little green self, coiled again on the very same log looking again at the very same spot of ground, no doubt hoping for a mouthful of something good to eat. He is the only snake I see for the rest of the night after the amethystine python. I should complain! Actually I saw four species of pythons tonight, and I could have seen six if I had encountered the black-headed and the spotted.

I spend the night in a bungalow at Portland Roads. An hour or two after turning in, I wake to go to the loo. In the dark, I open the door and feel around for a light switch. My hand suddenly touches something large, cold, moist—and alive! After yanking my hand back, I go find my flashlight and have a chuckle when I see a huge white-lipped treefrog clinging to the wall by the light switch. The huge beauty is about as big as my entire hand, an obvious reason why one of its common names is giant treefrog. I capture it and take several photos. Having giant treefrogs free-ranging in the house is a novel way to keep down the roaches—and a novel way to end a fantastic night.

I sleep in a comfortable double bed with a gossamer mosquito net draped all around, a necessity. Everywhere I have chosen to camp out I have not encountered mosquitoes, but where people live, mozzies flourish. In spite of having turned in so late, at 2:30 A.M., I wake up at about 7:30 and can't get back to sleep. I spend the day doing laundry, making phone calls, and attending to other chores. At 5:30 P.M., I resume road-cruising heading west, hoping to see more snakes.

The weather is blustery with clouds overhead, some wind, and no sun. Along the way there has been some scattered rain. I check on the green tree python at 7:15 P.M. It has already climbed down from its daytime retreat and repositioned itself as in the past two nights. This little snake must perceive some possible meal under the log and is willing to wait for a chance to strike and constrict it when the prey comes into striking range. Considering that the only energy this little snake expends is moving back and forth slowly between its night and daytime perches, plus what it uses up in metabolism, it isn't using much fuel to keep alive.

From the greenie I drive west about 12 more miles, mostly through heath scrub, hoping to see the sixth python of this amazing little park, the black-headed python, but after passing through the hot area for blackies, my eyelids are drooping and I have seen no sign of one. I pull off into the scrub and make ready for a night's slumber. Because I got so little sleep last night, I am really tired tonight.

I wake up after a good night's sleep, rejuvenated and mentally sharp. I whip up a breaky of oatmeal and honey, wash it down with a cup of Caro drink, and then sit thinking about what I am going to do during the remainder of my time in Australia. I decide to make a trip to Cairns and return in ten days. Most of the day I spend writing in my journal and reading. The weather is windy and deliciously cool.

I leave my camping spot at 4 P.M. and drive out the long narrow track toward the Pascoe River. En route I have the luck of the Irish. Not expecting any snakes, but sort of keeping my eye out for another taipan, lo and behold what do I see in the road in front of me? A big, dark snake stretched halfway across the track. It's a harmless black-headed python, *Aspidites melanocephalus.* This snake and its sister species, the woma (*Aspidites ramsayi*), are unique among pythons in several respects. Both are cylindrical, slender pythons with narrow heads that are not distinct from the neck, or only slightly wider, but foremost is their lack of heat-sensitive organs in the pits of scales surrounding their lips. These are the world's only true pythons lacking heat-sensitive pits. With their slender heads, the black-headed and woma pythons are also the only true pythons that actively burrow in soil. The lack of heat-sensitive organs is understandable in view of these snakes' diet, which consists mostly of cold-blooded lizards and snakes. They only rarely take birds and mammals. What I find most interesting about these two pythons is that they apparently are immune to the venoms of Australian elapid snakes, which they constrict to death, then ingest.

This is amazing. I have now seen six species of pythons in or near Iron Range National Park, and only one specimen of each. I've also seen three harmless colubrid snakes, but no venomous ones. From all that I have read about pythons, I believe there is no other place in the world with so many python species in such a small area. Iron Range National Park is a python trove.

Beyond the Pascoe River, I round a bend and come upon a frightening scene. In the middle of the road ahead of me, two huge Brahma bulls are engaged in a god-awful struggle that looks like a fight to the death. They are so wrapped up in their frenzy that I worry they may attack my campervan. I stop and lean on the horn, trying to break them up, but they pay me no mind. One bull has the other on the ground and is repeatedly butting him in the belly, trying to eviscerate him. The downed bull seems to be about done for. Each time the standing bull gores him, I hear a pitiful, pain-filled groaning grunt such as I might make if someone were pounding me in the guts. Dust flies, hooves stamp, and the standing bull freely savages the other. Finally, the standing bull stops and looks up, noticing me. He stands his ground a minute and I wonder if the campervan will be his next target.

Then the standing bull angles a few steps away from me, watching me intently. His focus now clearly on the campervan, he looks afraid of it. Then, amazingly, the downed bull gets up. He is *bigger* than the other bull. Then I see why he has been down. Apparently, while the two were butting heads, the larger bull backed into a barbed wire fence, parts of which now lie tangled up on the road, and had apparently been wrapped around the bull's hind legs. Now the larger bull trots off in pursuit of the smaller bull and they begin a terrible butting fracas in the eucalypt woodland. The larger bull is the stronger in these bouts, pushing the smaller bull backward at each bashing. Soon the smaller bull takes off in flight, with the larger bull following, but slowly. The larger bull won the contest, but I have no doubt that he fared much worse for the gut-pounding he took while lying on the road. It's a wonder he got up at all. Watching the violence of the two behemoths trying to kill each other leaves me sick at the stomach.

On my return trip from Cairns, I pass into Iron Range National Park about 2:30 and check on the site where my friend, the green tree python, was lying in ambush for three nights on my first visit. It isn't there, as I expect during daylight, but I search in the foliage above to see if I can find it coiled on a branch or liana. I never see it. At 3 P.M., a skinny, dark-colored goanna dashes into the deep grass of a wetland in front of me. I run back and spot it in the grass. It deftly climbs the only tree around, a stem about four inches in diameter, keeping the tree between itself and me. It is obviously an arboreal animal, with its long and thin legs and arms, narrow body and head, and long, prehensile tail. It is black, dorsally, with tiny little light yellow specks, one series forming a faint neck ring. I identify it as *Varanus kiethhornei*, a rare arboreal monitor lizard.

After dark, I drive slowly for what seems like hours, peering along the beam of a new, super-dooper hand-held spotlight I purchased in Cairns, which runs off of the campervan's cigarette lighter. I find absolutely nothing. I drive down the Chili Beach Road—nothing. I drive back and forth between Portland Roads and the Chili Beach Road—nothing. Then I drive in low four-wheel drive all the long way back to where the green tree python had been hunting—but he is not there. I get out and spot around, but can't find him anywhere. The only animal I do find is another lovely white-lipped treefrog about chest-high on the side of a rainforest sapling. I hope my greenie found a mouse and is happily hanging above ground tonight over some other mouse trail in the deep forest.

Next morning, I drive to Portland Roads and visit with Sandy Woods and Greg Westcott who manage the bungalow I rented on my last visit. Greg tells me that just the year or two before he moved to Portland Roads, the region was densely populated by a very venomous snake, the death adder, *Acanthophis praelongus*. Now there are none. There were so many death adders in those days that at night people were in danger just walking up the road without a flashlight. Then, in not much more than a single year after the arrival of the first cane toads, the death adders completely disappeared. Greg is disgusted with the way the native ecology of Australia is being degraded by the cane toad, as well as being lost to human development.

Over the next week, I walk the rainforests, hunt in the open eucalypt woodlands, and explore every road and track, but see no other pythons except one water python one night in a dry river course. My time in Iron Range National Park has come to a close. I drive to Chili Beach and find a nice, breezy place under swaying coconut palms where I relax until 3 P.M. As I pull out for an early road cruise, a police car from the settlement of Lockhart River passes me and I wave. It has just grown dark and I have begun spotting for green tree pythons and amethystines, snakes I'd love to photograph, when a car comes up fast behind me. The driver stops abreast of me and says that policemen in a police car not far behind have just arrested a chap for catching a snake. I have permits to photograph snakes, but I think it prudent not to be spotting in the woods when the police car comes up behind me, so I pull off the road and make camp for the night.

I learn later that within minutes of this encounter, the policemen did, in fact, arrest a man at Chili Beach for possessing an amethystine python in a bag in his car. Mick and Claire Blackman, the park rangers here, have both told me of the problem they have with Australians (and foreigners, too) who come here and poach animals of all kinds, especially the green tree python. Apparently there is good enforcement and arrests are being made. How can you expect to have a national park if people molest the flora and fauna and remove them? Why can't people be content to do as I am doing . . . finding and photographing wild creatures I love and then leaving them to be free in the wild?

As I drift off to sleep I review why I must now leave this paradise. I encountered most of the snakes I saw in Iron Range National Park the first week I was here, right after some substantial rains that occurred before I arrived. During the first week, little rain fell and for the past two weeks, none at all. When I first got here three weeks ago, there was no road dust on the roadside vegetation, but now everything is heavily coated and choking plumes of dust follow me everywhere I go. I have been here during August and September, the last month of the Australian winter—and the dry season—which will continue for at least another month through the end of October. Although October is the equivalent of April in the northern hemisphere, it is so hot and dry that reptiles and amphibians are inactive until the rains come in late spring, November and December. Besides, I have run out of the time I have budgeted for my stay in Australia.

On my last day in Iron Range National Park, I spend the afternoon in rainforest along a creek, reading and writing. While sitting in the campervan with the back doors wide open, I keep hearing little splashes. When I finally look up, I am amazed to observe that the noise is coming from two-inch-long fishes that are migrating upstream. They are jumping a small, six-inch cascade of water that drops over roots. They look for all the world like tiny migrating salmon. I sit fascinated for some time, counting them. In the space of a couple hours, I estimate that 200 little fish make the passage up the creek through the "falls." I wish I had a little dipnet so I could capture one and identify it.

At about 6:45 P.M. I take off on my last snake road-cruise in Iron Range National Park. The magical hour of dusk, when snakes crawl, is upon me. I drive back down the Old Mission Road and look for carpet pythons, which are said to commonly cross here, but see none. Then I top the crest of a high hill and slowly cruise for a mile or two through a big patch of rainforest that grows along a substantial river, hoping to see either an amethystine or green tree python. No luck. I next head west out of the park, road-cruising through the last patch of rainforest until about 8 P.M. I stop at one of the crossings of the Claudie River and wade up and down the stream peering into the bushes with my headlight, but still see nothing. Then I eat a can of chili and beans and two fresh ears of corn on the cob that I roast in their husks. At 9 P.M. I begin cruising in low four-wheel drive again spotlighting for snakes in the bushes. It is very dry and growing too cold for snake activity.

I turn on the AM radio and pick up a station that I can get only at night, which originates from Port Moresby in Papua New Guinea. Music is playing, and then it is interrupted and I hear voices talking excitedly and simultaneously. Only half listening and intently looking down the spotlight beam, I hear an incredible scenario like Orson Welles' famous Invasion of the Martians radio program. When I first hear, " . . . airplane crashed into the World Trade Center . . ." it doesn't register that I am hearing a live news flash. I hear some more excited talking and begin paying closer attention. The voices sound familiar. I am listening to a live CNN broadcast that is patched in to the radio. As the reception fades in and out, and amongst the static, I learn about the developing tragedy. Soon I hear, "My god, another plane has just crashed into the other tower of the World Trade Center."

I can't believe my ears. I drive west up out of the lowland rainforest of the park to the highest point of the road that I can find so I can get good reception. Then I turn off the road into the bushes and sit transfixed, listening to the developing story. All the rest of the night I am glued to the car radio. Most of the night I lie listening, not believing what I am hearing. I hear it all, as it is happening and being reported, from the collapse of both towers of the World Trade Center, to the plane crash into the Pentagon, to the revelation that four commercial airliners have been hijacked by terrorists, that one plane goes down in Pennsylvania somewhere, and that all air traffic is suspended throughout the country. I get the same sick feeling I had watching the two bulls trying to gore each other.

It takes me two days to drive to Cairns in hopes of making plane connections home to Florida. En route I have lots of time to think. I have spent much of my adult life trying to teach people to discover—and cherish—the beauty of nature, that unusual animals such as earthworms and lizards, frogs and turtles, even spiders and snakes, have great intrinsic beauty and value. Moreover, such living creatures deserve to be treated better by us than they are.

Then I think about all the horrors that mankind has perpetrated on mankind in my short life: World War II, the Korean War, the

Vietnam War, Khmer Rouge atrocities in Cambodia, genocide in Rwanda, genocide in Bosnia, the Palestine-Israeli conflict, and terrorism, just to name a few. The list goes on and on and still the horrors continue. If we can't even learn to treat our fellow man with respect, how can human beings ever develop a greater appreciation of other creatures?

.

22
OKEFENOKEE ALLIGATORS
Congratulatory Bellows

IT IS AUTUMN AND I AM FOOTSORE AND HEARTSICK. PEACEFUL
wilderness is the calming salve I need to ease the physical and emotional
travail of the past 42 days. When I get to the Okefenokee Swamp, I rent
a canoe and paddle a couple of miles up Cedar Hammock Trail. White
water lilies, glistening neverwet, and blue pickerelweed pop up in all
directions above the still surface of the reddish-black waters. Here
and there floating islands of peat support brilliant yellow sunbursts
of marsh marigold. I nose the canoe onto one of the herb islands, lie
back with my feet dangling over the sideboards, and let the peace and
beauty pervade me. My problems begin to vanish. Fresh air, clear blue
sky, wide-open space, and no people—it is heavenly!

Lolling there for about 30 minutes, I have my eye on some
foraging white ibises when suddenly two strong sonic booms blast
the swamp and startle me into nearly capsizing. The frightened ibises
fly off in a panic. I feel like cursing aloud for being unable to escape
human impacts in the middle of the Okefenokee Swamp, but at that
very moment the alligators capture my full attention.

Seven weeks earlier, in the predawn light of September 2nd,
1984, I had set out on foot from Louisville, Kentucky, to retrace John
Muir's 1,000-mile walk to the Gulf. Having just lost my job of fifteen

years I needed some wilderness to calm my anguish. I thought that the best way to put my troubles behind me was to immerse myself in the remnants of the wilderness that Muir had passed through. Using Muir's journal as a guide, I traveled over the same track and on the same dates as America's most famous conservationist, 117 years later.

Things didn't turn out as I expected. On the very first day I got a rude awakening. The dirt turnpikes that Muir had traveled were now two-lane paved roads with no shoulders to walk on safely. All day, walking into traffic on the hard macadam, my attention was riveted on avoiding high-speed vehicles that repeatedly forced me to jump into brambles and roadside junk. This preoccupation with my personal safety was to last the entire trip.

For all 42 days, my journey was a chronicle of man's inhumanity to nature. The deep, green sea of bossy oaks and virgin hardwood forests described by Muir were gone from Kentucky and Tennessee. I couldn't walk up "the leafy banks of the Hiawassee . . . with its surface broken to a thousand sparkling gems" because that "most impressive mountain river" had long been drowned behind dams. And more than 90 percent of the vast Coastal Plain longleaf pine forest was clearcut and replaced with agriculture and sterile tree farms. None of Muir's wilderness remained along my transect through the eastern US. Sick at heart, I detoured into the Okefenokee Swamp of south Georgia to seek relief.

Immediately following the sonic booms, from every direction sonorous roars explode from about 30 alligators. I had no idea there were so many gators around me. I sit upright in the canoe, reveling in the most spectacular chorus of alligator sounds I've ever heard. Their deep-throated bellowing goes on for a long time, nearly five minutes. This is highly unusual behavior; alligators rarely vocalize outside their springtime breeding season. For an additional five minutes, each time the bellowing begins to die down, I am able to fire it up again by making loud snoring sounds of my own. In those ten minutes, all my woes vanish. I ask myself, "What is it about wilderness that is so life-giving, so healing, so uplifting?"

Back at the University of Georgia research trailer where I spend the night, I catch a Jacksonville newscast in which the news anchor reports that sonic booms from the space shuttle *Challenger* returning to earth today were heard as far north as Jacksonville. I muse to myself that a whole swamp heard them, too, and I fancy that the gators were saluting a fellow earthling for such a high achievement.

During the last ten days of my walk, I try hard to ignore the four pulp mills at the mouth of the St. Marys River, the center-pivot agriculture, planted sand-pine desert, and open-pit landfill on Brooksville Ridge, and the recent horizon-to-horizon clearcutting of the flatwoods and cabbage palm forests in Gulf Hammock. At Cedar Key, Muir's and my final destination, I squeeze between tourist pubs to get to the seashore and end my walk by ceremoniously dipping my foot in the Gulf of Mexico, mentally awash in the irony that we can leave the tug of gravity to explore space and yet take such poor care of the planet we live on.

Standing alone amidst the thumping beat of one pub's band and the noisy crowd inside, the answer about wilderness comes to me. It was suggested by Muir, himself, whose last printed words about wilderness were, "Presently, you lose consciousness of your own separate existence: you blend with the landscape, and become part and parcel of nature." I don't feel part and parcel of the havoc wreaked on nature that I saw on my walk, but in that swamp with those bellowing alligators I lost my anguish in the beauty of my surroundings. I really did blend with the landscape and I did feel part and parcel of nature. It was a grand and uplifting feeling. Love of wilderness has got to be in our souls. Muir couldn't live without wilderness. Neither can I.

But what is wilderness without all of its parts? Wilderness begins with the rocks and soil of the earth, but it is incomplete without its living components of trees and groundcover plants—and animals. The alligator is a wonderful example of a species saved from the brink of extinction. It shows us that with only a little attention to its well being by humans, a species can save itself and even become a valuable renewable natural resource.

When I first came to north Florida to live in 1961, alligators were so scarce that I didn't see one alive in the wild until the mid-1970s. Not long afterward, in 1987, the alligator had become so abundant in Florida and Louisiana that it was pronounced fully recovered by the US Fish and Wildlife Service and removed from the federal list of endangered species. Today the alligator supports a hide and meat industry, providing income for hunters and merchants and products for consumers. And it also gives aesthetic pleasure to the recreational wildlife viewers and nature lovers like me. The alligator example shows us that simple management actions can even bring species back from the brink of extinction, and maybe allow us to preserve the whole of wilderness. A wilderness without alligators is not really a wilderness. Nor is a wilderness without rattlesnakes, kingsnakes, indigo snakes, Red Hills salamanders, alligator snapping turtles, treefrogs, and earthworms.

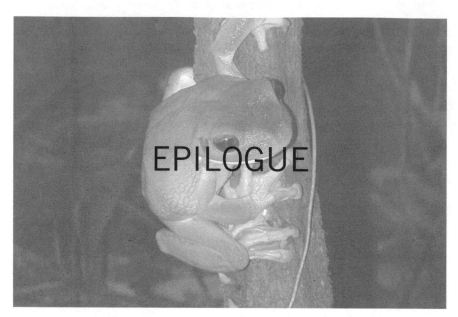

EPILOGUE

I HAVE AN ENORMOUS INTELLECTUAL CURIOSITY ABOUT, AND a fondness for, all the creatures of the world that most people loathe or don't appreciate as they do mammals and birds. My fascination and even love for certain species grew out of my close acquaintance with many of them. For example, during eight years of research on the eastern diamondback rattlesnake, I cut open a total of 776 carcasses that were brought in to me by hunters who had killed them. I carefully examined all the internal organs, paying special attention to the reproductive tracts. In females, I learned how oocytes grow, when enlarged ova pass into the oviducts, how many ova are in each oviduct, how the fetuses develop in oviducts, and when young snakes are ready to be born. In males, I investigated how the testes swell during mating season. I cut open the single lung, which runs from the mouth two-thirds of the way down the body, looking for a bizarre, wormlike parasite called a pentastome. I cut open the gastrointestinal tract and carefully examined it for the remains of food. Stomach items were often quite putrid-smelling, and quite different from feces, which I carefully pulled apart looking for the enamel crowns of the teeth of mammal prey items.

They say familiarity breeds contempt, but in my case, the

opposite was true. The more familiar I became with this venomous snake that is so feared by most humans, the more I came to appreciate it. By becoming intimately familiar with its body parts and functions, I saw that it was a highly organized living machine with as many sophisticated physiological functions as I have. I also could see that, whereas I possess two lungs, this species has lost one of the two lungs it inherited from its lizard ancestor and so better accommodates the long, slender body that it now has. I could see that it possessed all the organs and tissues that I possess, including a heart, liver, kidneys, spleen, stomach, intestines, gall bladder, ribs, muscles, eyes, teeth, a mouth, anus, and red blood cells.

I marked and released about 200 eastern diamondbacks in the wild on several study areas, and then followed many of them for several years by means of radiotelemetry and learned their secrets of survival. I came to expect, and celebrated, their spring emergence from the same underground overwintering sites spring after spring, amazed that every year they found the same stumpholes in hundreds of acres of dense groundcover in rolling terrain. I watched males search for females at breeding time and witnessed a male court and successfully copulate with a reluctant female. I followed a gravid female for many months, watching her find food to fuel the growing fetuses in her body and avoid death in winter's cold. I lay on the ground on my stomach all day writing notes and photographing her giving birth to 14 young. She spared my life when I became so preoccupied with the emergence of her young from their soft egg capsules that I failed to notice that her head had been within biting range of mine for untold minutes. My daily presence had made me so familiar to her that she did not consider me a threat and I probably had not been in any real danger. I came to love these snakes as dearly as any pet dog or cat I ever had.

What makes you hate or love an animal depends on how you view it. If you own a flock of sheep in Montana, the coyote is a sneaky scavenger and bloodthirsty lamb killer. But everybody loves the unlucky coyote of road-runner cartoons. We don't enjoy excessive grumpiness in our grandfathers, but we laugh at the grumpiness of Popeye or Elmer Fudd, the little old man of Bugs Bunny cartoons.

The cottonmouth moccasin is grumpy, and I don't find its behavior objectionable, because I understand it. A cottonmouth encounter on a field trip at first repulses my students. When they first see one coiled and mouth-gaping, they are scared. They back away and stare at it, wide-eyed. I hear horror in their voices when I move in to pin the snake and pick it up. In fact, people are so spooked about snakes that they are likely to divert my attention during crucial moments when I need uninterrupted concentration. Before I attempt to catch any venomous snake, if I am in the company of other people, I sternly request everyone to keep quiet while I am in harm's way.

When the cottonmouth is first in hand, it invariably squirts a foul musk from glands at the base of its tail and the next reaction students display is disgust at the smell. But then I explain what the musk is all about (it elicits that same disgust in predators) and I assure students that the snake is clean and the musky odor will soon disappear. Their expressions become much more relaxed and they become curious with the snake secure in my grip. Soon everybody is crowding around to feel the rough dorsal scales and the contrastingly smooth belly scales. They are especially attentive when I gently open the snake's mouth, display its fangs, and squeeze out a little venom.

By the time I release the snake, the students' attitudes have changed dramatically. They go home with less fear and disgust because they have learned, firsthand, a number of true facts about the animal and its ways of dealing with its life. Somehow this familiarity reduces fear and loathing, and sometimes even generates appreciation where there was none.

That people are fascinated by things they fear is well demonstrated by our love of storytelling. Who doesn't remember the scary stories of early childhood, when parents or older children try to startle the listener with an approaching monster's loud, "Gotcha!" We fear sharks, spiders, and snakes, yet we flock to the movies to see *Jaws*, *Arachnophobia*, and television "documentaries" about venomous snakes and enormous crocodiles.

Unfortunately, shockumentaries, as I call them, focus on sensationalism: a rattlesnake striking at the camera or a crocodile charging out of its holding pond after the presenter. The real story, the real beauty, of these animals is rarely told because producers believe that the audience just wants to be titillated by the proximity of danger. Ironically, however, and despite the overworked sensationalism in television programs, animals once feared and hated may become less so simply because the human audience is repeatedly exposed to them.

I think we need more familiarity, more understanding, and less fear. Our unbridled population growth and environmental impacts are causing many animals that people loathe and fear—the creepy crawlies and things that go bump in the night—to decline or even go extinct. I think this is a sorry trend. As a biologist—one who studies living things—my viewpoint goes beyond simple empathy for the creatures I like and beyond appreciation of their potential utility. I no longer just see "gold in them thar critters" in the form of proteins that might cure cancer, for instance. We have a kinship with all living things that, I believe deeply in my soul, not only should fill us with respect for other creatures, but also should make us morally responsible for their well being. Here's how I come to this conclusion.

Human beings, and all the animals and plants on planet earth, share a fabulous evolutionary journey. We all have come to survive on the globe through the same kinds of evolutionary responses to nature's challenges down through the eons. Most amazingly of all, we all share the same ancestors. Consider this. Each of us has two parents, four grandparents, eight great grandparents, and so on. We have 2^X ancestors at any time in the past, X being the generation in question. If you want to know how many of your ancestors were alive ten generations ago, the answer is 2^{10}, or 2,048. Did it ever occur to you that you have 2,048 great, great, great, great, great, great, great, great, great grandparents? That figure does not include all the more recent ancestors between you and the tenth generation.

Calculating that a human generation turns over every 25 years (four times a century), you are descended from 2,048 people who were alive in about the year 1750. The number of people you descended from just 20 generations ago is an astounding $2^{20} = 1,048,576$! That means you have genes in you from over one million people who were alive about the year 1500. If you are descended from Italian immigrants, there were over a million Italians living in 1500 that you can call "great (times 20) grandparent." The population of Italy in 1500 has been estimated at about twelve million. So you could claim descent from eight percent of all Italians alive in 1500. How many Romans at the time of Julius Caesar, then, might you be descended from? Possibly all of them.

Carry this simple math project further. A hundred generations back, 2,500 years ago, you could be descended from most of the people alive in Europe. Going back 1,000 generations, your great grandparents 25,000 years ago may have been most of the *Homo sapiens* living in Eurasia. At 10,000 generations ago your ancestors were most of the people alive in Africa a quarter million years ago, right around the time that *Homo sapiens* was evolving from our immediate ancestral species, *H. erectus.* Taking this model to the extreme, and relying on the best dates that can be estimated from fossils, you can easily calculate approximately how many generations back in time that you are related to the common ancestor that gave rise to any living species and you. Of course, generation times may have been different in times past, probably shorter, but the point I am trying to make is that at some juncture in the past, every amphibian, reptile, mammal, and other animal alive today shares a common ancestor with you, and with me.

That being true, all life is equal in terms of its long evolutionary path to the present. All living things got here the same way that we did. All living things, therefore, have as much right to live on this planet as we do. There ought to be a credo that applies to all life, that all living things, not just human beings, possess the right to life, liberty, and the pursuit of happiness.

Of course we, like other predators, must consume and otherwise utilize other creatures. Predation in the form of herbivory and carnivory is a naturally evolved process among species. In a world without modern humans, population regulation is partly maintained among species by predation. As populations of primary consumers (herbivores that eat photosynthetic plants) burgeon, predators either switch prey species and consume more of the more abundant resources, or multiply and put increasing predation pressure on primary consumers by means of more predators. Likewise, predator populations do not burgeon much beyond food supply without experiencing starvation, and ultimately, reduced numbers. This is what is behind the so-called balance of nature.

The difference between then and now is that one species, we humans, have evolved brains with high cognitive powers and intelligence which have enabled us to develop technologies that aid us in overcoming predators, food shortages, diseases, and short life spans. We now are increasing in numbers astronomically beyond the natural checks and balances that regulated our ancestral populations, but we are not so smart as we think. We may have tamed electricity and magnetism for our use, traveled to the moon, and discovered and harnessed the power of atomic nuclei, but our cultural traditions hold us back from effectively dealing with our global population explosion and many of its consequences such as environmental pollution.

The big problem for human beings, as I see it, is culture. We do not change culture as rapidly as we acquire new scientific knowledge about the world around us, and as we develop new technologies derived from this new knowledge. Culture does not keep up with science, and this is a bad thing. For instance, medical advances in the past century have given us much lengthier and healthier lives, but it has also fueled our population explosion. Cultural traditions, for another example, hold us to old ideas about having children, such as the Catholic Church's refusal to condone voluntary birth control. Even when presented with the facts, people obeying their cultural traditions rarely limit their families to two children.

It is the rare human who voluntarily curbs his or her profligate consumption of energy and goods. We continue to pollute water and air. We are champions of the "get rich quick" syndrome, at the expense of the planet and other life forms on it. So how in the world can we find the time or motivation to change our cultural or even personal attitudes about all of the creepy-crawly critters I love? These creepy-crawlies, in fact, comprise most of the biodiversity of the Earth.

To be honest, on a global, national, or cultural level, I don't really believe it will be possible to make broad-reaching changes before much of the world's biodiversity is lost. Global pollution and climate change—fueled by human population growth and resource consumption—are proceeding at too fast a pace for cultural attitudes to change sufficiently to halt the increasing impacts we are inflicting on other life forms on earth.

If we cannot become magnanimous enough to moderate our activities so as to insure the perpetuation of the rest of the world's creatures—our cousins, actually—I see little hope that our descendents will have much of the natural world left to enjoy. The only hope we can give our fellow creature cousins, as I see it, is whatever we can do on their behalf at our own personal level. If you are reading this, chances are that you have perused some, or much, of this book. You have shared some of my first-hand experiences with many of the creatures I love. If the accounts I have written about earthworms, frogs, salamanders, turtles, and snakes have piqued your interest or brought you any pleasure, then I have made a small contribution to their survival by elevating your awareness about them and their plight. Hopefully, the next time you see a snake in your yard, maybe you won't blindly kill it. Maybe you will stop to assist a turtle crossing a road somewhere. Or maybe you will get pleasure from viewing the herps of the world as I do. And for me—and them—it may not be enough to save a species, but it is a good start.

BIBLIOGRAPHY

Chapters 1–4

Klauber, L. M. 1972. *Rattlesnakes: Their Habits, Life Histories, and Influence on Mankind.* 2nd ed. Univ. Calif. Press.

Martin, W. H. and D. B. Means. 2000. Distribution and habitat relationships of the Eastern Diamondback Rattlesnake (*Crotalus adamanteus*). Herpetological Natural History 7(1): 9–34.

Means. D. B. 2006. Chapter 6. Vertebrate faunal diversity of longleaf pine ecosystems. Pages 157–213 *in* S. Jose, E. J. Jokela, and D. L. Miller, eds. *The longleaf pine ecosystem, ecology, silviculture, and restoration.* Springer, New York, NY.

Means, D. B. 2008. Diamonds in the rough, natural history of the Eastern Diamondback Rattlesnake. (In preparation.)

Rubio, M. 1998. *Rattlesnake: Portrait of a Predator.* Smithsonian Institution Press, Washington, DC. 240 pp.

Chapter 5

Krysko, K. L. and W. S. Judd. 2006. Morphological systematics of kingsnakes, *Lampropeltis getula* complex (Serpentes: Colubridae), in the United States. Zootaxa 1193: 1–39.

Means, D. B. and K. L. Krysko. 2001. Biogeography and pattern variation in the Kingsnake, *Lampropeltis getula*, across the Apalachicola Region of Florida. Contemporary Herpetology 2001(5): 1–33. http://www.calacademy.org/research/herpetology/ch/ch/2001/5/index.htm

Chapter 6

Ernst, C. H. and E. M. Ernst. 2003. *Snakes of the United States and Canada.* Smithsonian Press, Washington, DC. 668 pp.

Chapter 7

Gunzburger, M. S. 1999. Diet of the Red Hills salamander *Phaeognathus hubrichti*. Copeia 1999: 523–525.

Gunzburger, M. S. and C. Guyer . 1998. Longevity and abandonment of burrows used by the Red Hills salamander (*Phaeognathus hubrichti*). Journal of Herpetology 32: 620–623.

Means, D. B. 2003. Notes on the reproductive biology of the Alabama Red Hills Salamander (*Phaeognathus hubrichti*). Contemporary Herpetology 2003(3). http://www.contemporaryherpetology.org/ch/2003/3/index.htm

Chapter 8

Gloyd, H. K. and R. Conant. 1990. Snakes of the *Agkistrodon* complex, a monographic review. Society for the Study of Amphibians and Reptiles.

Wharton, C. H. 1969. The cottonmouth moccasin at Sea Horse Key, Florida. Bulletin of the Florida State Museum, Biological Sciences, 14: 227–272.

Chapter 9

Barrett, G. W. 2001. Predation on the hispid cotton rat (*Sigmodon hispidus*) by snakes and owls. Georgia Journal of Science 59(2): 94–100.

Layne, J. N. 19745. Ecology of small mammals in a flatwoods habitat in north-central Florida, with emphasis on the cotton rat (*Sigmodon hispidus*). American Museum Novitates 2544: 1–48.

Chapter 10

Ernst, C. H., J. E. Lovich, and R. W. Barbour. 1994. *Turtles of the United States and Canada*. Smithsonian Institution Press, Washington, DC. 578 pp.

Pritchard, P. C. H. 1989. *The Alligator Snapping Turtle: Biology and Conservation*. Milwaukee Public Museum, Milaukee, MN. 104 pp.

Chapter 11

Robison, H. W. and R. T. Allen. 1995. *Only in Arkansas: A Study of the Endemic Plants and Animals of the State*. The University of Arkansas Press, Fayetteville, AR. 121 pp.

Chapter 12 and 13

Campbell, J. A. and W. W. Lamar. 2004. *The Venomous Reptiles of the Western Hemisphere*. Cornell University Press, Ithaca, New York. 2 volumes.

Lee, J. C. 1996. *The Amphibians and Reptiles of the Yucatan Peninsula.*
    Cornell University Press, Ithaca, N. Y. 500 pp.

Chapter 14
Glaw, F. and M. Vences. 2007. *A Field Guide to the Amphibians and
    Reptiles of Madagascar.* 3rd ed. Vences & Glaw Verlag, Koln,
    Germany.

Preston-Mafham, K. 1991. *Madagascar: A Natural History.* Facts On File,
    Inc. New York, N. Y. 224 pp.

Chapter 15
Means, D. B. 2001. Just batty. International Wildlife 31(5): 28–29.

Means, D. B. 2001. Living on the Ledge. FAUNA 2(6): 1–7.

Chapter 16
Chaloupka, G. 1999. Journey in time; the 50,000-year story of the
    Australian Aboriginal rock art of Arnhem Land. Reed New Holland,
    Sydney, Australia. 256 pp.

Mulvaney, J. and J. Kamminga. 1999. *Prehistory of Australia.* Allen and
    Unwood, St. Leonards, New South Wales, Australia. 480 pp.

Chapter 17
Schwaner, T. D. 1991. Spatial patterns in Tiger snakes (*Notechis ater.*
    Elapidae) on offshore islands of Southern Australia. Journal of
    Herpetology 25(3): 278–283.

Schwaner, T. D. and Sarre, S. D. 1988. Body size of tiger snakes in
    southern Australia, with particular reference to *Notechis ater serventyi*
    (Elapidae) on Chappell Island. Journal of Herpetology 22: 24–33.

Chapter 18
Greer, A. 1997. *The Biology and Evolution of Australian Snakes.* Surrey
    Beatty & Sons Pty Ltd., Chipping Norton, New South Wales,
    Australia. 358 pp.

Walls, J. G. 1998. *The Living Pythons: A Complete Guide to the Pythons of
    the World.* T. F. H. Publications, Inc., Neptune City, N. J. 256 pp.

Chapter 19

Cogger, H. 2000. *Reptiles and Amphibians of Australia*. 6th edition. Reed
    Books, Sydney. 775 pp.

Doughty, P., B. Maryan, S. C. Donnellan, and M. N. Hutchinson. 2007. A
    new species of taipan (Elapidae: *Oxyuranus*) from central Australia.
    Zootaxa 1422: 45–58.

Chapter 20

Masci, P. and P. Kendall. 1995. *The Taipan: The World's Most Dangerous
    Snake*. Kangaroo Press, Kenthurst, New South Wales, Australia.

Chapter 21

Barker, D. G. and T. M. Barker. 1994. *Pythons of the World, Vol. 1*.
    Australia. Advanced Vivarium Systems, Inc., Lakeside, California.
    171 pp.

Chapter 22

Lockwood, C. C. 2002. *The Alligator Book*. Louisiana State University
    Press, Baton Rouge, LA. 130 pp.

McIlhenny, E. A. 1976. The alligator's life history. Miscellaneous
    publications, Facsimile reprints in herpetology, Society for the Study
    of Amphibians and Reptiles. 117 pp.

Neill, W. T. 1971. *The Last of the Ruling Reptiles: Alligators, Crocodiles,
    and Their Kin*. Columbia University Press, New York, N. Y. 486 pp.

INDEX

CP refers to the color plates in the insert.

Abala, Mexico, 105
Aboriginal people, 138, 141, 142
Aboriginal rock art, 144, 145
Aburga, 150
Acanthophis praelongus, 208
Adams, Craig, 165
Africa, 13, 141, 147
Agkistrodon bilineatus, 107
Agkistrodon contortrix, 107
Agkistrodon piscivorus, 61–69
Alabama, 28, 55
Alabama Red Hills physiographic
    region, 56
Alabama red hills salamander,
    52–60, **CP13**
Alaska, viii, 30
Alice Springs, 184
Allen, E. Ross, 32, 47
alligator, 15, 67, 213, **CP31**
Alligator Peninsula, 47, 48
alligator snapping turtle, 75–81,
    CP1
Altamaha River, 50
Ambanizana, 127
American egret, 15
Amerindians, 4
amethystine python, 147, 203, 208
anaphylactic shock, 165
Anchorage, 30
ant, 58
Antananarivo, 118
anthill python, 197
Antilles, 115
antivenin, 4
Apalachicola kingsnake, 33, 35, 36,
    CP14

Apalachicola Lowlands, 32, 34
Apalachicola National Forest, 31,
    82, 83
Apalachicola River, 32, 78, 80, **CP1**
Appalachian Mountains, 56
archon, 50
Arkansas, 66, 85
armadillo, 89
Arnhem Land, 148, 153
arthropods, 28
ashy downs, 173
Asian clam, 80
Aspidites melanocephalus, 205
Aspidites ramsayi, 205
Atherson Tablelands, 196
Atkinson, Jimmy, 75
atyid shrimps, 168
Aucilla River, 77
Audubon Magazine, 26
Australia, 13, 115, 133, 138, 141,
    154
Australian Reptile Park, 163
aye-aye, 119, 125

balance of nature, 220
Ballarat, 139
Bamaga, 144
baobab tree, 118
barn owl, 72
barramundi, 168
barred owl, 72
barrier island, 34, 48, 66
Bat Cleft, 131–137
Bay of Antongil, 119
beetle, 58

behavior
    aggressive, 62
    aggressive feints, 192
    alligator bellowing, 213, 214
    body-bridging, 67
    cobra crawl, 63
    coil up, 64
    flatten body, 64
    mouth-gaping 62, 218
    musk squirting, 67
    shammed aggression during
    blocked flight, 64
    snake-bluff, 62, 63
    tongue-flick, 72
    vibrate tail, 64
Berrill, Peter, 135
Big Cypress Preserve, 50
billabong, 138, 175
biodiversity, 115, 222
bioluminescence, 90
bird, 67
Birdsville Cutoff, 175
bison, 25
black and white ruffed lemur, 125
black bear, 30
black-belly salamander, **CP3**
black needlerush, 15
black racer, 19, 72
black tiger snake, 154–161, **CP24**
black-headed python, 204, 205
Blackman, Claire, 208
Blackman, Mick, 208
Blaney, Rick, 31
blotched kingsnake, 32, 35
Blount Island, 47, 48, 49
blue indigo snake, 38
boa constrictor, 104, 115
Boa constrictor, 115
Boiga dendrophila, 125
Boiga irregularis, 125, 133, 203
Bolivia, 115
Boophis, 122
Bosnia, 211
Bourne, Andrew, 139

box-thorn bush, 156
Britain, 84
British coast, 9
Britton, Al, 162
Bronx Zoo, 93
bronze frog, 53
Brookesia peyrierasi, 123
Brooksville Ridge, 214
brown bear, 30
brown mouse lemur, 119
brown tree snake, 48, 125, 133, 134, 203
brown-chinned black racer, 34
brush turkey, 201
Bufo marinus, 115, 201
Bufo woodhousei, 88
bug, 58
Bugs Bunny, 217
bullfrog, 68
burrow, 22
    crayfish, 55
    earthworm, 84
    mole, 91
    muttonbird, 159
    red-hills salamander, 58
    shrews, 91
    tortoise, 28, 41
    trap-door spider, 53
Bush administration, 36, 37
bushmaster, 93–101, 112, **CP18**

Caesar, Julius, 220
Cairns, 189, 205, 210
Cairo Messenger, 26, 27
Cambodia, 211
camel cricket, 52
Canada, 86
cane toad, 135, 201
canebrake rattlesnake, 67
cannibalism, 48, 67, 136
Canoochee River, 43
cantil, 107
canyon, 163
Cape Barren goose, 157

Cape Barren Mountains, 161
Cape York Peninsula, 142, 143,
    147, 184, 194
carabid beetle, 56
caribou, 30
carpet python, 135, 201
Carr, Archie, 66
Carr, Marjorie, 66
Carter, Cecilia, 139
cascabel, 103, 106, 108, 110
Casterton, 139
catfish, 68
cattle egret, 72
Cedar Hammock Trail, 212
Cedar Key, 214
centipede, 30, 52, 54
Central Queensland Speleological
    Society, 135
Cereopsis novaehollandae, 157
Challenger spacecraft, 214
Chaloupka, George, 150
chameleon, 118
Channel Country, 174, 182
cheetah, 29
Cheirogaleus medius, 119
Chichen Itza, 102, 117
Chicxulub, Mexico, 114
children's python, 197
Chili Beach, 197, 200, 202, 207,
    208
Chili Creek, 203
Chondropython viridis, 156
Chumpion, Mexico, 115
Cincinatti Zoo, 57
clampstick, 18, 19, 157, 175, 181,
    185
Claudie River, 199, 209
Claxton Enterprise, 27
Claxton Rattlesnake Roundup, 27
Clemmys insculpta, 83
climate change, 222
Clinton administration, 37
coachwhip, 72
Coastal Plain, 86, 213

coastal taipan, 183–193, **CP4**,
    CP33
coatimundi, 115
cobra, 198
cockroach, 58
coelomic fluid, 90, 91
Coen, 184
co-evolutionary see-saw, 72
Coluber constrictor helvigularis, 34
Colubridae, 195
common kingsnake, 31, 67, 72
compression bandage, 165
Cook, Andrea, 197
Cook, David, 61
Cooktown, 183
Cooper's hawk, 72
copperhead, 107
coral snake, 47
Corbicula fluminea, 80
cordgrass, 15
cotton rat, 16, 70–74, **CP16**
cottonmouth, 14, 61–69, 72, 107,
    218, **CP15**
Couper, J. H., 50
coyote, 217
Crack of Doom, 131
cracking clays, 174
crayfish, 54
Cresham, Rebecca, 141
Cretaceous, 141
crocodile, 29, 144, 218
    saltwater, 163, 197
Crotalus adamanteus, 1–5, 6–12,
    13–21, 22–29, 112
Crotalus durissus, 103
Crotalus tzabcan, 103, **CP20**
Ctenosaura similis, 115
cultural traditions, 220
curl snake, 177
curtains, 140

Dall sheep, 30
Darwin, Australia, 184
Darwin, Charles, 84

Daubentonia madagascariensis, 119
Dauphin Island, 48
Davidson, Max, 148
De Bry, Theodore
death adder, 208
Decatur County, 27
declining populations, 23
defensive behavior, 122
Demansia, 164
Dendrelaphis calligastra, 198
Desmognathinae, 55
Desmognathus brimleyorum, 87
Diamantina Development Road, 175
diatomites, 56
Diaz-Bolio, Jose, 102
didgeridoo, 148, 152, 153
dingo, 144
Diplocardia meansi, 87–92, **CP28**
Diplocardia mississippiensis, 83, 86
Diprotodon australis, 140
Discophus antongili, 119
Ditmars, Raymond, 93
DNA, xi, 69, 103, 122
dolly varden, 30
DOR, 31, 32
dreamtime, 138
drying ponds, 67
Drymarchon couperi, 38
drymos, 50
ducks, 25
dusky salamander, 53
dwarf chameleon, 123
Dynamic Figures, 151

earthworm, 58
eastern brown snake, 179
eastern cottontail rabbit, 16, 67, 72
eastern diamondback rattlesnake, 1–5, 6–12, 13–21, 22–29, 61, 72, 108, 114, 174, 216, 217, **CP10, CP26**

eastern indigo snake, 38, **CP21**
eastern kingsnake, 32, 36
eastern tiger snake, 155
eau vive, 127
echidna, 124
Egernia whitii, 159
eggs, 55, 56, 67
    elapid snake, 158
    quail, 73
Eglin Air Force Base, 50
Elapidae, 158
embryos, 56
emu, 146, 147
endangered species, 215
Endangered Species Act, 36, 60
England, 9, 156
envenomation, 28, 62
environmental pollution, 220
Eocene, 56
epinephrine, 165
Ericaceae, 194
Escambia River, 39
Eucalyptus forest, 119, 129, 150, 185, 208
Eulemur fulvius albifrons, 121
Europe, 153, 220
Evans County, 27
Evans County Wildlife Club, 27
Everglades, 128
Everglades National Park, 50, 69
extinction, 49, 114, 215

fat-tailed dwarf lemur, 119
fer-de-lance, 94, 104
feral hog, 53
Ficus tree, 168
fiddler crab, 15
fierce snake, 173, **CP27**
fiercey, 173–182
Finca Kinchahau, Mexico, 110
fire, 51
    bushfires, 184
fish-scale gecko, 126, **CP11**
Fitzgerald Rattlesnake Roundup, 23

Fitzgerald Wild Chicken Festival, 27
Fitzginger, Leopold, 50
flatwoods salamander, 38, 129
Flinders Island, 161
Flinders Ranges, 155
Florida, 9, 14, 65, 210, 215
Florida kingsnake, 32, 34
Florida panhandle, viii, 31, 32, 39, 50, 65
Florida panther, 129
Florida pine snake, 38, 129
Florida State University, 31
Fluothane, 19
Fort Caroline, 6, 9, 10, 12,
Fort Caroline National Monument, 10, 11
Fort Stewart Military Installation, 38, 43, 45, 50
fox, 89
Franklin County, 47
French fleet, 7
French Huguenot, 9
Frenchmen, 7
frilled lizard, CP6
Fudd, Elmer, 217
Furcifer pardalis, 120, 121

Gadsden County, 27
galah parrot, 139
gasoline in burrow, 22
Gates, Gordon, 84
gazelle, 29
Geckolepis maculata, 126
geese, 25
Georgia, 65, 83, 213
Georgia Department of Natural Resources, 27
Georgia Game and Fish Commission, 5
Giant Horse rock art, 146
giant southern toad, CP2
giant treefrog, 204, CP30
gibber plain, 173, 177

girlie stick, 164
glasswort, 15
Glenelg Highway, 139
glutinous secretion, 91
goatsucker, 106
Goetze, Karl, 197
Gondwana, 118, 141
gopher frog, 23, 38
gopher tortoise, 22, 25, 38, 39, 47, 49, 129
Gopherus polyphemus, 39
Grady County, 26
grasshopper, 159
gray rat snake, 72
great horned owl, 72
Greek Fates, 93
green tree python, 156, 198, 204, 207, CP29
green tree snake, 186
green treefrog, 132, 136, 202, CP22
green-backed mantella, 122
Greene, Harry, 94
Grim Reaper, 193
grindstone, aboriginal, 149
grizzly bear, 30
ground beetle, 52
ground sloth, 140
Guam, 133, 203
guano, 131, 137
Gulf County, 32
Gulf Hammock, 214
Gulf of Mexico, 48, 66, 214

Habitat Conservation Plan, 60
Hardy, Dave, 94
Hatchetigbee Formation, 56
hatchlings, 55
Hatteras Island, 48
heat-sensitive pits, 199, 203, 205
hedgehog, 124
Helen House, 21
Hemicentetes semispinosus, 124
Hermann, Eddie, 28
herpetology, viii

herpeton, viii
herpetophilia, 29
herpetophobia, 26, 29, 184
herptiles, viii
Hiawassee River, 213
Highton, Richard, 58
Holbrook, James Edward, 50
Homo erectus, 220
Homo sapiens, 153, 220
Hopkins, Bubba, 22
Hopkins, Milton N., 22
horehound, 156, 159
howler monkeys, 101
Hubricht, Leslie, 57
Hunter River, 163
Hurricane Isadore, 114
Hyslop, Natalie, 39

Ibalido, 125
Illinois, 65
Inca, 74
Incidental Take Permit, 60
India, 13
Indian Ocean, 118
Indiana, 65
indigo snake, 36, 72, 129
inland taipan, 173, **CP27**
insects, 23
Instituto Clodomiro Picado, Costa
    Rica, 94
intelligence, 220
iridescence, 203
Iron Range National Park, 184,
    189, 194, 198, 207
Italians, 220
ivory-billed woodpecker, 129

Jackfork Sandstone, 87
Jacksonville, 11, 214
Jerusalem cricket, 30
Joe Taylor, 14
Jones, J. P., 26
Juncus romerianus, 15

Kakadu National Park, 148
kangaroo, 13, 145
katydid, 120
Kavanagh, Clive, 135
kelp gull, 160
Kennedy River, 189
Kentucky, 67, 212, 213
kestrel, 72
Key West, 48
Khmer Rouge, 211
Kimberley, The, 162
king brown snake, 175
king cobra, 174
Klauber, Laurence M., 103
koala, 140
Komarek, Edwin, Jr. (Eddy), 84
Komarek, Edwin V., Sr., 84
Komarekiona eatoni, 86
Komarekonidae, 85
Korean War, 210
Krysko, Kenney, 34
Kukulcan, 102, 116, 117, **CP19**
Kununara, 162

Lampropeltis getula, 31
    L. g. brooksi, 32, 34
    L. g. floridana, 34
    L. g. getula, 32
    L. g. goini, 32
    L. g. holbrooki, 32
    L. g. meansi, 35, **CP14**
La Selva, Costa Rica, 94
LaBar, Ron, 31
Lachesis muta, 93–101, 112
Lake Bolac, 139
lamba hoany, 120
Lampropeltis triangulum, 106
land bridge, 200
Larus dominicanus, 160
larvae, 55
Latin America, 93
Laudonierre, Captain, 7, 10, 11
Laura, 142, 143, 189
Laura River, 146, 192

leaf-eating kangaroo, 141
leaf-tailed gecko, 121, 124, **CP17**
Lee, Julian C., 104, 105
LeMoyne, Jacques, 6, 9, 10, 12
lemur, 118
Lemur catta, 128
Lepilumur mustelinus, 119
Levriere, 9
Levy County, 46
Liasis amethestinus, 203
Liasis childreni, 197
Liasis fuscus, 202
Liasis maculosus, 132, 197
Liasis perthensis, 197
Liasis stimsoni, 197
lightning-ignited, 51
lion, 13
Liopholidophis lateralis, 123, 127
Litorea cerulea, 132, 202
Litorea genimaculata, 200
Litoria infrafrenata, 196
little bent-wing bat, 131–137, **CP22**
Little St. Simons Island, 13–21
live birth, 158
lizard, 23, 30, 67
loblolly pine, 59
logos, viii
London, 9
longleaf pine forest, 38, 39, 47, 59,
    82, 129, 213
long-tailed salamander, 58
Los Angeles, 146
Louisiana, 67, 215
Louisiana pink, 83
Louisville, 212
Lowery, George, 73
Lumbricus terrestris, 84

Macroclemmys temmincki, 75–81
Macropus rufogriseus, 140
Madagascan tree boa, 120, 123
Madagascar, 118–130, 141
Madtsoiidae, 141
Magee, Mimi, 138, 173

magpie, 139
Mahzucil, Mexico, 106
Malakiri people, 150
Mantella laevigata, 122
Mantidactylus luteus, 123
March burns, 73
Mareeba, 144
marine toad, 115
Maroantsetra, 119
marsh elder, 15
marsh hawk, 72
marsh marigold, 212
marsh rabbit, 16
marsupial cat, 168
marsupial cow, 140
marsupial lion, 140
Masoala National Park, 127
Mayan Indians, 109
Mayan Riviera, 104, 115
Mayan ruins, 102
Mayapan, 102
Means, Harley, 22, 75, 87, 93–101
Means, Ryan, 78, 87, 93–101
Megadrilogica, 85
megapode bird, 201
Mena, Arkansas, 87, 88
Merida, Mexico, 109, 111, 114
merlin, 72
Merritt Island, 48
Merritt Island National Wildlife
    Refuge, 50
metamorphs, 55
meteorite impact crater, 114
Mexico, 31, 102–117
Meyer, Art, 33
Miami, 128
mice, 23, 67
Microcebus rufus, 119
Microhylidae, 119
millipede, 58
Miniopterus australis, 131–137
Mississippi, 83, 86
Missouri, 65, 66
Mitchell County, 27

Mitchell grass, 174
Mobile Bay, 48
moccasin, 218
Modern Period, 152
mole, 67
mole salamander, **CP9**
mole skink, 38
Moler, Paul, 46
moose, 30
Morelia carinata, 165
Morelia spilota, 135
Morgues, James, 9
Mt. Borradaile, 148
Mt. Chappell Island, 155
Mt. Chappell Island tiger snake, 155
Mt. Etna Caves National Park, 134
Mt. Etna, Queensland, 131–137
Muhlenbergia capillaris, 13
muhley grass, 5, 13, 16, 20
Muir, John, 212
Muna, Mexico, 105
Musgrave, 144
Musgrave, George, 143, 153
Musgrave, Victor, 143
Mushroom Rock, 145
muttonbird, 155
Myrica cerifera, 16

Naracoorte, 139
Narracoorte Caves, 171
Naracoorte Caves National Park,
    139
National Geographic Explorer, 166
naturalistic painting, 151
Neill, Wilfred T., 32
Nepenthes mirabilis, 195
neverwet, 212
New Guinea, 152, 196, 200, 203
New Jersey, 31
New World, 4, 10,
North America, 10, 65
North Carolina, 48, 85, 86
north central Florida, 47
Northern Territory, 184

northern tree snake, 198
Norton, Terry, 45
Nosy Mangabe, 119–127
Notechis ater serventyi, 155
Notechis scutatus, 155
Nunnery, 103, **CP19**

Ocala National Forest, 50
Ochlockonee River, 32
ochre, 153
odor, repulsive, 67
Oenpelli, 148
Ohio State University, 58
Okefenokee National Wildlife
    Refuge, 50, 69
Okefenokee Swamp, 212
Oklahoma, 67, 89
oldfield mouse, 38
oldfields, 108
old-growth hardwood forest, 59
olive python, 166, 168, **CP34**
ophidiophilia, 36
opossum, 36, 89, 139
Opp Rattlesnake Roundup, 26
Opp, Alabama, 28
Oregon, 31
Organization for Tropical Studies,
    94
Origin of Species, 84
Orion, 161
Orizorictidae, 124
Orono, Maine, 84
Oryzorictus, 124
Osierfield, 22
ostrich, 147
Ouachita Mountains, 85, 87
Ouachita Mountain dusky
    salamander, 87
Oxyuranus microlepidotus, 173
Oxyuranus scutellatus, 183–193

Palestine-Israeli conflict, 211
paleteria, 106
Palorchestes azeal, 140

Pandanus palm, 186, 187
panther chameleon, 119, 121
Panzik, Harry, 31
Papua New Guinea, 210
Parker, Adrian, 148
Paroedura homalorhinus, 127
Pascoe River, 194, 206
passenger pigeon, 25
Pennsylvania, 83, 210
Penola, 139
Pentagon, 210
pentastome, 216
Perinet, 128
Peru, 74
Phaeognathus hubrichti, 52–60,
    CP13
pheromone, 98
Phrynohyas venulosa, 115
pickerel, 68
pickerelweed, 212
pig frog, **CP5**
pipefish, 152–153
Piste, Mexico, 104, 115
pit tags, 132
pitviper, 4, 93, 98
plague rat, 174, 177
plated lizard, 121, 122
Pleistocene, 141, 171
plethodontid salamanders, 57
Plethodontidae, 54
plumed serpent, 102–117
poison eggs, 36
Popeye, 217
popsicle man, 108
population decline, 35
population explosion, 220
porcupine, 124
Port Moresby, 210
Portland Roads, 195, 197, 204, 207
predator eradication, 36
prehensile tail, 57
prescribed burn, 51
Procoptodon goliah, 141
Pseudechis australis, 175

Pseudonaja textilis, 179
Pseudoxyropus hetururus, 127
ptarmigan, 30
Puerto Morelos, 114
Puffinus tenuirostris, 154
pygmy rattlesnake, 47
pygmy sunfish, 67

quail, 26
quail eggs, 36
Queen of Angels Hospital, 146
Queensland, 131, 142, 183, 184
Queensland Parks and Wildlife
    Service, 132
Quetzlcoatl, 102, 116, 117, **CP19**
quoll, 168

raccoon, 89
radiotelemetry, 20, 40, 61, 72, 94,
    97, 197, 217
radio-tracking, 83
radiotransmitter, 20, 40
rain frog, **CP8**
rainbow serpent, 147–153
rainforest, 108, 116, 128, 166, 171,
    197, 200, 208, 209
Raleigh, Sir Walter, 9
Rana clamitans, 53
Rana daemeli, 200
Ranidae, 200
rat, 23, 67
rat snake, 19
Rattus villosissimus, 174
ravines, 52, 55
Reagan administration, 37
red rat snake, 72
red-cockaded woodpecker, 38, 129
red-shouldered hawk, 72
red-tailed hawk, 72
Relais du Masoala, 119
reptile poachers, 132
Reynolds, John, 85
Rhacophoridae, 122
Ribault, Captain Jacques, 7, 8

rice tenrec, 124, 125
Rich Mountain, 85, 87, 88
Rich Mountain giant earthworm, **CP28**
rimstone pool, 140
ringtail lemur, 128
Rio Lagartos, 115
River of May, 6
Riversleigh, 171
road cruise, 88, 175, 201, 204, 209
rock art, 150, **CP23**
rock glacier, 87
Rockhampton, 131, 183
Romans, 220
rough-scaled python, 162–172, **CP25**
Rural Georgia newspaper, 27
Rwanda, 211

St. Augustine, 7
St. Catherine's Island, 45
St. John's Bluff, 7, 8
St. John's River, 6, 47
St. Mary's River, 214
St. Vincent Island, 48
salamander, 68
salt marsh, 15
saltbush, 174
saltwort, 15
San Antonio Rattlesnake Festival, 27, 28
San Jose, Costa Rica, 94
sandhills habitat, 50
Sands, Noel, 132, 135
Santa Monica Mountains, vii, 30
Sanzinia madagascariensis, 120, 125, 126
Savannah, 38
Schwaner, Terry, 158
sclerophyll forest, 184
scorpion, 30
scorpion-eating snake, 115
screech owl, 72
scrub python, 203

sea oxeye, 15
seahorse, 152
Seahorse Key, 66, 69
serendipity, 55
sharp-shinned hawk, 72
shingleback, **CP7**
shortleaf/loblolly pine forest, 47
short-tailed shearwater, 154
shrew, 67
Sibon fasciatus, 104
Sigmodon hispidus, 70–74, **CP16**
silicious mudstones, 56, 57
sisal, 128
skunk, 89
slash pine, 59
slatey gray snake, 195
slimy salamander, 58
small-scaled snake, 173
Smith, Becky, 46
Smith, Meredith, 141
snail sucker, 104
snails, 58
snakebite, 1, 2, 94, 162, 164, 174
Snakes of the World, 94
snakestick, 115
snapping turtle, 67
snowshoe rabbit, 30
soda straw, 140
Song of the Snake, 158
South America, 29, 141
southeastern pocket gopher, 38
southern California, vii, 30
Southern Cross, 161
southern hognose snake, 38, 129
spadefoot, 68
Spaniards, 6
Spanish soldiers, 7
Sparganophilus meansi, 86
spear grass, 185
speckled kingsnake, 32
speleothems, 139
spider, 58
spiny tenrec, 124
spiny-tailed iguana, 115

spotted python, 132, 133, 197
spruce grouse, 30
squirrel, 67
Strickland, Danny, 27
stalactite, 140
stalagmite, 140
Stapleton, Seth, 36
State Amphibian of Alabama, 58
Stegonotis cucullatus, 195
Steinheimer, Kathy, 14, 21, 104–115, 118–130, 187
Stenophis, 125
Stenorrhina fremvillei, 115
Stevenson, Dirk, 38
Sthenurus, 145
Stimson's python, 197
Stoddard, Herbert, 73
Stone, Ian, 94
striped newt, 38
Sumatra, Florida, 62
sunfish, 68
superb dragon, 162
Suta suta, 177
Suwannee River, 39
Swansea Bay, 9

Tacon, Paul, 152
tailing a snake, 181
Taipan Tribe, 145
Talimena Scenic Highway, 87, 89, 90
Tall Timbers Research Station, 14, 35, 47, 85
Tallahassee, 14, 35, 47, 55, 129
Tallahatta Formation, 56
tarantula, 30
Tasmania, 154
Tasmanian devil, 140
Telogia Creek, 32
Tennessee, 213
tenrec, 124
tepui, 29
termite mounds, 195
Texas indigo snake, 49

Texas, 65
The Tombs, 127
Thomas County, 27
thorn forest, 104, 108
Thousand-mile Walk to the Gulf, 212
threatened species 39, 46, 53, 59
Thylacoleo carnifex, 140
ticks, 158
tiger, 13
Tikit, Mexico, 110
timber rattlesnake, 61, 72
Timucuan people, 10, 12, **CP12**
toepads, 122
Toltecs, 116, 117
tomato frog, 118
Torres Strait, 152, 196
tortoise, mechanical, 28
transmitter, 61
trap-door spider, 53
tree snake, 171
treefrog, 68, 115
Trezise, Steve, 189, 193
Trinidad, 93
tropical kingsnake, 106
tropical pitcher plant, 195
trotline, 75–81
Tula, Mexico 117
Tulum, Mexico, 115
turtle, 68
tzabcan, 103

United States, 86
University of California, Berkeley, 94
University of Georgia, 39, 214
University of Maine, 84
University of Maryland, 58
Uroplatus fimbriatus, 121
US Fish and Wildlife Service, 25, 36, 39, 55, 59, 60, 215
US Forest Service, 37
Uxmal, 102, 105, 117, **CP19**

Varanus keithornei, 207
Varecia variegata, 125
venom
    elapid, 164, 190
    rattlesnake, 73
vertebrate animals, 28
vertebrate food webs, 74
Victoria Cave, 139
Vietnam War, 210
vine snake, 171
Virginia, 65
Volcan Arenal, 99
vomeronasal organs, 198

walkabout, 142
Warrego Highway, 173
water lilies, 212
water moccasin, 61
water python, 202
waterfall, 169
watersnake, 68
wax myrtle, 16
Wayne County, 50
weasel-sportive lemur, 119
weaver ants, 195
Weigel, Arnie, 165
Weigel, John, 163
Westcott, Greg, 207
Western Australia Parks and
    Wildlife Department, 166, 172
western cottonmouth, **CP32**
western taipan, 173
Wewahitchka, 32
Whigham Rattlesnake Roundup, 23
whipsnake, undescribed, 164
white cockatoo, 139

white-fronted brown lemur, 121
white-lipped treefrog, 196, 204
White's skink, 159
white-tailed deer, 25, 26
wild turkey, 25, 26
wildebeest, 29
Wildlife Conservation Society, 45
Winding Stair Mountain, 87, 89
Withlacoochee State Forest, 50
wolf spider, 53, 54
woma, 205
Wonambi naracoortensis, 141, 150
wood frog, 200
wood stork, 72
wood turtle, 83
Woodhouse's toad, 88, 89
Woods, Sandy, 207
World Trade Center, 210
World War II, 210
worm fiddling, 83
worm grunting, 83
worm noodling, 83
Worrell, Sir Eric, 158, 163
Wright, David, 138, 162, 173
Wyndorah, 173

Yalsihon, Mexico, 115
Yam Figure, 151
yellow mangrove snake, 125
Yucatan Peninsula, 102–117

Zonosaurus madagascariensis, 121, 122
Zygomaturus trilobus, 140

Here are some other books from Pineapple Press. For a complete catalog, write to Pineapple Press, P.O. Box 3889, Sarasota, Florida 34230-3889, or call (800) 746-3275. Or visit our website at www. pineapplepress.com.

Florida's Rivers by Charles R. Boning. Provides an overview of Florida's waterways as well as detailed information on sixty of Florida's rivers, covering each one from source to end, and introducing plants and animals endemic to each. Includes maps and color photos. (pb)

The Springs of Florida, 2nd edition, by Doug Stamm. The deepest and largest known springs in the world are found here. The photographs are the result of hundreds of hours under water. This new edition is completely updated to serve as a guide to Florida's many spring parks and their inhabitants. (hb, pb)

The Everglades: River of Grass, 60th Anniversary Edition, by Marjory Stoneman Douglas with an update by Michael Grunwald. Before 1947, when Marjory Stoneman Douglas named the Everglades a "river of grass," most people considered the area worthless; she brought the world's attention to the need to preserve the Everglades. In the Afterword, Michael Grunwald tells us what has happened to them since then. (hb)

Everglades: An Ecosystem Facing Choices and Challenges by Anne E. Ake. The Everglades ecosystem is in trouble, and it's all about the water. Plant and animal populations are declining at an alarming rate. The quality of life for people in south Florida is also at risk. Can we save the Everglades? You can decide for yourself after reading this book. (hb)

Easygoing Guide to Florida, Volume 1: South Florida and *Volume 2: Central Florida* by Douglas Waitley. Nature is indeed wonderful, but some of us would like to enjoy it with minimum effort. To make this series, a site must be beautiful and easy to reach, must not cost a lot of money, and must not require a lot of exercise to enjoy it. In southern Florida we visit east coast beaches, interiors scrub, and more. In central Florida we experience wetlands, rivers, and longleaf pine forests, among other natural delights. (pb)

Florida's Living Beaches: A Guide for the Curious Beachcomber by Blair and Dawn Witherington. Beginning with the premise that beaches are alive, this complete guide is organized into Beach Features, Beach Animals, Beach Plants, Beach Minerals, and Hand of Man and includes descriptive accounts of 822 items and over 900 color photos. (pb)

Dangerous Sea Life of the West Atlantic, Caribbean, and Gulf of Mexico by Edwin S. Iversen and Renate H. Skinner. Learn how to avoid dangerous creatures—and how to administer first aid just in case you are unable to avoid them. Includes sections on species that bite, species that sting, species dangerous to eat, pests that harm swimmers, toxic mucus-secreting species, and fish beak and processing injuries. (pb)

Florida's Birds: A Field Guide and Reference, 2nd edition by David S. Maehr and Herbert W. Kale II. Illustrated by Karl Karalus. Now with color throughout, this guide includes sections on bird study, bird feeding, bird habitats, threatened and endangered species, exotic species, and bird conservation. Each section has been updated and 30 new species added. (pb)

Those Terrific Turtles by Sarah Cussen. Illustrated by Steve Weaver, photographs by David M. Dennis. You'll learn the difference between a turtle and a tortoise, and find out why they have shells. Meet baby turtles and some very, very old ones, and even explore a pond. (hb, pb)

Alligator Tales by Kevin M. McCarthy. Color photos by John Moran. True and tongue-in-cheek accounts of alligators and the people who have hunted them, been attacked by them, and tried to save them from extinction. (pb)

The Young Naturalist's Guide to Florida, 2nd edition, by Peggy Sias Lantz and Wendy A. Hale. Provides up-to-date information about Florida's wonderful natural places and the plants and creatures that live here—many of which are found nowhere else in the United States. Now available in a newly designed and updated edition. (pb)